DISCOVERED IN A SCREAM

A Story of Survival & Healing

Names of some people and places have been changed

My story is true

Ben Nuttall-Smith

Discovered in a Scream, 3rd edition
copyright © Ben Nuttall-Smith 2019

First published as *The Chameleon Sings*, Trafford Publishing, 2005
Revised Edition, *The Chameleon Sings*, Trafford Publishing, 2007

Author: Ben Nuttall-Smith
         www.bennuttall-smith.ca

Publisher: Rutherford Press
            www.rutherfordpress.ca
For information, contact:
            Rutherford Press
            PO Box 648
            Qualicum Beach, BC, V9K 1A0 Canada
            info@rutherfordpress.ca
            www.rutherfordpress.ca
            Printed in the United States of America and Canada

All rights reserved. No part of this book may be reproduced in whole or in part, materially or digitally, including photocopying, without the express written permission of the author or publisher.

ISBN (paperback) # 978-1-988739-38-0
ISBN (ebook)   # 978-1-988739-00-7

Cover illustration, *Finchingfield,* by Ben Nuttall-Smith

Book design by George Opacic

Acknowledgements

To my primary and principal editor, companion and loving partner, Margot Thomson, for warmth, encouragement and understanding throughout the telling and retelling of this story.

To my son who stood by me with support and encouragement through some very tough periods of my life when I felt otherwise alone. Without his maturity, love and understanding, this story might never have been told.

To my story editor, Sylvia Taylor, for recognizing missing pieces and helping bring them to light.

To David C. Manning, men's group leader on the Sunshine Coast for recognizing me when I needed a good ear.

To the many friends who have loved me and supported me throughout my battle with this monstrous task. Special thanks to Anna Baidoun, Nora Sterling, Bernice Lever, Margaret Hume, Barbara Schillinger for dedicated reading and suggestions.

Last but not least, to my good friend and publisher, George Opacic, whose patience, encouragement and help have gotten me to this final stage in sharing my story.

Thank you, thank you, thank you, and much love.

Ben Nuttall-Smith

INDEX

One: Fairies, Witches, and Birds In the Thatch   1937 - 1940

Two: Parachutes, Spies, and Bogeymen

Three: Bombs, Boarding Schools and Deep Dark Secrets

Four: Change of Name; Change of Nationality   1945

Five: Running the Gauntlet

Six: Bell-Bottom Trousers 1950   1953

Seven: Sparks and Sputters 1953   1955

Eight: Bed Sheets and Matches   1955

Nine: Searching For the Fountain of Life   1956 – 1968

Ten: Hearts and Flowers and Fleurs de Lis   1969 – 1973

Eleven: New Horizons

Twelve: Broken Promises – Shattered Dreams

Thirteen: "Recovery is the process of discovering who we are."

Epilogue   No More Running

WHEN LIFE HANDS YOU LEMONS,

MAKE LEMONADE

Tanganyika,

British South-East Africa

June 1933

Discovered in a scream

When I was born, a hyena laughed. My mother screamed and cursed me for the pain. A black hand slapped my pink bottom and made me cry. Then my mother loved me and passed me to a wet-nurse to be fed.

One

Fairies, Witches and Birds In the Thatch

1937 - 1940

Willets Cottage

In 1937, Finchingfield was, in fact, still is, a picture postcard village near Braintree, Essex, fifty-four miles northeast of London. At the centre of the village, a green rises from a duck pond with a footbridge, a motor bridge and a war memorial. Up the hill toward Horsham stands the 14th century church of Saint John the Baptist.

We lived in Willets Cottage, on the Causeway in Duck End. Though our roof was not thatched, many of those surrounding us were. Smoke curled from chimneys adding the scent of wood and coal smoke to the perfume of open fields, farm horses, rabbit pie and Yorkshire pudding. From our bedroom window, my three-year-old sister Naomi and I, eleven months older, could stand on tiptoe and gaze across the road to pigs, cows and chickens.

We had a privy at the top of the garden. Close behind it stood an ancient wooden windmill. Because we had no fence nor hedge to separate our garden from the field, my sister and I could jump in the hay, roll down the hill and play hide-and-seek right up to the top hedges behind the windmill.

An old man in a raggedy coat is doing something behind the hedge. Naomi and I draw close but not too close.

"Hello children. Would you like to see my birdie? ... Don't be afraid."

We run home. It isn't a birdie.

"Don't be silly children", Mommy says, "that's only the farmer walking his dog. He wouldn't hurt you. He loves children. Now, go back out and play."

When we heard the birds building nests beneath the eaves, I teased my sister. I told Naomi the birds were coming to our bedroom to peck out her eyes 'cause she was "sugar and spice and all things nice". I'd be safe, "Little boys are made of slugs and snails and puppy dogs' tails". If my sister cried loud enough, Mommy would spank my bare bottom with the hairbrush.

I got spanked for climbing the apple tree, too. After a spanking and time crying in my room, Mother held me and rocked me until my sobbing subsided. Such moments of love and undivided attention were wonderful, and I looked for them more and more. If pain was the only way to assure undivided love from my mother, then I was willing to make the sacrifice necessary to win her love. At an early age I learned to equate pain with love.

Naomi was born in London. That made her more English than I, born on safari in Tanganyika. Mother said a hyena frightened her while I was being born, so I came into the world laughing. I always got fits of the giggles when being told off, which was most annoying to those doing the scolding. Also, according to Mother, since I was born in Africa, I had to be boiled in a pot for several days just to make me blonde. The fairies delivered Naomi so she was perfect.

"Never pet a rat! Rats bite."

I pet a rat in the garden. Antiseptic Dettol stings like hot fire. Daddy kills the rat with the garden spade. Mommy pours Dettol on my finger. I cry. Naomi screams.

Mommy scolds. "A rat is not a pussy cat. A rat is a rat. Hold still!"

My father (Mother called him Freddie or Darling) was "so terribly tall" and was forever bumping his head on the beam above the door into the kitchen. He was blonde like my sister and me and quite slim. My mother, Alicia May, was fabulously beautiful. Heads turned wherever we went. Both parents smoked *Players Navy Cut* from a silver cigarette box on the living room table by the fireplace. And they drank *Gilby's Gin* with fizzy water squirted from a silver-handled seltzer bottle.

Except for clicking away at his typewriter, I can't remember my father working at anything in those early years. Mother had an allowance from Denmark. Perhaps my dad wrote newspaper articles or stories about country life or bunny rabbits or the fairies in our garden. Apart from cricket matches and tennis, I can never remember either of them being away, until the war came to spoil everything. Everything was secure and safe … for the time being.

When it was hot, my sister and I took off all our clothes and ran around in the garden naked. Once, when I was very small, I rambled into the village and was brought home by a red-faced Bobby.

Often we took turns giving each other rides in the wheelbarrow. Another favourite activity was lying on our backs in the hay, looking up at the animal shapes in the clouds. Wherever Naomi and I went, our Springer spaniel, Buller, came with us. He chased cats and rabbits and rolled in cow pies.

Grass snakes slither; worms wriggle. The big worm in my hand makes me think of that man behind the hedge. I think of chasing my sister with the worm but throw it away instead. Worms aren't fun any more.

We played "babies" but not when grown-ups were watching. I could never be the baby. Anyone who ever saw a doll knew only girls could be babies. Boys just turned up in a gooseberry patch. Boys were never given a bottle and were never supposed to cry. Still, I wanted to be cuddled and loved, just like a girl baby.

We had neither running water nor electricity at Willets Cottage. We went to bed by candlelight. In the morning, my father emptied our chamber pots in a hole behind the privy.

As for bathing, my sister and I were kept clean at the big kitchen sink, where a drainpipe ran out to a deep, dark hole at the back of the house. A barrel caught rainwater that flowed off the roof of the garden shed. My sister and I would stand up on bricks to see all sorts of wiggly creatures, swimming around and up and down.

When it rained, my dad taught us to read books and write letters. Mother played piano and sang songs that made us laugh.

Because we loved singing and listening to music, we seldom minded rainy days. We wound up the crank-handled gramophone and listened to Paul Robeson and Noel Coward. Then, after Naomi and I went to bed, my parents and their friends often sang around the piano. It was wonderful to lie awake, all comfy and cozy, just listening.

Men with slobbering lips and giant worms chase me through the mud until I get stuck up to my waist. "Mommy! Daddy!"

Nobody comes to save me. It is ugly, horrible. I scream awake. The moon shines through our bedroom window. My pillow is clammy cold.

Gypsies

We seldom went alone into the village. When we did, it was to go to Mrs. Turner's greengrocer shop with a big woven basket which Naomi and I carried between us. On the way, we stopped to see chickens and pigs and to listen to the humming in the telegraph poles. Sometimes, from the garden gate, we'd watch Gypsy bands as they travelled through Finchingfield on their way north. Gypsy caravans were brightly painted and pulled by shaggy horses. Buckets, chairs, pots, pans and cooking utensils jangled and clanged as Romany men in colourful shirts and jingly hats drove their loaded wagons past Duck End to their campground near the woods, not far from home. Mothers, grandmothers and Romany children walked behind with dogs and goats. Gypsy dogs were often dressed up and did tricks to entertain the villagers.

During the day, Gypsy men mended villagers' pots and sharpened knives and scissors. They played concertinas and mandolins and violins and sang and laughed and spoke rapidly in Romany while little dogs barked and mothers called for their children.

Naomi and I went with our dad to have his axe and garden spade sharpened. Dark-skinned Gypsy children stared at Naomi and me – fair as lilies. We were never allowed to get as dirty as they seemed to be. Their mothers forever cooked over open fires, and their fathers and grandfathers did magic tricks with colourful flowers and puffs of smoke. Some village people went to the Gypsies to have their fortunes told. But we were warned not to get too close – the Gypsies might steal us away.

When the Gypsies set their bonfires at night, farmers locked up their chickens, goats and pigs. Naomi and I fell asleep to the hubbub of their happiness, which echoed loudly until late into the evening.

One of the Gypsies sang songs while playing a concertina. Although I couldn't understand the man's language, I got caught up in the sheer joy of his music.

I wanted a concertina. My fifth Christmas, 1938, my parents gave me one, and I squeezed out my own happy and not-so-happy melodies. Despite the fact that my raucous noise got so annoying that I had to practice in the field or behind the tool shed, I nevertheless insisted everyone – my parents and Naomi – attend my recitals. Our dog, Buller, would run off and hide.

In those days before the war, men other than the gypsies passed through our village. They lived off the land and carried their scant belongings in a large handkerchief slung over the shoulder. They snared rabbits, skinned them, and cooked them over open fires. With branches and grass, they built shelters among the roots of trees. In good weather, they slept in haystacks. They searched for berries, dug up turnips from farmers' fields, and liberated chickens and eggs from their hen houses. They cooked everything in pots, with nettles and dandelions. The aroma was delicious. One of the men taught me how to blow my nose without benefit of handkerchief. My dad laughed when I demonstrated but Mother didn't think it was clever at all. "Guttersnipe."

Others traveled in caravans, sometimes singing as they went. They were the odd-job men with their barrows and carts. Some sharpened knives; others collected rags, bones and scrap metal. Rags were used for making paper. Bones made knife handles, toys and ornaments. The grease from bones was used in making soap. Naomi and I always ran out to greet the knife grinders and the travelling salesmen.

Rags and bones. Rags and bones.

Any old rags and bones.

Knives to grind. Knives to grind.

Scissors, axes, knives to grind.

Toodle-lumma-luma. Toodle-lumma-lumma. Toodle-i-ay.

Any um-ber-ellas, any um-ber-ellas to mend today?

The Bully

Finchingfield had a bully who loved tormenting smaller boys and girls. When grown-ups weren't looking, he chased us with stones, horse-droppings, and stinging nettles. If he caught us, he twisted our arms behind our backs and made us repeat bad words.

One day, he caught my sister and told her, "Swear to Jesus, you're a shit-maid!" I threw a stone at him; he let my sister go and chased me. Naomi and I ran home. Luckily for us, it wasn't far. Our legs were shorter than his but he couldn't run for beans. He was worn out before he got to our front gate.

In the middle of Finchingfield is a pond fed by the River Pant, which is really a stream. Under the footbridge, Naomi and I fished for "gollywogs" which was our name for tadpoles. Usually, there weren't any gollywogs in the pond. The swans ate them all. On sunny afternoons, we took a bag of breadcrumbs to feed the swans. If we got too close, hissing swans chased us. Then we dropped our bags of crumbs and ran home.

Punch and Judy bashed each other noisily in the puppet show by the pond. All the children came to watch. Punch whacked Judy. Then he threw their baby down on the ground. Everybody laughed and clapped.

Billy and another bully catch me all alone under the footbridge. Billy takes my fish net and twists my arm behind my back while the other boy puts his face right up to mine and growls: "Tell us what you know about the hairy cock."

I don't know the answer, so Billy pulls my pants down and pushes me in the mud.

Fairies and Little People

One day, crossing the footbridge, I saw an "enormous" fish and ran home to tell my dad. The next morning, the fairies left a packet of fishing hooks in one of their circles in the garden.

My dad helped me dig for worms. Off I went to the bridge, pole and string and baited hook in hand. Before long, a sudden tug pulled the rod from my hand. The enormous fish swam off, line and pole in tow, never to be seen again.

The little people were elves, gnomes and leprechauns who sometimes played tricks like hiding Daddy's watch or Mommy's lipstick. When they came to play with us in our bedroom under the eaves, our parents sometimes caught us out of bed. I'm not sure about my dad, but Mother didn't believe us when we told her about the fairies taking things. She couldn't see them, of course, and smacked our bottoms really hard for lying. When my sister and I came down with German measles, Mother hired a nurse to look after us. Nurse kept the fairies away. I still looked for them when we went for walks in the woods. I looked for them at the bottom of the garden. But they never came back.

I can still picture the elves. They were smaller than my sister and I. Though they didn't look like the pictures of fairies with wings we'd seen in books, we knew they were fairies. They seemed older than we were: much older. Their clothing was ragged and colourful. They all wore tiny cloth shoes with pointed toes and hats with small feathers.

The fairies laughed and chatted in happy, bright voices. They sang nonsense songs in a strange language. We tried to join in and ended up falling down in fits of giggles.

Their laughter was high pitched, like Christmas bells. Sometimes, they flew to the window to see if grown-ups were coming. When they danced around Naomi and me, we danced with them. Then they would spin in a circle and disappear in a puff of sparkles. Sometimes, they got really small and slipped through the crack under the door.

Childhood was an adventure in all kinds of weather. On winter mornings when we woke up to snow, we went on long walks and got buried in enormous drifts. Then the snow melted and we got stuck in the mud. In summer, we went with our parents to pick mushrooms in the cow fields. Or we picked blackberries and wild gooseberries. Then on a most exciting day, Dad hitched the caravan to the family car for our trip to the seaside.

Oh, how I remember my first view of the ocean. When we reached the top of a hill I felt such wonder at the beauty of the blue sea, and miles and miles of long, sandy beaches. With spades and buckets, we dug in the sand. Our dad helped us build gigantic castles. We got sunburns that blistered and peeled and Mom had to rub our backs and legs with Vaseline.

The fairies left money in a wishing well in Wales. Naomi and I bought ice cream and liquorice all-sorts with it, and Dad bought petrol for the drive home. I sensed, even then, that it was bad luck to take pennies from a wishing well. Our lives would change because of it. Of course, Naomi and I never did tell.

But things did begin to change.

The Witch of Finchingfield

Across the road from Willets Cottage, where Naomi and I peered over the garden fence to an exciting world of beggars, gypsies, milkmaids, umbrella menders, shepherds, horseback riders, and urchins with runny noses, there lived a spinster who, in our childish eyes, was truly a witch with a big, black cat named Satan. She was stooped over and very, very old. Her lips sucked into her mouth so that her nose and chin looked Punch-like. Her nose had a wart at one side, and her hair hung in stringy white strands halfway down her skinny body. She walked with a knobby cane and smelled of incense, sweat and pipe tobacco.

The witch lived in a wee house all alone. If ever she caught us, we knew she would eat us. It was a known fact among the children in the village that she had a big pot in her kitchen where she boiled all the little ones she could catch. Holding a basket of apples or a jar of liquorice all-sorts, she sometimes called to my sister and me. We ran shrieking into the back garden and hid behind the tool shed.

Our parents never asked us why we hid. Naomi and I never spoke of the old woman, even when she held out an empty bucket to my dad on his daily trip to and from the village water-pump. Dad would bring a whole bucket for her, then return for more for us.

Naomi, and I picked mushrooms only when we were with our mother. She knew which ones were good and which ones were poisonous. The best ones grew in the cow pasture where the red-eyed bull stood guard. With permission, we could go by ourselves to pick blackberries along the edge of the cow field.

One lovely day, with three buckets full of juicy blackberries, our faces and fingers stained purple, we were suddenly interrupted by the thumping and wheezing of the red-eyed bull as he charged across the field. Terrified we ran to the fence. We tried to help each other over the stile. I went first.

Before I helped her up and over, I told Naomi to hand me the buckets of berries. I hadn't yet learned "ladies first". Besides, I knew it was my red cardigan that attracted the bull. By this time, Naomi was crying. As I climbed back up to urge her on, she climbed up too with two of the buckets. The bull stopped quite close. His eyes blazed and his nostrils bellowed steam as he stood his ground, stomping and snorting, preparing to charge.

Naomi had just passed me the first full bucket when a rough voice from behind me bellowed, "Oi! W'at you two doin' stealing moi berries? 'and 'em over."

The bully!

Quickly, I put down the bucket of berries. Naomi stopped crying and picked up the other two buckets. "You can't have them." Just like the bull, she stood her ground. Then, as carefully as she could, she passed me the two buckets.

Suddenly, I felt stinging nettles on the backs of my legs. I dropped both buckets and turned around.

The bully was on top of me, stinging me all over my bare arms and legs. Naomi climbed over the stile, screaming, "Leave my brother alone!" So the bully chased her down the path with his nettles.

At that moment, the witch appeared, shouting and waving her stick in the middle of the path. My sister ran back to me. We were in a terrible state. We burned from the nettles. Our buckets lay on their sides beneath the stile. All the berries had fallen into the mud. But the bully was gone, running across the field, as fast as his legs would take him.

By the time we gathered our senses, the witch was upon us. "That guttersnipe! I'll be paying Mrs. Bates a visit, just you see. She'll give that Billy what for." My sister and I wanted to run, but we couldn't.

"Here, let's rub some of this on those wee legs of yours and on your arms." The witch took dock leaves growing by the stile, and rubbed my sister's legs with them. I took some, too and soon the sting went away. "You'd better get home now before your mother finds out you're lost."

We took more dock leaves and continued rubbing while we ran home as fast as we could. Mother stripped us, washed us, and put us to bed.

The next morning, we found three buckets on our front door stoop, brimming with fresh blackberries.

My dad said, "The fairies picked them". I wasn't so sure.

That afternoon, he took a blackberry pie across the road. As for us, at teatime we ate big slices of blackberry pie, slathered with fresh, thick cream.

Two

Parachutes, Spies, and Bogeymen

The Ack-Ack Emplacement

One day, our dad came home in soldier's uniform. He had volunteered for the Home Guard. He looked smashing in khaki. I was so proud of him.

Our Finchingfield constable, "the Bobby", rode his bicycle through the village and up our way blowing his whistle. That told my father to throw on his uniform and get to the village on the double, where he caught a lift to his post at the anti-aircraft battery on the hill.

Sometimes an airplane flew over low enough for us to see the red, white, and blue circles on the wings. When we saw the pilot, we waved. Sometimes the pilot waved back. Some airplanes had double wings and sputtered and banged.

When planes buzzed low over us, we had a lot of fun. The older men shook their fists in the air and patted each other on the back and laughed. In those days, no one thought of shooting at anyone. Dad said, "This is a silly war. It'll be over in a few weeks."

Dad started going to the battery more often. He had to watch and listen for enemy planes. The lookout post had a big chart showing the shapes of the different types of aircraft. My father spent hours studying the chart and keeping a lookout with his binoculars.

Since 1938, Naomi and I had been attending the Montessori Class at St. Christopher's Preparatory School in nearby Braintree. When we weren't in school, Dad took us to his post on the hill. He let us sit up behind the double gun called an "ack-ack". The place was exciting, with its trenches and sandbags to climb around and jump from. Some of the older men didn't want us there because our dad told them to watch their language.

One day, when Naomi and I were having fun chasing around the sandbagged gun emplacement, an airplane flew over low. Amidst the usual shouting and scurry of activity, we heard a whistling sound, then, a loud "Whoomph!" Sand and rocks rained down on us. The ack-ack pounded out its "Pom! Pom! Pom!" Dad shouted, "Children, get down in the trench. Now!"

That time it wasn't a game. From then on, whenever the policeman came riding his bike and blowing his whistle, our dad went to his post alone. We stayed home.

FATHER GOES TO WAR

We almost never went for walks with our parents any more. Instead, while Naomi and I spent time in our room under the gable, they played tennis or shouted at each other downstairs.

One night, we heard a crash, and Mother screaming, "There won't be any more money from Denmark. Get a job or join the bloody army".

He shouted back, "You know the army won't take me with my bad feet."

Another plate smashed against the wall. "Damn you. The least you can do is try." The front door slammed.

Naomi and I sat at the top of the stairs, shivering. "Get back to bed, you two", Mother screamed at us, "before I come up there with the hairbrush".

Silently, we cried ourselves to sleep.

Next day, Daddy was gone.

He was gone for a very long time.

Weeks later, when we saw my dad, he was wearing a different uniform. As we ran to meet him, he got down on one knee, put down his packsack, and lifted both of us into his arms.

Mom and Dad hugged and kissed, right there in the middle of the road. I tried to pick up my father's pack. I could barely move it. He picked it up and slung it over his shoulder as easy as could be. My father was the strongest man in the world.

Soon Mom said, "Why don't you children go to Mrs. Turner's for me? I'll write out a list." I really wanted to stay and visit with my dad, but I also knew that he and Mom wanted time alone. So, with the shopping bag between us, off we went to Mrs. Turner's greengrocer shop.

This time we didn't dawdle. We ran through the village up to Mrs. Turner's. Out of breath, we told her the good news that our dad was home. Mrs. Turner gave us a big glass of sweet lemonade, reminding us to drink slowly or we'd be sick. The walk home with a heavy basket took a long time, even though it was mostly downhill.

The next few days were like old times. We went for long walks. Dad took us up to visit his old buddies at the anti-aircraft station. He managed to buy some petrol and took us for a ride in "Bessie", our 1928 Morris Oxford. But this time, we had to stop at roadblocks and show papers. The next day, we left the car at a horse and carriage stable in the village.

Months later, when we next looked at Bessie, she was up on blocks in the buggy stall at Swan House, covered in cobwebs and straw. Her tires were gone as well as half her motor.

My father's visit was all too short. Just a few days later, in the morning, a soldier came to the door. A lorry waited outside. Naomi and I ran out to see. Dad squatted down in front of us with his pack, "You children look after Mommy. I must go away for a while," He stood and hugged Mother extra long, then someone offered him a hand to jump into the back of the lorry.

Everyone waved goodbye. "Don't you worry, sweetheart," one of the soldiers called out, "your soldier boy'll be back in no time." Then off they drove in a cloud of dust. My dad was gone.

Later, Mother told us that Dad had gone to fight in the war in Africa. Almost overnight, we were too old for "Mommy and Daddy". They were both gone and we had "Mother", and a father who no longer came when we called in the night.

I didn't think of deserts and tanks. I saw only jungles, savannahs and giraffes like those I'd seen in my baby pictures from Tanganyika.

I wanted to go with my dad.

Brave English Soldiers

In the weeks to come, hundreds of evacuees from France, Belgium, the Netherlands and Denmark, fleeing bombing and Nazi occupation, passed through Finchingfield, on the way north. They traveled in busses and in the backs of open lorries. They lined up to use our privy, then sat in the hayfield next to our house and ate bag lunches.

Mom – almost "Mommy" but warmer for now than "Mother" – took charge of the local first aid post as part of civil defence. She busied herself with Red Cross nurses, changed bandages, and talked to evacuees. Because she had gone to school in Denmark, France and even Germany, Mother sometimes spoke in languages we couldn't understand.

For the most part, the evacuees were mothers with small children, and elderly men and women. We heard one panicky English lady tell Mom the Germans were coming.

Whenever we fell and scraped ourselves, Mom used Dettol to kill "Germans". Naomi and I had been sick with German measles. We really didn't understand what kind of "Germans" could be coming to make people so afraid. I imagined giant ugly creatures with green arms and long spiky fingers. For all the geography Dad had taught us, I didn't know Germans were people.

As we no longer attended St. Christopher's Preparatory School and Montessori class, someone's mother or older sister bussed Naomi and me and several other children to another school in Braintree. We attended what the English would now call a "state school". (In North America, this would be "public school.")

Private or public, the teachers were often bad-tempered. The bigger children got caned on their hands, and the little ones got paddled on their bottoms. In adjoining classrooms, divided by a big, windowed partition, we all stood to sing "God Save the King" and recite the "Our Father – Thy king-dum-cum, thy wilby-dun, ... deliver us from eagles. Amen".

Sometimes we sang a hymn such as "Onward Christian Soldiers" or "Gladly, the Cross-Eyed Bear".

And we prayed for the brave English soldiers, who got killed for us every day. We also knitted for the soldiers. I produced a khaki scarf for a midget.

The German Pilot

The day finally came when Mom picked us up at the school bus and, instead of taking us home, she took us to Swan House, a small farm on the other side of the village pond where all our things had been moved. The house had its own well with a water pump. It had an indoor toilet, but its bucket had to be emptied every day by the gardener.

Floss Halls was a cleaning lady from the village who came to 'do' for my mother by cleaning and washing. She told funny stories about people and animals that made Naomi and me laugh. Sometime around that move, my birthday came. Finally I was big enough to get a red scooter. Now I could ride to and from Mrs. Turner's greengrocer shop and glide most of the way home with a basket hanging from the handlebar. Coming down that steep hill, I rode the brake. There were very few cars on the road.

Best of all were the barn and two horses. Joyce was Mom's mare; Nellie the pony was Naomi's and mine. Now and then, the gardener hitched up the little surrey and Mom, Naomi, and I went riding down country lanes. We fed our pony green apples from the big apple tree in the orchard, juicy carrots from the garden, and sugar lumps which we took from the kitchen – when Mom wasn't watching.

Late one afternoon, while we rode our horses, Joyce threw Mom. Because her leg was badly hurt, Mom rode Nellie, and led Joyce by her halter all the way home. Naomi and I walked.

A doctor bandaged Mom's leg and a nurse had to come look after all of us. She wasn't the nice young nurse we had when we were sick in bed at Willets Cottage. This one was much older and grouchy. My sister and I spent a lot of time in the barn, playing in the hay and brushing Nellie. When the gardener came around to empty the toilet bucket and clean out the horse stalls, we let him brush Joyce. When the nurse called us, we often hid in the hayloft and pretended not to hear.

One sunny afternoon, I climbed up the apple tree and tried to reach a big green apple that had grown just far out enough that I couldn't quite grasp it. Naomi called my attention to airplanes buzzing at each other in the sky. A German bomber and an RAF Spitfire were coming down with smoke trailing behind them. From my niche in the apple tree, I watched everything. As soon as white puffs appeared in the sky, I climbed down. Close by, I could see one of the parachutes. Beneath its strands a German pilot slowly dropped, swinging back and forth. Before he landed, Naomi and I ran into the house to tell Mom – she was already on her way to the village green.

Nurse ordered us to stay in the house. Then she ran off to call the Home Guard, screaming, "The invasion! The Germans are coming!" People had been talking about a German invasion for weeks. Maybe this was the start of the invasion.

As soon as she disappeared, my sister and I ran out to have a closer look at all the fuss. While the German clenched his injured arm to his chest, Mom had a look at his leg. He must have smashed into the war memorial when he landed. He was very close to it and his parachute was tangled on the monument.

Mom said something to one of the other ladies. Next thing, we were all going home with the pilot supported between two men. Mom offered him a chair at the kitchen table.

"These little blonde angels must be yours," he said to Mom in English as he ruffled my hair. " For a moment, I thought I'd landed in heaven."

While Mom busied herself with cotton wool, Dettol and bandages, villagers gathered in our kitchen. They must have been surprised to hear the visitor speaking English.

The stranger smiled at my sister and me. "I say, I haven't had a proper cup of tea in ages."

"I'll put the kettle on", Mom replied as she limped over to the sink pump and filled the kettle.

"What the devil happened to your leg?" the German asked.

"Ach! Herunterfallen." (I fell.) Mom's answer surprised everyone.

"Sie sprechen Deutch?"

"Da ich ein Kind war." (Since I was a child.)

Smiling, the parachutist returned to English. "I read at Cambridge before joining the Luftwaffe."

Just then the nurse returned, followed by a rather out-of-breath policeman. "We're just about to have some tea. Would you care to join us? It won't take long." Mom invited the bobby and nurse to sit down.

"Oh, I'd love a cup", replied the constable.

The nurse just stood and glared at my mother. "I'd rather not." She turned and walked out. A moment later, she came back, only to say, "I'll be back for my wages, if you don't mind, when Jerry's not here."

With that, she was gone.

After the German left with the bobby and a couple of the Home Guard, we all went off to the First Aid Post in Spring Mead. There Mom spoke to the other three Germans. One of them had bitten off part of his tongue and couldn't reply.

Spies and Nasty Bits

Shortly after the parachute incident, many villagers snubbed us. When we went out for walks - which was not often any more - people moved to the other side of the road or turned away and whispered in small groups.

When part of a German airplane crashed in a field just behind our home, the curious villagers came to see and one of the children walked over to Naomi and me and said, "Your mother's a bloody German spy." Angrily, her mother told her, "I told you to stay away from them".

Scared, I raced home and asked Mom if she was a German spy.

"Of course not. Sometimes we sing little songs I've taught you in Danish or German or French. Or that little African song we used to sing. Some people don't like what they can't understand or anyone who is different. Never mind them. They're just guttersnipes."

Despite what Mother had said, I promised myself I'd never speak any language but English.

Funny, I don't remember being afraid despite the adult hysteria going on at the time. I only remember a sense of excitement. Perhaps I was too young to be really afraid. The one German I'd met so far seemed a friendly enough chap.

At school in Braintree, we learned Scottish dancing and sang "God Save the King", "Rule Britannia" and "Land of Hope and Glory". We learned that the world belonged to the English, who had "civilized the savage nations." Also we heard stories about good King John and Oliver Cromwell and found out that Napoleon was a madman, just like Hitler and Mussolini and that Japanese bloke.

Some of the older children dressed up and sang songs by Sir Arthur Sullivan. I was six or seven when I first was exposed to "For He Is an Englishman" from *HMS Pinafore* and to *The Mikado,* where everyone had silly names.

We were fortunate indeed we had "chosen" to be English.

Swan House had a cellar containing a large coal box and several old wooden tea crates. The cellar was full of cobwebs. Naomi and I were terrified of that place. One night I woke up screaming. I had walked into the dreaded cellar. German spies, little men with sharp teeth, reached out at me from the coal box.

Frequently, we saw Mom crying. Both Naomi and I said, "If only Daddy were here." Finally, Mom grew exasperated when we asked, for the umpteenth time, "When's Daddy coming home?"

She replied, "Your father's dead." Her tone was so cold we didn't ask again.

Naomi and I walked to the far end of the orchard and cried. Mom came out to find us. She hugged us both and we all cried.

The next day, the gardener made a hutch. Soon we each had a rabbit to look after. We fed our bunnies dandelions and grass and watched them get fat. Sometimes we took them out and let them run around on the grass. One morning when we went to feed our bunnies, the hutch was empty. We called all over - until the gardener walked out of the barn with two freshly skinned rabbits and brought them to Mom at the kitchen door.

We had often seen skinned rabbits hanging outside the butcher shop, but we hadn't expected to see our own bunnies dead like that. The gardener had been our friend. Now we stayed out of his way and hid when we saw him coming. Mom's involvement in the killing made me less trustful of her, too.

I don't remember eating rabbit pie or rabbit stew. Then again, Mom may not have told us what we were eating.

One night an incendiary bomb dropped on our barn. The horses screamed. When Mom ran outside, the air raid warden sent her back into the house. Flames shot up everywhere. One of the horses was killed outright; the other was taken by the Home Guard.

Next day, some village children ran past our house and sang, "Serves you right. Your horse is dead." I hated them for their horridness. Worst of all, everything I loved was being taken from me and Mother would no longer comfort Naomi or me.

I climbed as high as I could into the apple tree. When Naomi called me, I pretended I couldn't hear her. I wanted to be caught and spanked and loved. But Mother didn't bother with me at all.

Indeed, I wished I were dead. I fantasized my own funeral although I'd never attended a funeral nor known anyone who had died. Perhaps I remembered the funeral in *Little Women* and how sad that scene made me feel when we saw the film and our own world was falling apart. Sometimes I'd hum the theme music and cry myself to sleep.

My funeral would be like this: The day would be rainy and cold as they lowered my coffin into the deep earth. Mother would cry and cry. But there would be nobody to hold her and comfort her. Then she would know how lonely I had been and how much I wanted her to love me. No one would be able to stop her constant sobbing. She would beg me to come back. But I wouldn't. I would go off to be with my dad and the angels. Mother would be alone, and it would serve her right.

Eventually, Mom came and called me down. I knew I was in for a good spanking. Instead, she just hugged both of us – for a long time.

Not long after that, while we played in the schoolyard, at recess or lunchtime, an airplane came out of the clouds and dove at us. Everyone screamed; there was a lot of noise. Something or somebody knocked me down. My leg hurt. Cars and ambulances arrived and Mom came to pick us up. A bullet from the Nazi strafe plane had grazed my knee. I was lucky I hadn't been killed.

I had to get stitches in my knee. The doctor said I was a brave, wounded soldier. I felt very proud to be a wounded English soldier. Naomi and I didn't go back to school for weeks after that.

After staying home for my knee to mend, we were sent to the two-room school in Finchingfield. Though a glass partition divided the classes, we all assembled for singing and Highland dancing – jig and reel – point-toe-heel-skip-turn. Arms flung high. I loved Highland dancing.

Three

Bombs, Boarding Schools and Deep Dark Secrets

The Headmaster's Parrot

Soon after the incendiary bomb incident, Mom got a job in a sausage works, then in a munitions factory. The other workers called our mother "Mrs. Lah-de-Dah". She, who had been brought up with everything fine – with maids and a gardener and cleaning women and a trust account from Denmark to pay for it all – now had to work with the class of people she so often despised.

Naomi and I were sent off to an old English mansion that had been turned into a Catholic boarding school run by teachers who hadn't had the "good fortune" to be called into the army or to serve as officers in His Majesty's Royal Navy or to be shot from the sky in flaming Spitfires. The men and women who taught at *Saint Whatsername* were a miserable collection of rejects. Every one of them seemed to hate children.

From the smallest to the oldest boarder, we were given castor oil regularly, whether we needed it or not. This gave me bad stomachaches and sometimes the runs.

We had regular bath nights, but more than five inches of water was unpatriotic. We younger children lined up for our three-minute bath in the same water that ten before us had used. The water was usually cold and filthy. One matron washed our necks and ears; another rubbed us vigorously with a soggy towel, inspecting our bums to make sure we had rid ourselves of all the newsprint ink from sheets of newspaper we used to wipe ourselves. (Toilet paper was a luxury I only discovered when we came to Canada.) One word of complaint and we got whacked on our bare bums by a matron with a bamboo cane. Even babies got whacked. Being naked invited whacks. Nakedness was badness. If you talked while naked, you must have said something bad, something dirty.

Mother wasn't happy when she came to see us. Naomi and I received terrible school reports. We were homesick. We weren't making friends. Often we lined up to get caned on our hands for all sorts of things we did wrong or didn't do at all. Despite our age difference, my sister and I were placed in the same form; as a result, we were way ahead for some subjects and behind in others.

While our form prepared for First Holy Communion, Naomi and I were not to participate. The school didn't have our baptismal certificates. Grandpa, a priest in the Church of England, had Christened us while we were still babies. But that didn't count. While the other children attended catechism, Naomi and I were sent to scrub pots and to sweep and dust and set tables.

I wanted to learn what the other children were being taught. So I borrowed the little *Catholic Truth Society* booklets from the back of the church where we went regularly for Mass and Benediction. I read the booklets sitting on the toilet and faithfully returned each one when I finished reading it. I read all about purgatory and popes and Protestants and the English Catholic martyrs and how God loved me.

One day we were taken on a field trip to visit one of the old mansions where Jesuits hid from soldiers in their secret "priest's holes" behind hidden doors and under carpets. This made me think I could be a martyr some day. Everyone would love me, then, and say nice things about me.

In the middle of a daydream, I was called from class to go to the headmaster's study. Those of us who had never before entered the headmaster's "sanctum sanctorum" (Holy of Holies) regarded the place with awe and dread.

As I approached the door, I heard an awful fuss. I knocked, my knees shaking. I could barely stand.

"Come."

I opened the door a crack. There, in a huge cage, a macaw climbed about, beak and claw, screaming obscenities at a large orange cat which sat grinning like Alice's Cheshire on the back of a green chesterfield.

From behind a huge desk, the headmaster scowled. He was thin as a string. His face, blanched like a plant grown in deep shade. He had bushy white eyebrows. Mutton chop sideburns flared out beneath a mop of unruly white hair.

His voice sounded hoarse, like he had cobwebs in his throat. "Milne, empty your pockets." Wondering why, I obeyed – and surrendered a couple of *Catholic Truth Society* booklets.

Whatever else I possessed didn't matter. The headmaster called in one of the teachers, a miserable old woman with teeth like tumbling tombstones. Her hair was all wrapped up in a tight bun and stuck through with huge knitting needles. While she glared at me, her hands pinched at one another like quarrelsome crayfish.

The headmaster pulled a light bamboo cane from the umbrella stand behind the door and swished it a couple of times through the air. He seemed to enjoy my terror. The woman sniffed loudly. At a signal from her boss, she grabbed me by the hair, pulled my pants down, and forced me, struggling, over the arm of the chesterfield.

"The more you struggle, the worse it's going to be," she hissed. The moment of stark terror while I waited for the caning to begin seemed like forever.

Then it began. I screamed.

My scream nearly drowned out the macaw's screech.

Others who had been "whacked" had warned me not to make a sound. That meant more licks. But I wasn't able to follow that advice. Nor was I able to sit down for a long time. Naomi was also implicated. She got caned too, along with a couple of others. But I was considered the ringleader of this band of thieves. So I stood for my meals at a table by myself, hating that cursed parrot.

The headmaster said we had stolen many books, at great loss to Holy Mother Church. The school had been so good to us heathens, and we'd dishonoured its trust. I was a thief. I'd end up in the fires of hell. This was a foretaste. "As your backside burns, think of hell."

Uncle Sigvard

Whether we were expelled or Mother pulled us out, that school was no longer suitable. And because of the war, Mother could no longer look after us, nor could she afford to send us to any more boarding schools. Naomi and I went to live with our Uncle at Ealing, in the heart of West London.

Sigvard was Mother's half-brother. Sometimes, he lived like a millionaire, despite the war. Other times, he was church-mouse poor. At one time before the war, he had headed his own film studio in Hollywood, California. Apart from working on a variety of inventions to do with film and x-rays, he was a cameraman for Ealing Studios. My uncle was pudgy but not fat. He had very wavy hair and a cigarette forever dangling from moist lips, which had bubbles of spittle at the corners. His sky blue eyes could see right through me, and his hands forever pulled me to his smoky tweed jacket. The pockets contained sweets he slipped to me one at a time with a wink.

Mother asked her brother to get her a job in film. She was sure she could be a movie star. But, despite many promises, Uncle Sigvard didn't get her what she wanted.

When we first moved to London, we were sent to a local school, even rougher than the last boarding school. I thought I was fitting in quite well, but Mother complained we were starting to sound like the London guttersnipes. Boys played warplane "dog fights" in the schoolyard. We were all Spitfires; no one wanted to be a Messerschmitt. Aiaooow! Pta! Pta! Pta! Pta! When that school was bombed, we were glad. We borrowed books from the mobile library and stayed home.

Living with my uncle was a whole new adventure. Not only did he take me with him to shoot film, he put me into some movie "co-op spots". I once got to sit on a barrel eating a banana made of a sugary paste. There weren't any real bananas during the war. Uncle Sigvard also took me to movies and bought me sweets to eat during the film while he smoked his cigarettes. Naomi usually stayed at home with or without a sitter.

While living with my uncle, I got to be in Cubs. Uncle Sigvard knew Lord Baden-Powell and had been a Scout leader. At that time, Boy Scouts acted as air raid wardens and as organizers for recycling drives. We Cubs collected newspapers, string, and foil from cigarette packages for the war effort. I remember a Cub outing where we camped overnight in a farmer's barn and played parachutes, jumping in the hay. My uncle was one of the overnight leaders but we had nothing more to do with cubs or campouts after that one outing.

My Uncle Sigvard was one of the few people anywhere who still owned a car. Driving for pleasure was not allowed. One day, he had to make one of those "necessary" trips – to film for the War Department, or something like that. He returned home by bus. The government had labeled his car "unnecessary", put it up on blocks, and removed the tires and rotor arm. If the Germans had invaded at that time, they would have had a hard time finding ground transportation.

Trevor was probably sixteen or seventeen when he came to live and work with my uncle. I envied the attention Uncle Sigvard now showed his assistant, attention that once had been mine. Even though Trevor was kind to my sister and me and sometimes gave us money and ration tickets to go out and buy sweets, I hated him. Instead of sweets, I often bought *Boys Own* magazines – a popular magazine full of stories and pictures for boys.

From the fireplace mantle - where Trevor left piles of change - I took half a crown. When questioned about my newly found wealth, I said I found it on the street. Trevor knew I stole his money. But my uncle took my side and let me keep the silver piece. I was one up on Trevor.

A mother and her daughter, who had escaped to England from one of the Nazi-occupied countries, came to spend a couple of days with us. The little girl spoke no English. She slept in the same room with Naomi and me, and cried all night. I hated the intrusion. Here was someone else demanding my uncle's attention. I felt unsympathetic towards the little "crybaby". I shushed her. Fortunately, I couldn't say mean things to her; she couldn't understand a word I said. I just wanted her to stop crying.

Farting Through Gas Masks

For Londoners during the 1940 – 41 Blitz, clear skies meant a restless night. Thick cloud, once so depressing, promised relief and a night's sleep.

Whoever went out at night, walked in darkness. White lines on curbs, trees, lampposts, and even on the mud guards of busses helped us to find our way without bumping into things. Just a tiny crack in people's curtains provoked the air raid warden to shout, "Put that bloody light out!"

There were sandbags all over London, trenches in the parks, and sticky paper strips criss-crossed on all windows. Sandbags and trenches were to provide shelter and protection from blasts and bullets. Sticky paper was to lessen the danger of flying shards of glass.

For us kids, daylight air raids offered welcome breaks from boring lessons. With the first wail of the siren, we walked single file and in silence to the cellar, or to the space under the stairs, or to the civic air raid shelter. Headmasters and Matrons counted heads then checked us off against school registers while teachers stood in the falling dust and bits of plaster to lead us in rousing choruses of "One Man Went to Mow" and "Hitler Has a Bunion" as we did our best to drown out the screaming bombs and sounds of destruction above us. I'll never forget the old man who sat in the dark in one London shelter, hardly able to muster the breath necessary to whisper, "Don't forget your gas mask."

We carried our gas masks wherever we went. We soon discovered we could make excellent farting noises by blowing hard through our gas masks. Since so many of us were farting during gas drills, the teachers couldn't sort out anyone in particular for punishment until we were ordered to "Take those bloody things off!"

In the shelters, people often sang. Where there were electrical plugs, some regulars brought a wireless and we listened to George Formby, Gracie Fields, Vera Lynn, "It's That Man Again" (ITMA), Tommy Handley, Henry Hall, Tessie O'Shea, Mrs. Mop, and Claud and Cecil. As counterpoint to this, we kids ran noisily about and got underfoot, while bossy grown-ups yelled at us to settle down or to blow our noses.

When we lived on the outskirts of London near Croydon and didn't have a cellar, we had a shelter in the back garden. Measuring about 5' by 8', the pit was covered with corrugated tin and sandbags then heaped up with earth. The shelter contained bunk beds, food, and other supplies to keep us through long raids.

As often as not, garden shelters held only muddy water and, perhaps, a floating doll or teddy bear or bits of soggy clothing; reminders that children had spent drier days playing house or doctor. I don't think we ever used our garden shelter except for keeping vegetables. Very few people had refrigeration. We certainly didn't. Some people lived in partially bombed-out houses with blankets and sheets hung for privacy. We visited friends of my uncle who lived with dust, dust, dust and mouldy, cracked ceilings. In the public shelters when we did have to go to them, I remember the smell of sweat, wet and soiled nappies (diapers), and the stale reek of fish and chips in old newspapers.

We children were warned a lot, about many things. "Don't pick up lost toys, packets of sweets, or model airplanes." The Germans had dropped – or so we were told – innocent looking, explosive materials into parks, fields and city streets. As soon as unsuspecting children picked them up – bam!

Mother absented herself more and more, sometimes for two or more weeks. Instead of attending school then, Naomi and I spent many happy hours reading. Because Uncle Sigvard had no faith in the shelters, he refused to go to them. Londoners had been trapped in the tube stations and other underground shelters. Some had drowned in sewage when pipes burst.

Underground tube stations had bunk beds, three high. Families undressed in public, played cards, chatted, sang, and yelled at kids to stop chasing up and down the platforms while trains whistled in and out of tunnels. Mothers searched for missing children. Sometimes children, lost, homeless and terrified, searched station to station for mothers, grandparents, aunts, uncles.

Uncle Sigvard took me one day to see where London's homeless lived. Several times he reminded me that, if it wasn't for him, Naomi and I could be living in the London tubes, scrounging for food with the other lost children. I knew I had to be extra good and always do what I was told.

We sat up during the air raids and talked. We opened the curtains and watched the fires around us. Sometimes, I accompanied Uncle Sigvard and Trevor onto the roof while they did their filming.

We saw German bombers in their daylight raids and in the beams of searchlights generated from parks all over London. I watched aerial dogfights between Spitfires and Messerschmitts high above the barrage balloons. I remember German bombers trying to destroy King's Cross Railway Station nearby.

During the times of the bombing, dogfights, crumbling buildings and great loss of life, I felt safe with my uncle. Not only that, I felt truly, gloriously alive. It all was "bang-on", "smashing".

I was unaware of the pun.

One night, during a particularly heavy raid, part of the flat was blown away. In the midst of a terrifying nightmare, Trevor grabbed me by an arm and pulled me from my bed. Just a few feet away, the floor had ceased to exist. From the pit below came flames and screams and flying dust.

After the loss of our flat in Chelsea, my uncle moved to "digs" near Croydon. Our new home was really an unused shop with rooms in the back. There Uncle Sigvard and Trevor mixed huge vats of molten lipstick, which they then poured into moulds. (My uncle had invented a new smear-proof lipstick and was producing it to sell to cosmetics shops.)

Trevor drew cartoons in lipstick all over the walls and I began to admire him. Trevor and Uncle Sigvard argued over something about the war and Trevor joined the RAF. He came to visit in his Airforce uniform and he and my uncle went out to a party with some of their friends and came home very drunk.

Trevor was shot down over the North Sea. The first time I saw a grown man cry was when my Uncle Sigvard wept for Trevor. Perversely, I was glad my competition was gone. For a while, Uncle wanted to be alone. Naomi, now seven, and I, eight, took long walks and spent a lot of time watching the planes take off and land. Some aircraft arrived with wings all shot up or on fire. One day a Spitfire almost touched our heads as it came in for a crash landing. It burst into flames against a big old tree in a park.

We always avoided the local boys and girls who ran ragged through the ruins, picking out souvenirs and pieces of shrapnel. When I found a bullet casing that made a super whistle, a big boy knocked me over and took it from me. A workman confronted Naomi and me and ordered us to stay out of bomb sites.

Bomb sites weren't the only dangerous places. Barrage balloons, weighing fifty to sixty pounds, were flown all over London to protect against dive-bombing and low-level attacks. Each balloon was moored to a wagon by a thick steel cable, strong enough to destroy aircraft that collided with them. In a wind, balloons sometimes broke away, dragging thousands of feet of steel cable. Messerschmitt 109s flew in ahead of bombing raids to shoot down the barrage balloons. I remember seeing helium-filled balloons in flames and firemen trying to save the houses in their fiery paths.

Soon we all moved to a flat near Hampstead Heath in Northwest London. I don't remember going to school there, only that Naomi and I spent hours every day exploring the area.

After she finished at the munitions factory, Mother got a job riding motorcycle dispatch in London. Following that, she worked as an ambulance driver, on call for air raids. As soon as a siren sounded, off she went. Before the "all clear" and for some time after, she dodged bomb craters, racing past burning buildings, falling debris and smashed busses while picking up wounded firemen and civilians, and rushing them to emergency wards.

When she went to work as an examiner for the British Censorship Office, she was absent for great lengths of time.

EDUCATION BY CANDLELIGHT

My ninth Christmas went by with barely a mention. We had little money and food. We seldom got milk; what there was of it, often went sour. When Mother was home, she put the sour milk in cups on the window ledge until it turned into custard. Then we ate it with sugar. The best part of getting fresh milk was taking the cream from the top. This we put it into a jar and shook until it turned into real butter. We drank the buttermilk that remained, sweetened with vanilla and sugar.

Despite the inconveniences of war, people managed to enjoy life. We laughed a lot. Uncle Sigvard had a wireless. Every night after supper, we sat close and listened to the BBC news. Later, when the Yanks came, we quickly learned the songs they sang in the pubs. "Roll me over in the clover." Mother sang them louder than anyone. She and Uncle Sigvard outdid each other with limericks and raunchy jokes.

Since we weren't going to school, Mother gave us poems to memorize and recite in front of company. My earliest introduction to Robert Service was *Bessie's Boil*. Mother had a delicious sense of humour. Some of the poems she encouraged me to memorize were not the sort a child would normally learn in school. But they were fun.

Mother gave me a fondness for language, and an ear for accents and dialects. She taught me the beauty of speech and gave me the capacity to remember good jokes as well as the fearlessness to tell them even if they shocked the listeners. Language became my private gem collection. Tact, I had to learn on my own, the hard way.

When Mother and my uncle went to a pub in the evening, Naomi and I – we shared a bedroom – sat up reading until we heard them come in, singing at the tops of their voices and shushing each other not to "wake the children".

Quickly, we snapped out the light. We were "sound asleep" when they came in to check on us.

After lights out, we read by the light of a candle on the floor between our beds. One night a candle tipped over and made a small burn on the floor. When I tried to fix it with shoe polish, it only looked worse. Luckily for me, the flat was bombed before the landlord or anyone else discovered it.

We were never happy when we spent a weekend at a faraway flat back in Chelsea with "Aunt Robbie", an old lady who wasn't really our aunt. Uncle Sigvard always wrote down our bus travel instructions to ensure we wouldn't get lost. Aunt Robbie was a widow from the Great War; worse, her only son had been killed in a jungle, fighting another enemy, the Japanese.

The woman was terribly lonely. She wore her hair tightly bound under a net, never smiled, and heaved sighs at every move. Her skin looked grey, her varicose veins showed big and deep purple, like a road map on her legs, and she snored like an old horse. Worst of all, she smelled of stale pee. Naomi and I had to sleep crammed into the same bed with her.

One day, when we arrived to keep her overnight company, her building was gone; in fact, the whole street was gone. With mixed horror and relief, we made our way back to Wimbledon, very late.

I had grown to love my uncle. At a time when the world was becoming increasingly violent and frightening, he provided security and affection. As Mother turned away, Sigvard gave me sweets, took me to movies and made me feel loved. Above all, he gave me the hugs I so sorely missed and needed. That he was a pedophile would be totally beyond my seven year-old scope of understanding. Affection that turned violent and painful would endure for much of the coming three years. The alternative of life on the blitzed streets of London was more than I could endure.

The secrets I promised to keep would remain suppressed until they returned to destroy health, career and marriage many years later.

For What We Are About to Receive

There came a time when Mother, having packed our few belongings into two small cardboard suitcases, said "Give Uncle Sigvard a hug. I've managed to find a good school for you both. I'm sure you're going to love Holly Hall."

My uncle gave us both a bear hug. He gave me an extra squeeze and a wink as he slipped a guinea into each of my trouser pockets. I was rich indeed, but sad at the prospect of another boarding school.

Holly Hall School (can't recall the actual name) was divided, according to forms, into boys' and girls' sides. At meals, Naomi and I sat at opposite ends of the hall. When I could, I caught Naomi's eye during grace and wiggled my fingers in her direction. The headmaster droned out the grace in Latin. I don't think any of us ever knew the meaning of the words. He recited the prayer as if he didn't know the meaning of the words either.

Benedicite.

Benedicite

Benedic Domine nobis et donis tuis quae ex largitate sua sumus sumpturi et concedi ut abiis salubriter enutriti tibi debitum obsequium praestare valeamus, per Jesum Christum Dominum nostrum mensae caelestis nos participes facias rex aeternae gloriae. Amen

We all responded "Amen" and sat down. Those whose turn it was to dish out the food did so. We passed each plate of sausage meat and mash until all were served. Sometimes we chewed our way through "twice-slaughtered" mutton (meat was killed once by the butcher, then again by the cook). After the headmaster rang a little table bell, we "dug in like hounds". During most meals a senior boy or girl read to us while we ate in silence. There was to be no talking during meals. We listened to such classics as "Tale of Two Cities" and "Oliver Twist", a chapter at a time. Sometimes readings were taken from Butler's Lives of the Saints. Following the main course came dessert, which was often tapioca. We associated tapioca with St. Simeon, the "pillar hermit" who lived on top of a column for thirty years, stood on one leg for a year and tied a rope around his waist so that his lower body rotted and became infested with maggots. Then he ate the maggots, proclaiming, "Eat what God has given you."

I was miserably lonely for my mother and for my sister whom I seldom got to see. Once again, my sister and I were behind in everything. For a variety of misdemeanours, such as trying to make contact with each other, Naomi and I were sent to "Coventry", which meant nobody was allowed to speak to us.

"Milne." I jumped from a refectory hall daydream with a start. Had I been discovered waving at my sister during grace? "Milne. Come get it or you'll lose it."

"Psst. That's you. You've got a parcel."

I started up to the head table and beckoned to Naomi to join me. I was handed a parcel, said "Oh, thank you", and turned to open it with my sister.

"You may open it right here, Milne."

Between us, Naomi and I opened the parcel: socks we had needed but somehow felt cheated receiving, several chocolate bars (an unheard-of luxury), and a letter. We were allowed to keep the socks which had our names sewn in on tags. The headmaster checked the letter for spending money, which would be held for safekeeping. The chocolate was to be shared with everyone (at a later date). We never saw it again.

The letter came from Mother. The chocolate was a gift from our "new father". We were told to work hard at school. Nothing else. After being given "sufficient time" with it, Naomi and I had to yield up the letter – for safekeeping.

We were dismissed to our separate tables. From there, we went to recreation, which was always organized games, then study hall until bedtime.

I just had to find out about this "new father". Who was he? What had happened to the father I'd known so long ago? Days turned into weeks. Still, there was no word.

Every Sunday afternoon we had to write letters to our mums. We also could write to our dads, provided we had their army addresses. We were allowed to write to other relatives only under special circumstances, such as when both parents were dead. Never were we to correspond with anyone else. The cost of paper, envelopes, and stamps was taken out of the pocket money that was held for us. Every week, Naomi and I faithfully wrote to Mother.

Our letters were returned to us with spelling and syntax errors circled in red. If we mentioned we were not well - or anything else negative - the sentences got crossed out until there was little left. Sometimes, when we had to rewrite a letter several times, we couldn't get it in on time for the post. Or we ran out of our share of writing paper. Staff supplied envelopes and addressed them from an office list.

There were no more letters from Mother. I liked to think she too had her paper rationed.

I still had the money from my uncle tucked away under my clothes beside my bed. I knew his address, so I decided to write a secret letter and find a way to buy an envelope and stamp and post the letter from the letter pillbox near the school.

That night, letter written, I lay awake working up the courage to get out of bed. Eventually, I put on my clothes. Then, ever so quietly, opened my drawer and felt around for the two guineas so carefully hidden weeks and weeks before.

I took everything out of the drawer and put each item of clothing carefully back. The money was gone. Then I heard footsteps. I leapt into bed and pulled the blanket up over my clothes. For a long time I lay there, waiting for the bed check and dorm inspection. Next morning I awoke fully dressed.

One Sunday afternoon, Naomi and I were called down to the grand hall. We had a visitor. Uncle Sigvard greeted us with a whispered "How would you two like to come to a pantomime?" We must have burst with excitement as we both forgot the rule against running in the school and tore off to fetch our coats.

On that glorious Sunday with our uncle, we sat in a huge auditorium, where "Buttons" introduced us to an actor who, with a flash of magic smoke, changed before our very eyes into the evil giant. The production of Jack and the Beanstalk was enthralling. I never discovered how such magic was done.

After the performance we walked and talked about magic beans and golden eggs. I forgot about the one issue I wanted so desperately to discuss. While we traveled by taxi to have tea with a friend of my Uncle, I remembered the letter still tucked in my pocket. I took it out and showed it to my uncle. He read it with a laugh. "Why do you think I came for you?" he asked, mysteriously. "I have telepathic powers. I knew all about your letter. When did you write it?"

"Several weeks ago."

"Of course! I've planned this outing for weeks now. As for your mother, she'll be coming for you very soon; you mark my words."

The day was perfect.

Partying - Burning

After tea, Uncle's friend packaged sandwiches and cake. Into a bag he popped corked bottles of ginger beer, some apples, and some sweets – all for us to take back with us to...

"Don't you worry about a thing," he said, winking to Uncle Sigvard . "We know all about boarding schools."

We said our goodbyes and happily went with our uncle to catch the bus to return to school. He came with us. At the stop before the school, we got off the bus and began walking.

At the bottom of the school grounds, a gate led into a wooded area. It was strictly out of bounds, but a wonderful place for hiding away when solitude was needed. Uncle opened the gate. We found a hollow in an old tree where we secured our bag of goodies. Then we turned back to the gate.

"We'll say cheerio here," he said. He gave Naomi a hug, then put his arms around me and squeezed very hard.

"I miss you very much, my Paddie" he said.

"I miss you, too."

I meant it. Anything was better than boarding school.

Just about every boarder at Holly Hall School - once a school for boys, now co-ed because of the war - knew that the scullery door, which led to the back of the building where the ashes and slops were kept, was never locked. The kitchen staff who also boarded at the school went out at night and frequently returned in the wee hours. Banging into pots and pans as they crept in long after blackout, slightly the worse for wear. Towards the end of term, certain senior students put up fancy barricades to ensnare the unwary returnees in a tangle of noisy utensils.

To be sure, we ate the following day's meals with great care. Some form of terrible revenge might be taken out on us by an angry cook or embarrassed scullery maid. Those unfortunates, usually intermediate students, whose turn it was to help out with kitchen cleanup, were always given an extra mountain of greasy pots to scrub. It didn't matter that intermediates were far too young to have taken part in the previous night's trickery.

Almost every student at Holly Hall School had a torch; this was common fare for reading under covers after lights out. For every torch that was ever confiscated, another was found and hidden. The huge freestanding bedding closet in the hallway outside each dormitory provided a common hiding place for contraband items. These were stashed on top and as far back as one could possibly reach, with a boost from a chum or with the aid of a chair. Objects placed there by peers were generally respected as private property. Everyone took turns boosting others up to reach for snacks, torches, and, of course, cigarettes and matches that had been pilfered on weekend visits home. Even the monitors respected our right to a safe hiding place, which they themselves had enjoyed as intermediates, even as juniors.

Monitors were selected from the senior boys and girls who had survived the years of initiations, detentions and caning, and who were now only too ready to help ensure such traditions continued. Monitors had the right to paddle juniors – even intermediates – for minor infractions rather than reporting us to staff for canings. Some of us were paddled for very minor infractions such as not giving way on a stairway or bumping into them when monitors or seniors rushed faster than we to classes. I don't know if the girls were paddled, but we boys certainly were. For punishment, we were summoned to appear before a group of monitors, then ordered one by one to touch our toes while whacks were administered. Nobody ever dared cry; it was a group thing. We had to be brave together.

Anyway, seniors were not in the habit of boosting one another up to search in high places. They had much better things to do with their time. They left us lesser creatures at peace once we learned the rules and showed them the respect due to their position in the institution's hierarchy.

After our visit with Uncle Siegvard, Naomi and I had a plan to retrieve our bag of goodies from the hollow tree in the woods. As soon as possible after lights out, we would meet outside the scullery door. It was simple to bunch up our blankets to make it look as if we were in bed.

I crouched shivering behind a dustbin as one of the seniors stood just outside the door having a lengthy smoke. The smoker was joined by another senior who pulled a large bottle of beer from his dressing gown pocket. The two stood in the shadows sharing beer and cigarette. Finally they went inside. Naomi nearly bumped into them in the hallway. She was giggling with excitement when she reached me.

Just as the two of us started off, we were stopped in our tracks by a light shining right at us. To our relief, the light came from one of two girls from my sister's dorm.

"Put out that bloody light." The voice came from the boy who occupied the bed next to mine.

The next thing we knew, there were nine or ten of us – boys and girls from both dorms. We all made a dash for it, careful not to step in puddles or bump into wooden posts or trip over rope erected to replace the iron railings which had been removed for the war effort. They were supposedly being dropped as bombs on Nazis far across the English Channel or made into Royal Navy ships to help protect North Atlantic shipping lanes. Perhaps they were being made into bayonets to rip open enemy stomachs in hand-to-hand combat. (One of our favourite boy games.) Or, saddest of all fates, they could have lain rusting in heaps next to a factory in England, never to be used for anything as useful as killing people.

The moonlight washed the grass with silver as we streaked toward the copse at the bottom of the hill. Out of breath and with much giggling and hushing, we all arrived at the hiding place where Naomi and I retrieved our prize. This was to be the price for some short-lived popularity within our own groups.

We sat on stumps or stood against the tree and shared our feast. One of the boys passed around a cigarette – a "dog's end". We competed to see who could muster the mightiest drag and hold it down the longest. This sent one or two first time smokers into fits of coughing and slaps on the back, accompanied by much laughter. Someone farted. More laughter. This started a barrage of farting and meowing noises. One of the girls imitated the voice of the matron: "Give me the instruments with which you are making those rude noises." More fits of laughter.

Our hilarity was brought short by the wail of the air raid siren. Since everyone had to be ushered into the lower hallway under the stairs, our absence surely would be discovered. On the other hand, we conjectured, maybe we wouldn't be missed. Fat chance of that happening. Since it was too late, we might just as well stay and sneak back at the "all clear".

We watched the searchlights combing the night sky, heard the "room-room-room" of German bombers, and saw lines of tracer bullets from the antiaircraft battery nearby. Shells spattered about us like fireworks. When we heard the shrieks from the fluted fins of falling bombs, we instinctively dropped to the ground.

With each explosion, the earth shook. My fingers dug into the dirt. I heard the high-pitched scream of a large, oil-filled incendiary device – and held my breath. It slammed into a rise, much too close for comfort. A furnace burst open; smoke and flames leapt into the night sky.

I wet my pyjamas, swallowed hard to lessen the lump in my throat, and fought back my tears.

Nearby Naomi cried. "Won't do. Won't do."

Then – silence.

Eventually, I heard an "all clear". Once more, silence reigned. Someone cried. Another said, "Oh, shut it, will you?" Still another giggled, "Oh, shit! I'm shot!" Two or three snickered nervously at the alliterative joke. Most people, however, kept quiet. My hand bled where I'd scraped it while grappling with the ground.

Then someone pointed. "Look! The bloody school's on fire!" Sure enough, flames leapt from the upper story.

"We'd better get back."

"We're for it now."

"Oh, bloody hell."

"Would you shut up."

We made our way to the back courtyard. Already, a bucket brigade was in full progress as fire engines clanged their way up the driveway.

"What the devil are you doing here? Get around to the front of the school with the rest of your form." It was one of the teachers. What had been drizzle became a downpour. We moved quickly. Before long, we realized that it wasn't rain descending on us but water from the fire-hoses.

"Where have you lot been? The whole staff's been looking for you."

Eventually, we all assembled in the chapel in pyjamas and dressing gowns and blankets. In a daze, I heard the headmaster addressing the raggle-taggle student body. He muttered a few words about some of the unfortunate victims who'd been caught by the suddenness of the attack.

My sister's dormitory-mates had not managed to evacuate on time. A number of children and one staff member had been sent to hospital. Fortunately, they were expected to be up and about within a few days. Several dormitories were gone as were some staff sitting rooms, classrooms, and part of the refectory. But the library and chapel had been saved.

Teachers, head staff, and a number of seniors were black with grime from helping to put out the blaze. Several had bandaged hands and arms. They received congratulations for their excellent effort in saving most of the school from utter destruction and stood for a round of applause.

Then the hammer fell. "A number of you will be going home. Some will be transferred to other schools. As for the truants, those of you who spent part of the evening having a jolly old time at our expense will kindly step forward."

Slowly, shamefully, we made our way to the front of the chapel. We stood in silence. "You may all stand here, so the rest of the school might see you in your disgrace."

Time ticked painfully.

At the appointed time, bamboo struck flesh. As each teary-eyed face reentered the hall and met mine, my stomach sank another foot. I felt like throwing up. "All your fault," a former *best friend* muttered as he passed me. Then Naomi went in. Stroke after stroke descended on her. I tried to block out her screams.

"You!" the headmaster bellowed at me. "Do you realize we had people looking for you in that blaze? I'm going to make you wish ... Take down your bottoms."

I backed away, shaking my head in refusal. The matron stepped forward and grabbed me by an ear. She threw me onto the table and grabbed me by both wrists, holding me firmly so that my entire upper body was face down. I kicked wildly as the headmaster yanked my pyjama bottoms to the floor. Someone else had to come in and hold my feet before the caning could begin.

Four

Change of Name;

Change of Nationality

1945

Khaki Soldiers Singing

Khaki Songs

One day, a pimply-faced Canadian soldier came to take us to our new home in Sussex. Too young to shave, but brimming with importance, he declined to answer our questions.

Through the countryside of pillboxes, checkpoints, and barricades, he flew the jeep over bumpy roads as if we weren't there. Maybe he was late. We hung on, dust blowing in our faces. Our two small suitcases slid and banged from side to side as we swerved around corners.

The kid spoke up only when he delivered us to Mother. "*Voilà Madame, vos deux enfants.*" Then he squealed off in a cloud of dust.

Naomi and I suddenly had to get used to our new names. My first name was to be Benoît – no resemblance to Paddie, and our new surname was Bertrand. Benoît Bertrand. Already I hated the name.

It was September 1943. We were taken into Horsham and registered in the Catholic school. Transportation was not provided to Catholic school students. We were to walk the two miles to school and the two miles home, without dawdling. Furthermore, we were forbidden to accept rides from servicemen, be they British, Canadian, or American. Broadbridge Heath was a small village, an hour's walk from Horsham, within easy reach of Aldershot where the Canadians were stationed.

On the road, we passed khaki lorries filled with khaki soldiers singing khaki songs. When it rained – which it did often – lorries and jeeps roared past, soaking us with muddy spray. Our only reward for this came when Canadian and American soldiers driving by in convoys tossed us sticks of gum. But Mother always made us spit the gum out. "Get that disgusting wad out of your mouth!" Then she'd make us empty our pockets.

We often saw tanks on the road. I loved tanks and dreamed of being taken for a ride in one. I never was. Housewives hated the tanks, especially the American ones. They drove over lawns and flowerbeds and knocked down fences. Housewives, hands on hips, would come to their front doors and ask sarcastically, "Hello, Duckie. Are you dropping in for tea?"

When it wasn't raining, we walked through fields where blackberries grew in hedgerows. We stumbled upon soldiers and village girls "doing it" behind the bushes. "You wanna come watch?" While the girls yelled at us to "Get lost!" or "Fuck off!" we giggled and ran.

We witnessed mock battles as soldiers ran through hedgerows and in and out of clumps of trees, throwing small bags of flour at each other.

The home of the Canadian Army Overseas was at Aldershot, in Hampshire.

The entire area of Hampshire and West Sussex was a practice ground for D-Day.

As we walked home from church one Sunday morning, planes swooped low over us. Instinctively, my sister and I dove into a ditch. Covered in smelly mud, we had to undress at the back door before entering the house. The smell of manure made Mother sick.

Mother got sick a great deal of the time, so my sister and I had more and more to do in and around the house. It soon became obvious Mother was going to have a baby.

Naomi and I weren't allowed to play with the neighbourhood "guttersnipes". We spent our spare moments in and around the garden air-raid shelter. I found the nose cap of a bomb in a crater near our house. Many of the kids collected bits of shrapnel, incendiary bomb fins, and spent bullet casings. So the nose cap was a real treasure. With a large iron ring on its conical tip, it was at least eight inches in diameter and weighed several pounds. I could have traded it for gum and sweets. Mother confiscated the souvenir.

Food was severely rationed but we made do. I don't remember complaining much.

Mother sent us to the butcher with money, a note, and ration tickets. Sometimes, the butcher slipped a small packet of liver in with the salty sausage meat. Mother told us we'd learn to love liver "whether you like it or not".

People got together in groups to raise a community pig and share the benefits of saving scraps. We deposited our kitchen slops in a bucket, and a woman came around with horse and cart to collect. Since everything was valued, nothing was wasted. Sheep grazed on the commons and in the parks. I remember rabbits and chickens in many back garden pens. People fed their pets dandelion leaves until cuddly bunnies got big and fat. Then the bunnies disappeared.

Every home had a victory garden. After the milkman came by, we raced out to pick up the horse dung steaming in the morning air. At school, we grew carrots and radishes and beetroot and potatoes. Our teachers took us on outings to pick berries for jam. We also picked crab apples for jelly and rose hips for the syrup that mothers gave to babies.

At night, soldiers walked through Broadbridge Heath singing at the tops of their voices. They stopped to relieve themselves against bushes and fences and dropped empty beer and whisky bottles in flowerbeds. Warnings were posted by military police: "Drive with care; the child you hit may be your own". People complained, "Bloody Yanks! Overpaid, oversexed, and over 'ere."

Christmas, 1943, brought parcels from Canada, with clothes and food and knitted booties and baby gowns. Naomi and I were invited to meet "Santa Claus" at the Canadian Forces base. We sat on wooden chairs in a huge Quonset hut and sang carols and received bags of sweets. Santa Claus appeared with an obviously false beard that kept slipping, and a continuous "Ho! Ho! Ho! Merry Christmas!" that we had never heard before. Our concept of Father Christmas was an elfin character that resided mainly in our imaginations.

Some children were invited up to receive presents from Santa's sack. Naomi and I weren't called.

Babies and Doodlebugs

March 23, 1944, just as an air raid siren sounded, Mother determined it was time for her twins to be born. "Put on the kettle, get out clean towels and cotton wool, and scrub your hands."

Since the midwife wouldn't come during an air raid, Mother sent Naomi next door to get help. Nobody came.

At just under eleven years of age, terrified, I helped bring twins into the world. I'm not sure what I did, but I fetched hot water and towels and mopped up. There was blood and yelling. The house shook, maybe from what was going on within, maybe from a 'tip-and-run' bombing raid lost in a fog. Finally, a nurse arrived from the village. I was sent off to bed. Next day, our back garden air raid shelter, which we never used and which always had ankle-deep water in it, lay in ruins.

I told my friends at school about the miracle of the birth. They sang in my honour:

Tra, la, la boom-ty-ay,

Ben's mum had twins today.

They sucked her tits away.

Tra, la, la, boom-ty-ay.

On April 25th, 1944, Louise, Nicole, Naomi and Benoît, all declared to be the "children of François and Alicia Bertrand", were baptized according to the rite of the Roman Catholic Church at St. John the Evangelist in Horsham. The

Bishop of Pella, without asking either of us any questions to find out what we knew or didn't know about the Catholic Faith, confirmed Naomi and me on the same afternoon.

I can't remember when we made our First Communion.

In the weeks and months to come, I learned to change babies, wash nappies and prepare bottles. Naomi and I did everything but cook. We sang duets and exchanged silly jokes while washing and drying dishes and played with the babies on a blanket on the back lawn.

"Mairzy doats and dozy doats and little lamzitivy."

We splashed one another or flicked the tea towel at each other's bare legs. The sound of our fun exasperated Mother, who needed peace and quiet. When she told us off, we'd burst into uncontrollable fits of giggles.

That summer, beginning in June, "doodlebugs" – "buzz bombs" (V-1 rockets) – began sailing over Sussex, on their way to London. The doodlebug was more terrifying than all the big bombers had ever been. It "put-putted" slowly overhead. We dropped whatever we were doing and watched until the jet engine suddenly stopped. We had fifteen seconds from the time the droning ceased until the powerful blast that followed. We lay flat, covering our heads and praying we wouldn't be hit with flying shrapnel. Some large chunks would flatten houses. Mostly, those that didn't reach London left sizeable holes in farmers' fields.

Once in a while, Spitfires and Hurricanes flew up alongside and touched their wings to the square-end wings of the bombs to redirect them so they'd explode over fields to the south of us rather than over London. In horror, we watched one brave RAF pilot touch the wing of a V-1. As it exploded, it reduced his plane to a shower of flaming shrapnel.

About 8,000 doodlebugs were launched at Britain; over 2,000 of these hit London, killing more than 6,000 people and destroying about 500,000 homes.

June 6th, 1944, the sky was blackened with the hundreds and hundreds of aircraft heading south towards France. For some days before that, there had been more movement than usual of tanks, lorries, jeeps, and the amphibious lorries called "ducks". All moved in the same direction. But the hustle and bustle didn't last long. One morning, we awoke to sudden quiet.

No more rumbling of military machinery. Even the soldiers were mostly gone; the camps seemed deserted. Some girls wept in the streets. Mothers cheered. People looked toward the sky as it filled with aircraft of all sorts, including towed gliders all headed for the French coast.

The invasion of Europe had finally begun.

We stayed home from school and listened to the wireless for news from the beaches and from the small towns along the Normandy coast. The Fifth Symphony blared its V for Victory over the airwaves as BBC announcers proclaimed the people of Europe would soon be free.

We'll meet again. Don't know where. Don't know when...

Waiting In Line

Eventually, we moved back to London to await word from Canada House concerning transportation to Canada. This time, my uncle lived on Gray's Inn Road near King's Cross Station. That is where we went to stay.

While on standby notice, we couldn't leave the flat for more than short walks. The living room was always strung with washed nappies and baby clothes, which got soaked and wrung out in the kitchen sink. The flat was so crowded my sister and I had once more to share a room. This was far better for me than having to sleep with my uncle. Mother slept in uncle's room with the babies. Uncle Sigvard slept in the living room on a cot. More often than not, he stayed over with friends.

Again, Naomi and I stayed out of school. In our rediscovered freedom, we explored Wimbledon Common. The V-2 rockets terrorized Londoners. A flash of brilliant light followed by an explosion would cause us to duck to avoid shattered glass and dust from the shock waves that often followed. At home, we'd stand in the dark and gaze at the glowing skyline.

One morning, after much begging, my uncle gave my sister and me money for our first ice cream cone ever. We arrived just as the blast from a rocket destroyed a queue of over a hundred people. We saw a flash. Then we heard a whoosh and a thunderous explosion that echoed on and on. At one slap of a giant hand, the long line of men, women, and children flattened like a wall of playing cards. My sister and I had been protected from the blast by the buildings that stood between where we waited in line and the carnage around the corner.

A woman ran towards us. "Oh, thank God you're all right." She grabbed my sister. Neither of us knew who she was. A policeman came to lead the confused woman to an ambulance.

The money still in our sweaty palms, we ran back to Uncle's flat. Screams and shouts, whistles and racing ambulances echoed through the night.

The next day, ambulances were still picking up pieces of men, women and children. Glass and debris had flown outwards in all directions. A huge building had been wiped out, leaving one enormous crater.

March, 1945 — Sailors In the Icy Water

One night, long after dark, a female Canadian Naval officer "Wren" came to fetch us for our journey to Canada. We sat in the back of a blacked-out lorry with several other families. Children were allowed one small suitcase apiece. Mother was permitted two, one for herself and one for the two babies; these had been packed since shortly after our arrival in London. We weren't to bring anything but the clothes on our backs and our gas masks. Gramophone records, books, toys, paintings, all had to be left behind, to be sent on, or not, at some later date.

At Canada House, we assembled in a large room as more and more people arrived. When night turned to day, Navy Wrens served sandwiches and tea. Night fell once more and people sprawled out on their luggage. Babies cried; people lined up for washrooms. "Hey! Wait your turn." "But I gotta go." The air was filled with cigarette smoke. Some were thinner than we were and dressed in rags. Many just sat and stared at nothing, as though blind. Others chatted in strange languages.

In the middle of our second full night, we were roused and led out single file to be loaded into busses with blacked-out windows. Someone said we were heading to Portsmouth. Someone else said we would be going by train to Liverpool. Another reminded us that no one could know how or where we were going; word might get out and we'd all be sunk before we sailed past the South Irish coast, where the entire fleet of German U-boats sat waiting to blow us into the frigid March waters. Relieved at such "cheerful" news, we enjoyed dark bumpy roads. Someone began singing:

> *"Old Hitler has a bunion,*
> *A face like a pickled onion,*
> *A nose like a squashed tomato,*
> *two legs like broomsticks."*

Someone else chimed in:

> *"Hitler has only got one ball;*
> *Goering has two but very small;*
> *Himler has rather sim'lar*
> *But poor old Goebells has no balls at all."*

Another favourite was the song that the Yanks sang as they marched through the villages before D-Day:

> *"This is number nine and the baby's doing fine*
> *Roll me over, lay me down and do it again."*

As more people joined in, we felt cheerful for the first time in days. But when the driver passed along word to "pipe down, Jerry might be listening", we hushed up for a long time. Babies stopped crying.

At last we were led off the busses and into a large empty shed awash with puddles and reeking of oil. In pouring rain, we went in small groups up a gangplank to be welcomed aboard the RMV *Rangitata* (a New Zealand Kiwi name) – a converted oil tanker.

As the wife of a major with four children, Mother was awarded the privileges of an upper cabin and service at the captain's table. Most of the other passengers spent their time seasick in cramped quarters.

As soon as we sailed out of sight of land, we were summoned to lifeboat drill. Each of us was assigned a spot in a lifeboat. There we were instructed to sit, wearing our life jackets and carrying our ever-present gas masks. We were ordered away from our lifeboats and back to them several times, until deemed speedy enough to be seaworthy. Then we went for steaming mugs of hot cocoa and biscuits, "cookies" in Canadian.

While many on board ship were seasick, Naomi and I enjoyed our adventure. We hid behind the stacks and smoked Pall Mall cigarettes with a Canadian boy, sailing with his mother. He taught us the Canadian saying: "Aw, gee whiz, ma!" We tried it out on Mother – just once.

We heard stories of the Canadian prairies from sailors who had been brought up on farms where it took all day to ride on horseback from the front gate to the house. We were told how in winter it grew so cold that people spoke, then had to go inside for words to thaw out before they could be heard. We heard how in summer the mosquitoes grew so big they could pick up a cow and fly off with it - if someone didn't shoot the mosquito first.

Sometimes we hid in the lifeboats which always stood deck-level. Here we could observe without being seen. When caught, we'd be pulled out and sent running. Then we'd find somewhere else to play, away from bossy grown-ups.

One black night, shortly after sailing, Naomi and I and our friend from Canada sat in a lifeboat, peeking out from under loose tarpaulin, watching explosion after explosion as corvettes fired depth charges into the ocean. We should have been with our mothers below decks, but our mothers were too busy looking after babies so we weren't missed when the call to action stations came.

I saw ships on fire and heard men screaming in the water below our cutter. Sailors and lifeboats floated about on the icy sea amidst the flotsam and jetsam. They had struggled to the choppy surface through oil slick, debris, and frantic companions. People cried. Some were burned. Some were broken and bleeding. Nearly all were encased in oil.

In all this agony, our ship picked up no survivors. She couldn't. She would have endangered her own passengers and cargo.

As we raced along at full speed, I heard the distant thuds of bursting depth charges. I'd already heard adults say, "The U-boats are the wolf pack; we're to be sheep for the slaughter." In such tight quarters, gunnery could do little. The Royal Air Force could no longer help us out; we were probably too far beyond their reach, in that part of the North Atlantic World War II sailors called "The Black Pit".

The rescue ship had to be close by. But she couldn't come in all the way without an escort. Worse, Grand Admiral Karl Dönitz had instructed his U-boat captains to take no prisoners. The Nazis were in a death struggle as the Allies closed in to end the war.

On the deck below, a sailor remarked, "It's the graveyard watch." Another replied, "Yeah. Rightly named." I gazed out at the eerily glowing horizon. The sea stared back, cruel, heartless, and threatening. Suddenly, I felt seasick.

Only much later would we learn the frightening details of the danger we were in during that blustery March, 1945. In the months and years to come, those dangers would return to haunt us in countless subtle ways. Meanwhile, we children were awed, even excited, by what we were witnessing.

We had sailed from Liverpool on March 13th. We would not reach Halifax until March 24th.

Following "stand easy", we three rejoined our mums for supper. Naomi and I had our faces slapped. "Where were you two? I was worried, sick." We didn't tell what we'd seen. We never did.

Eventually, we docked in Halifax. For all the secrecy of our voyage, a newspaper reporter greeted us when we boarded the train in Halifax. Our picture appeared in *Le Soleil*, with a story in French, on the day we arrived in Quebec City, March 24th, 1945. The headlines in other Canadian papers, just a few days previously, read:

 "Convoy ships returning to Canada sunk by German U-boats, including the HMCS GUYSBOROUGH, LOST with 51 hands, March l7th, l945."

Wartime Crossing

Lifeboats deck level ready,

hiding place for hidden pleasures,

pilfered Sweet Caps and Spearmint gum,

beneath the canvas, hid from adult eyes.

We'd have our ears boxed, backsides booted,

depending on who caught us, if they did.

Played our dreams of Indians and birch canoes,

skis and all we'd heard from men on board

of miles and miles of prairie wheat,

cowboys, horseback Mounties, bears, wolves,

and mountains even taller than the Alps.

Enthralled, we did not hear the call to "action stations".

We were used to bombs and guns,

played bravado and were thrilled in our excited fear.

Then the hoot of ships' horns, running boots

and the thump-thump of depth charge "ash cans",

dropped to kill Donitz's boys,

slinking beneath the waves.

Peeking out we watched the flash and smoke

of battle on the frothy sea

and fired our finger guns

at submarines we could not see.

Nor could we stop to pick up sailors

screaming in the icy waves but plowed through

oil-soaked men who cursed us as they drowned.

When all was calm and we snuck out,

and when frantic mothers boxed our ears,

we said not where we'd been, nor what we'd seen.

Yet in restless sleep for nights and years to come

we'd shrink from blood-soaked hands

and see the scattered flames that brought them death.

Land of Milk and Honey

We came ashore in the dim light of early morning to be ushered into a large draughty shed in Halifax Harbour. The adults stood in long queues to have documents checked while the Canadian Red Cross doled out hot cocoa and buns. Then we were taken on busses to board a blacked-out train, cramped among crying babies and bossy mothers we didn't know. One woman screamed at nobody in particular, "Stop picking your nose, you dirty little bugger." I doubt anyone had managed a bath since leaving lodgings in London two weeks earlier. The air, blue with cigarette smoke, reeked of sweat, vomit and urine.

When we left the train in Quebec City, the day was already over. On the dimly lit platform, fresh air and light snow signalled our arrival in Paradise. Relatives greeted many with hand printed signs. Other passengers remained on the train to shuttle on to Montreal and points west. Two sisters and their two brothers had no difficulty recognizing their elder brother's new family.

Aunties Patricia and Madeleine and Uncles Louis and Emilien from our stepfather's family had two taxis waiting to take us to the family home – the upper level of a large house in Limoilou with bright lights beaming from every window. The Bertrand home was, to Naomi and me, a fairy-tale castle of magnificent proportions. With half a house for five adults, two children and two babies, this was more room than we had ever known. We were given towels and face cloths and invited to wash up. Then we were shown to our rooms. Naomi had a bed in our Aunties' room; I had my stepfather's bed across from my two uncles in another huge bedroom. Mother and the babies were given the grandparents' room. Biggest of all, this had been kept for special guests. I had never seen such high ceilings.

Patricia and Madeleine were short and slim, their voices high-pitched yet gentle. Emilien, hunched over with a limp, sported a perpetual smile. His eyes twinkled and he loved to tease. Louis, on the other hand, was silent and businesslike but as kind as his brother. Although they were bi-lingual, all four talked among themselves in rapid French. How they heard one another seemed a mystery.

Despite Mother's persistent refusal, Naomi and I were given clean clothes that had belonged to our uncles and aunts when they were our ages as if they had been saved especially for us. Mother insisted Naomi and I go to bed right away but Auntie Madeleine asked when we had last sat down to a proper meal. Mother was gently overruled. I went to the dinner table in knee britches and a warm pullover. Naomi wore a full-length dress, the babies wore new dresses, and Mother looked more beautiful than I'd seen her in a very long time.

The table was set with lace cloth and candles and we all had wine with our meal. The two sisters ran back and forth carrying heaped dishes, each outdoing the other in kindness. Naomi and I ate as if we had never eaten before, and we drank far too much wine. With all the excitement, we babbled constantly, forgetting the English rule: "children should be seen and not heard".

Mother looked embarrassed. Everyone else was delighted. We talked and talked about the boat trip and asked hundreds of questions about Canada. "Can we ski?" "Can we paddle up to Montreal and the Great Lakes in a canoe?" "Where do the Indians live?"

Aunties Patricia and Madeleine included Naomi and me in their conversations. They listened to each of us with great interest and quiet respect. Even when I wasn't talking and joining in, I felt included.

Following dinner, the Aunties wrapped Naomi and me in woollen scarves, and mitts, coats, and overshoes – surprisingly they fit – and the uncles took us for a walk in the cool night air. We could see first hand the high snow banks that lined the streets. On the way, my sister and I threw up our supper. We had to be taken home and helped into bed.

The next day, feeling much better, the Aunties fed us a breakfast of porridge, toast, butter, marmalade, big glasses of real milk, and oranges. Aunty Patricia reminded us to eat slowly and to enjoy. We were not used to such food and so much loving attention.

That day was devoted to sightseeing with Uncle Emilien and Auntie Patricia. Uncle Louis went to work at the bank; Auntie Madeleine stayed home with Mother and the babies to help them get settled. Uncle Emilien and both aunties had taken the day off work.

We went first by bus to see the Chateau Frontenac, where my stepfather had worked as a boy, and to the Ramparts with the huge sled run, where Uncle Emilien had been hit in the back and crippled for life.

The sled run had just ceased operation because of warmer weather. Despite that, I saw more snow than I had ever imagined. We explored the Plains of Abraham and the old city by horse-drawn calèche. After that, we visited the shop on Rue St. Jean where the aunts sold lingerie.

At the end of the day, we ate – and enjoyed a small glass of wine – in a beautiful restaurant. The bus ride back to Limoilou had people turning to see "*les deux jeunes émigrés de L'Angleterre*" (*the two young immigrants from England*). We didn't stop our excited chatter for an instant until we climbed the stairs, when Mother reminded us that the babies were sleeping.

In days to come, we took memorable trips to the shrine at *Ste. Anne de Beaupré*, with its 360° Cyclorama of Jerusalem on the day of the Crucifixion. With French lessons as we went, we visited *Les Laurentides*, where people went to ski, and *Les Chutes Montmorency*. On *L'Isle d'Orléans*, we ate bread, fresh baked in an outdoor oven. We also went to the Quebec Zoo.

One of the best experiences of all was a visit to *une Cabane à Sucre* where we ate *taffée d'éràble* (maple toffee) and pancakes smothered in real butter and maple syrup. There was so much to see and do that Mother had to remind us our holiday couldn't last forever. Adults had to work and children had to attend school.

Five

Running the Gauntlet

Maudit Bloke
(Damned English)

Auntie Madeleine took me to St. Patrick's School, "Home of the Fighting Irish", taught by the De La Salle Christian Brothers. Because our schooling had been so disrupted by the war, the Brother principal decided to place me in grade five, two years below my age level, for the balance of the term. He also informed my aunt I'd have to repeat the grade starting in September. Auntie gave me a bag lunch, a bus ticket, and a slip of paper with directions for getting home. Then she took Naomi to St. Monica's just down the hill from St. Pat's. My sister would be in the fourth grade which she also would repeat the following year.

To get his grade five boys interested in good literature, Mr. Sheahy read to us every Friday afternoon after recess. By the time I arrived, he was already halfway through Tom Sawyer. I enjoyed hearing the teacher read, even though Mother had introduced Naomi and me to Tom Sawyer and Huckleberry Finn while we were receiving so much of our education through the help of the London Mobile Libraries. When I mentioned this to Mr. Sheahy, he asked me not to show off by giving the story away before he'd finished in June. He told me I'd be wise not to talk more than I had to. I think he knew my accent would cause me trouble among the Irish boys.

Despite my enthusiasm for reading, I was far behind in Canadian history and arithmetic. The history I could read on my own but I needed extra help with multiplication, division and fractions. Whenever I opened my mouth to ask questions, "Please sir," the teacher would have to ask me to repeat the question and the boys would laugh at my English accent. Then they'd whisper "Bloke", "Limey", and "D.P." for displaced person. Fortunately, I made friends with Jimmy Scott who didn't mind the way I spoke and whose main interests were military history, science and mathematics. During lunch times, Jimmy did his best to help me get caught up in arithmetic and I managed to avoid schoolyard bullying by remaining inside.

Our seats were at the back of the class with the taller boys. Some had difficulty fitting into the grade five desks. I was thin but my legs stretched out in front as there was little room for my knees under the desk. Class bullies (there were a few) would step on my feet or kick me as they passed, then claim I had tried to trip them. I'd be made to stand until told to sit down. The bullies would turn and snicker while I tried very hard to ignore them.

In the days to come, Jimmy introduced me to the boys' choir. I also had a lot of fun exploring the Plains of Abraham with Jim and his younger brother, Peter. They lived with their mother in an apartment on Grande Allée, overlooking the Plains. Their dad was still overseas, as was my new father. Since their mother was out much of the time, we had lots of time to get into mischief.

One day, I helped Jimmy take a couple of shotgun shells apart and we rammed the powder into a model cannon with a wick. Then we put pellets down the barrel and fired the gun from the window. The explosion was terrific, and the apartment filled with smoke. Another day we dropped a water-filled balloon from the window onto some people on the street below.

Jim also owned a chemistry set. We experimented with hydrogen sulphide and had to leave the door and windows open to get rid of the rotten egg smell before his mother got home.

It wasn't long before Mother made me dress again in the clothes we brought with us from England. I looked more like a British schoolboy than a Canadian. Naomi was lucky. Her school required a uniform; even if she didn't sound the same, at least she looked like everyone else. In my short pants, knee socks [which never stayed up], and oversized sweater [which came from some grab box] I was as English as any English kid could be. In comparison, every other boy my age wore breeches that went to just below the knees, a parka, and a knitted toque.

The boys teased me, mercilessly. I was "Skinny", "Slim", and "Bloke". I shied away from rough-and-tumble. I couldn't catch a ball; I didn't know how to hold a baseball bat. I knew nothing about hockey; hadn't even heard of "the Rocket", Maurice Richard.

The violence of my past caught up with me in small ways. Whenever I was called to the principal's office, no matter what the reason, I had the terrible feeling I was about to be strapped, caned, or spanked. And when you look guilty, you probably are.

I tried making up for my weaknesses by asking and answering a lot of questions in class. That was not the tradition at St. Pat's; I had to be reminded to give other people a chance. Teachers were kind. Better yet, good food and loving care from aunts and uncles began to put meat on my bones.

Run Skinny Run

Transportation home each day required a transfer at the bottom of Boulevard St. Jean to the Limoilou bus. As I headed home on my own, a group of boys near the transfer stop called to me: "*Eh! 'ti gar.*"

I answered: "Sorry, I don't speak French."

That was a mistake. "*Un maudit bloke.*"

One of the boys pushed me until I fell backward over another boy crouched down behind me. Then they pounced. Blow after blow bloodied my nose and blackened my eye. A man came and pulled the bullies off me and asked questions in French. A bigger boy answered and pointed to me. The man cuffed me across the back of my head, and said, "*Va t'en!*" This I had no difficulty understanding: Get out of here.

I got out. Never mind the bus. I'd lost my transfer in the scuffle.

I ran in the direction of 18th Street and arrived home too late for supper. Mother was insistent I go without. People don't get picked on for nothing. I had to fight my own battles and if I lost a fight, I probably deserved what I got.

Later, Uncle Louis brought me up a sandwich and a glass of milk. Then he went back to the kitchen icebox to chip some ice for my swollen eye.

That night I had a terrible dream. I hid from Germans under my bed. I screamed and thrashed. Uncle Emilien shook me awake rescuing me from flames and mass murder. The next day, both uncles joked about my antics; nevertheless, they were concerned.

When Naomi and I left together for school, I had a "shiner". We caught the same busses as always and planned to meet at dismissal to return home together.

After school, I ran down the hill and waited at the gate to St. Monica's for my sister. Naomi did not show up. I thought she had left without me but she had been kept in, to catch-up on schoolwork. The Sisters were strict.

I boarded the next bus and got off at the same transfer point at the foot of St. Jean. The same gang of boys pushed and shoved one another at the bus stop. While everybody disembarked, I hid behind the last adults. The boys saw me and I made a run for it. Though I arrived home late again, I was in better condition than the day before.

That evening, Uncle Louis gave me a present. From now on I could use his bicycle to ride to and from school, and wherever I pleased. It was mine to keep. Auntie Patricia gave Naomi her bicycle. We had never owned bicycles before, but it didn't take us long to learn to keep our balance.

Naomi still preferred to take the bus to and from school. But I decided it would be far healthier and less expensive if I used the bicycle. Mother said I could keep the gift – at least for the time being.

A great many of the boys who attended St. Pat's were from Wolfe's Cove. The Cove was home to the Irish who landed at that point during the Great Potato Famine. For many years, the British had persecuted the Irish. The Brothers told tales of how the "Black and Tans" would break into Catholic homes and beat and smash in the pretext of looking for hidden arms. These were the Royal Irish Constabulary *na Dúchrónaigh*, British volunteers recruited from the prisons of England to carry out house-to-house searches and imprison those Irish who refused to belong to the Protestant Church of Ireland.

It was Ireland's troubles with the British that got me into trouble. Since I spoke with an English accent, I was the enemy.

One weekend, Naomi and I rode our bicycles along the waterfront near the Lévis ferry terminal. Someone shouted "Hey, Limey!" I recognized one or two scruffy faces from St. Pat's.

Naomi and I pedalled as fast as we could to the big hill that wound its way up to the far end of the Plains of Abraham. There we got off our bicycles to push our way up the hill. Halfway up, having taken some shortcut unknown to us, the Cove boys waited. Naomi and I turned our bicycles around and sped down the hill. The cove boys shouted after me, "Run Skinny run!" I pedalled faster and faster, my heart in my throat.

At the bottom, I misjudged the turn and crashed into a monument. Whose monument it was I am unable to say. The bicycle got the better of the deal. A kind passerby drove me home. I was in a terrible mess. Mother made us give up the bicycles.

LAC SERGEANT

As soon as school ended for the summer, we all headed to a rented cottage on Lac Sergeant. Aunties stayed with us while someone took over their shop for the summer. Uncles Louis and Emilien stayed in Limoilou during the week and came up weekends.

Meanwhile, Naomi and I rowed a "chaloupe" out on the lake and caught frogs and sunfish. We picked blueberries on the hill near an orphanage. The nuns at the orphanage seemed kind. But the flies and the smells from the kitchen brought back memories of boarding school.

Mother took sixteen-months-old Louise and Nicole and placed them naked on the sandy beach where we all sat to watch them play in sand and water as Naomi and I had played when we were babies. A prattle of women from the local parish escorted *Monsieur le Curé*, the parish priest, down the gravel road to our tiny wharf to inform Madame Bertrand that such an immoral exhibition could not be tolerated at Lac Sergent. Mother, using her most profane French, told Monsieur le Curé and his lady friends what she thought of them and their morality. They left in a huff.

Within half-an-hour, the local *Chef de Police* paid a visit. Once more but in a slightly jovial manner, Mother discussed the absurdity, tossing a few choice words into the conversation that shocked our aunties but brought delighted laughter from mon Oncle Emilien.

Still, the authorities won out. The babies wore little dresses while playing in the water. When we went to Mass on Sunday mornings at the local parish, Mother stayed home. "*Renégat damnée.*"

Back to School

All too soon, September came and summer holidays were over. The terrors of returning to school had to be faced once more. Though the war was over, many Canadian soldiers would not return for months. Worse, battles still raged in my mind. Often, while we played in the schoolyard, planes from the Air Force base at Valcartier flew over our heads. This inspired a terror in me worse than I had felt in England. Instinctively, I crouched down and covered my head. Of course, no one understood delayed emotional response. So I got scolded for "putting on an act".

The more nervous I became, the more I got picked on. Boys flew past me in mock raids and batted my head with their "wings". To their delight, I responded by covering my face with my arms.

In September 1945, I was still in grade five but with a different teacher. The Brother didn't show the same sympathy and protection that I'd received from Mr. Sheahy. I was openly laughed at in class, especially for using British rather than Canadian terminology and pronunciation. The Brother constantly corrected me. He strapped me for poorly done homework and for failing to memorize my Catechism answers. "How does God love you?" Whack!

I asked questions a boy my age had no business asking. The Brother told us about the terrible sufferings that awaited us in purgatory, even eternal damnation, if we touched ourselves in an "impure" way or if we allowed ourselves to have "impure" thoughts. "There are more souls in hell from sins of impurity than for any other sin". I was sure the Brother could gaze right through to my soul. I began wetting the bed and my bedwetting and the constant smell that went with me were a direct result of sins of impurity.

Soon we had to move. My enuresis was part of the problem, as was Mother's row with my aunties. The babies teethed on the dining room chair legs.

We moved to Sillery. Despite the upset at losing our aunts and uncles for the time being, I was delighted to discover that we were within walking distance of school.

As my aunties no longer were close by to baby-sit, Mother's patience with Naomi and me grew shorter. We only had one bathroom so bathing was limited. I went to school stinking of pee. I had to put my mattress over the front railing where people could see. In the winter months, my mattress got caked with ice. I had to turn it over many times until it got covered, not only with pee stains, but also with rust.

I don't remember how or when I stopped my bedwetting. Having nothing to drink after supper, then waking myself up with terrible nightmares and going to the bathroom may have helped. Eventually, Mother gave me a cover for my smelly mattress. Life improved.

We lived on Cremazie Street, in rooms above a store run by two elderly matrons. Afraid of moths, Mother decided to get rid of a full-length fur coat. She ordered me to take it downstairs and put it in the garbage in the alley. Instead, Naomi and I took it to the shopkeepers. The two old ladies were so delighted that, for many weeks, they supplied us with all sorts of candies and "junk": Pixy Stixs – straws full of tart sugar you sprinkled on your tongue; tiny wax Coke bottles with coloured sugar water inside; wax lips and wax buck teeth you could both wear and chew. There were jawbreakers - also known as gob stoppers – which you sucked until they turned different colours. And, best of all were the candy cigarettes, the mint ones with pink tips, as well as chocolate cigarettes and liquorice pipes.

They also supplied me with comic books, which I read in secret and traded. If Mother found comic books, she destroyed them, whether they were ours or belonged to friends. I especially enjoyed *Classic Comics*, as well as *Beano*, *Rover*, and *Hotspur*. Though I was less interested in *Superman* and other *Marvel Comics*, I read and traded them also.

We kept our loot hidden from Mother. Though we still fought over dishes and diapers and other housework, Naomi and I drew closer.

Since I didn't have any friends during that school year, apart from Jimmy Scott and his younger brother, I welcomed the school choir. Some Sundays, we sang at St. Patrick's Church.

Naomi and I walked to church every Sunday. One sunny day, my sister forgot to wear the obligatory hat or scarf, so she put a handkerchief on her head. We were both seized by fits of giggles, during which I pretended to sneeze, grabbed the hanky from her head, and loudly blew my nose.

On Monday morning, we each got called to the principal's office at our respective schools. I got the strap. As long as Mother didn't find out, we took everything in our stride and faced the world's inconsistencies together.

Nightmares and Other Antics

On weekends in the winter, we went to the Plains of Abraham and tobogganed on pieces of cardboard. On one long hill, an excellent bump sent the kids sprawling. Then someone discovered a hand sticking up out of the snow. Our "bump" was an old man who had frozen in a snowstorm. Even though I'd seen dead people before, I dreamt of that hand coming out of the snow to grab me by the penis.

Nightmares became a nuisance. My screams got loud enough to awaken the babies. Mother told me that, if I didn't stop trying to "get attention" in this way, I would have to sleep in the back shed. This didn't stop me. So Mother walked in and slapped my face when I screamed. That didn't help either. I also walked in my sleep. I strolled into my sister's room and tried to make Naomi "get out of my bed".

I was often punished for "foolish" antics. Once, when she got really furious, Mother gave me a black eye. I had to tell teachers and friends I had bumped into a door.

Naomi had her own share of grief. Mother threw her into an icy bath for not washing properly.

If we tried to defend ourselves when she slapped us, or if our hands rose, as they did in an automatic response to being swung at, Mother struck us with anything that lay handy. As most of her blows occurred when we washed and dried dishes, we frequently got hit with wooden spoons, but sometimes with pots and pans.

Though Naomi and I each found separate friends as time went on, we still went for long, exploratory walks together. Sometimes in the winter, when we returned home late and freezing cold, Mother locked us out. So I found a way to climb over the roof of a shed at the back of the shop; if my window wasn't also locked, I managed to get us in. Otherwise, we had to wait around until Mother unlocked the door. Either way, we were in for it, no matter our reason.

Mother asked me if anything ever happened when I was alone with Uncle Sigvard. I couldn't answer but shrugged my shoulders and stayed quiet. She became very angry and began to shake me and slap my face. I just shook my head and cried. Mother gave up in exasperation. If I told her, she'd hate me. She might even send me back to London.

From then on, I spent most of my time alone.

The child who is not supported or protected learns to be isolated and unsupported. He doesn't learn boundaries or how to avoid danger or how to protect himself. In seeking approval, he leaves himself open to ridicule and attack. Those who were supposed to protect me, such as my Uncle, abused me. My mother had no time for me. The aunties and uncles did not wish to interfere.

Y CAMP

At the end of the school year, Mother decided I could spend a couple of weeks at YMCA summer camp. Maybe this was a gift from the Bertrand family or from my stepfather. Uncle Louis gave me a sleeping bag. I can't recall if Naomi went to a girls' camp or stayed home. Camp in the Laurentians was a tonic. Not only were Jimmy and Peter there, I made new friends, too.

We all whispered and farted and snored and giggled during the first night. "Pipe down in there before I come in and smack the lot of you." There'd be silence for two, maybe three minutes. Then we whispered and farted and snored and giggled some more, until early morning light. After that, we just carried on – until time to get up.

I started to wet the bed again. But I wasn't the only one. Some days five or six sleeping bags were hung out to dry. Then one of the counsellors began getting us up at night, and we all felt better.

There were no girls within miles, apart from adult kitchen staff, so campers swam in the buff. During general swim, a group of us were playing Tarzan from a rope, swung out over the water. We were unaware of a hornets' nest until someone threw a stick into the bush. Wasps swarmed the waterfront. I had to be taken to the infirmary, placed on a rubber sheet, and bathed in milk of magnesia.

The camp scheduled a rest period after lunch – to be spent in our tents. This was a time for writing letters, reading comics or telling stories. Supposed to be a quiet time, it never was. One day, our counsellor, a boy in his teens, had us all laughing by jumping up and down on his bunk naked. He asked someone to pull his finger and emitted a loud fart. We split our sides laughing.

The following Sunday, Jimmy told his mother about the counsellor, and how we had all laughed and joined in. On Monday morning, the camp director called us, one by one, into his office. The counsellor had been sent home. The rest of us – all but Jimmy – were spanked.

When I was ushered in before the camp director and saw him sitting there with the miniature canoe paddle, known by most campers as "the board of education", he told me to lower my pants. I felt as though I would throw up. I just stood there and cried. It wasn't a cane but a paddle. I couldn't explain myself. I knew I had to get it over with. Surprisingly, the spanking itself didn't hurt much. What hurt more was when the director remarked on the smell of pee from my underwear. I tried to hide the fact that, despite being gotten up at night, I still wet the bed. I felt confused, dirty and terribly ashamed.

Later that morning, a new counsellor opened my sleeping bag and hung it out to dry while others from my tent were present. Jimmy and I were no longer friends.

Pirouettes and Hockey Sticks

While I was at camp, my stepfather, now Major François Bertrand, returned from Europe. Soon we moved to "L'Ecole d'Hotèlerie" – Canadian Vocational Training School for Veterans, at St. Paul l'Hermite, just east of Montreal. He had been commissioned to start the school having learned his trade at the Chateau Frontenac before the war. The place was a huge barracks, and almost everyone spoke French. Waiters in training served the meals. We had the best food and the best service because the major was big man on campus. My stepfather was shorter than I, much plumper but not fat. He was handsome with a small moustache. His English was impeccable. His men respected him.

Once again, something terrible happened to me – anal rape by a serviceman at the school – which I could only push from memory until a much later time.

We moved to a little house in Strathmore, thirteen miles to the west of Montreal and a stone's throw from Lac St. Louis. Naomi was registered to attend the English class at L'Ecole Ste. Jeanne de Chantalle close by. I was enrolled for grade six at St. Ignatius of Loyola in Montreal West. For our birthdays in May and June, we were given bicycles so we could ride to school. My trip each way was approximately thirteen miles (21 kilometres).

 On weekends, we sometimes cycled up Sources Road on the far side of the railroad tracks. The road ended at an old quarry, a favourite hangout for young couples and hot-rodders. On the bushes hung safes – "French letters", loaded and tied as trophies for all to see.

We rode our bicycles along the lakeshore, to Pointe Claire and Lachine. I spent many contented hours playing in the ruins of air force planes in the fields surrounding Dorval Airport. In the cockpits of those wrecks, I became an RAF pilot defending London from Messerschmitts and heavy bombers. Memories and imagination carried me back to dogfights I'd watched such a short time before.

We lived practically in farm country. Now tall and lanky, I dressed like other boys my age. Though my English accent was fast disappearing, Mother didn't permit sloppy speech; she made sure my sister and I spoke clearly and distinctly, often making us repeat our phrases until she was satisfied with our enunciation.

When the heavy snows came, I found it increasingly difficult to ride my bicycle the thirteen miles to and from school. My stepfather relented and gave me a train pass for the coldest months.

There was a community hockey rink in the park behind our house. Naomi and I received skates for Christmas. My sister learned to skate very quickly, but I spent most of my time keeping out of the way of the local hockey players and holding on to the boards. Gradually I strengthened my ankles enough to propel myself without mishap, except for local ruffians who enjoyed butting me over the boards and dumping me head first into snow banks.

Naomi soon had a group of friends to skate and spend time with. My best friend was Ian Knight, whose father was our Scout Master. Ian could figure skate better than any of the girls, who tried copying his pirouettes and jumps.

François Bertrand determined I would become the son fate denied him. "I don't want you playing with that "fifi" fancy-skater, at least not on the skating rink. Play hockey like a real boy for Christ sake."

Fat chance! As soon as I skated onto the ice with a hockey stick, I ended up in a snow bank or flat on the ice against the boards.

One day, a gang of rough kids chased me home. The front door was locked. The bullies beat me up on my front steps, while my mother and stepfather watched from the living-room window. He was furious that I didn't put up a fight. Definitely, something was wrong with me. He wanted a son to be proud of.

Ian did as well on roller skates in the summer as he did on the ice in the winter. Once, he let me try his roller skates. I attached the clamps to my shoes, tightened them with his skate key, and then stood. I moved slightly, my feet flew from under me, and I landed with a thump. Painfully, I removed the skates.

My one escape came through books. I devoured every book I could get my hands on. I read the Greek heroes and the Classics. I cried over Charles Dickens, Charlotte Brontë, and Jane Austen, explored with Mark Twain, Jack London, Robert Louis Stevenson, Jules Verne, Rudyard Kipling, and Sir Walter Scott. I curled up in corners at school, even stood in the school yard absorbing every Hardy Boy adventure I could borrow from friends or acquire as Christmas and birthday presents. At night, I read by flashlight under the bedcovers. I read until my eyes ached.

Some people are good with animals. I've always been good with children and babies. As one of the best baby-sitters on the Lakeshore, I made fair money looking after other people's kids. I changed and fed babies, read bedtime stories to toddlers, and wrote down telephone messages for partying parents. I was a natural. I also spent countless weekend hours pulling my baby sister, Jackie, through the snow on long toboggan rides.

Jackie was born in late November, 1947, a year and a half after our move to Strathmore. The twins, almost four years older now, hated getting stuck with their baby sister. Sometimes, to get rid of her, they initiated a game of hide-and-seek. Jackie covered her eyes, pressed her face against the wall, and shouted the few numbers she knew at two years of age. As soon as she ended with a breathless "*Cent!*" (one hundred), she ran off in all directions to find her older sisters. Louise and Nicole were not to be found; they had disappeared down the street to Majoleine's house. I took my sobbing sister to the park and pushed her tears away on the swing.

Discovering Girls

Grade Seven was the year for discovering girls. According to schoolyard boasting, every boy except me had "done it" with one of the girls near St. Ignatius. In an apple orchard some distance from the school, someone had put up a pup tent. I asked the girl with the most promising reputation if she would go into the pup tent with me. She told me I was sick, queer, and "wouldn't know what to do anyway."

One afternoon, after early dismissal from school, we sat around in a circle on the edge of the high-school football field. Boys and girls alike, lounged, sprawled, wrestled, watched, and pissed our pants with laughter.

The girl opposite me hiked her skirt up around her knees. She wasn't wearing panties! I looked around, hoping, praying that no one else saw what was happening to me. I laid my arms over my boner.

Little booklets of pornographic cartoons, depicting men with gigantic penises, penetrating girls tied to trees and demonstrating every perversity imaginable, were sold from under the counter at a corner store near the school. These books set my imagination awhirl. After masturbating in the school washroom and in the bathroom at home, I destroyed my booklets in dread that I might die and go to hell before getting the chance to go to confession. My life was a torture of shame and desire, imaginings and guilt.

"Sins of desire are as bad as sins actually committed." If you think about it, you've committed a mortal sin.

One rainy day, I was having a rough-and-tumble on the floor with the three babies when my stepfather barged into the room, jerked me to my feet, and checked my fly. Every button was done up. But I felt as ashamed as if I had done some terrible act. Sent outside to find companions my own age, I felt judged for what I might have done.

L'Ecole St. Louis de Strathmore

In September, 1948, I had one of three choices: Loyola High School taught by the Jesuits, a French school in Montreal taught by *Les Frères des Ecoles Chretiennes*, and *L'Ecole St. Louis de Strathmore* taught by *les Frères de l'Instruction Chretien*. I made my choice mainly to please my parents. Attending high school in Strathmore would save transportation costs and school fees. I would also have to become fluently bilingual. Maybe then I'd no longer be the phoney English kid with the French name who didn't belong in either world. I knew I was going to have a tough battle, but I was determined.

The battle began from the first day. In our history lessons, we learned about the cruel outcome of the Battle of the Plains of Abraham and the torture of the French and Hurons by the savage Iroquois and "*les maudits Anglais*". Frequently, we reenacted these battles on the playground - until I found excuses to remain in class, cleaning blackboards and brushes or catching up on corrected assignments. But this, by making me "*le petit pet*", only aggravated matters.

Despite difficulties, I gradually succeeded. By age sixteen, I knew as much French as a boy needed to use, at least for a place like Strathmore.

School learning proved to be simple – and simple-minded – rote memory: names and dates, countries and capitols, cities and towns, rivers and seas, times tables and rules of arithmetic, and Catechism and Missal passages. Endlessly, mind-numbingly, we recited everything. Serious thought seldom required.

In singsong fashion, we repeated phrases from lengthy lists, mathematical tables, and prayers in French and Latin. I became trilingual, by rote.

For me, the lessons dragged on. My Math got muddled, my geography parched, my history became odious, and my French grammar turned frustrating.

My memory was excellent. I could recite all the major prayers in English, French and Latin. I served Mass, with all the correct Latin responses. I even took part in a school play in French, which neither of my parents attended. Of course I was disappointed.

Grade nine proved more of a struggle for me. I had such a terrible time with geometry that I knew I'd fail. When I asked for extra help, no one had time.

I sensed unfairness. Mother had argued with Monsieur le Curé over his decision to tell the Town of Dorval to dump rocks along the sandy beach in front of the parish church. This was to discourage the "indecent sunbathers" from flaunting themselves there on Sunday afternoons. Also, at a meeting of the Legion of Mary, she disagreed with Monsieur le Curé when he informed the ladies that it was their duty to encourage their husbands to vote for Maurice Duplessis. According to him, a vote in any other direction would be "*un péché mortel*" (a mortal sin). Naomi and I, as children of "that sinful woman", were treated accordingly.

Then there was the issue of fifteen cents – the amount each of us took to Mass. Ten cents was for a seat tax and the other nickel was for the collection. Sometimes we shrugged when the men came to collect "*le dime*". If we also didn't put our nickel in the collection basket, we had a dime for the movie matinée at l'école St. Louis and a nickel for a packet of fizz. One of the ushers informed Papa François that his children were not paying "*le dime*". In short order, he brought us to account. Not only did we have to bring the missing money to Monsieur le Curé and receive a stern lecture, we had to go without pocket money for many weeks, to make up for our dishonesty. God needed those dimes and nickels.

The Whoopi-Cushion

I could always scrape up spare cash by shovelling driveways or mowing lawns or baby-sitting. And I always found people ready to take my hard-earned pennies, dimes, and quarters.

Alongside the chocolate bars and spearmint gum, Legault's store sold packaged "magic" tricks that guaranteed instant fame: "Fool your friends." "Be the first on your block." I bought chattering false teeth and a small round membrane that was supposed to enable me to throw my voice like a ventriloquist. I found itching powder, a ring that buzzed when I shook someone's hand, a bar of soap that turned the user's hands black, chewing gum that did the same to a person's mouth, and a chewing gum pack that snapped like a mousetrap when I offered someone a stick of gum. Two of the best tricks though, were a sugar cube that melted and left a spider floating in Mother's coffee and realistic doggy poo made out of plaster.

Naomi and I pooled our pennies to buy a whoopee-cushion. Mother thought it was an amusing trick. When one of the parish ladies visited, we hid the inflated "fart maker" under a cushion. It sounded off appropriately when the visitor sat down. The cost for our joke at the woman's expense was to be sent to our rooms for our "outrageous" behaviour. Later, when the woman left, Mother called us downstairs, and we all had a good laugh. This same lady had announced at a function at our house that she couldn't understand why her fingernails got so dirty when she came to visit. "Perhaps, my dear, it's because you scratch yourself" was Mother's reply. Mother always had a wonderfully wicked sense of humour - except when she was exasperated with her teenage children.

Another amusing incident involved our parish priest in Strathmore. A dozen or so men regularly ducked outside for a smoke during his overlong sermons. When Monsieur le Curé listed forbidden books and films or ranted on about mothers who prevented "God's gifts" – children – from entering the world, the number of men swelled to a crowd.

One Sunday, we heard a commotion of laughter at the front of the church. Monsieur le Curé left the pulpit and marched to the front door. Two dogs were copulating on the front steps. The parish priest was furious – with men and dogs both. In short order, town council posted notices that all dogs were to be kept on leash or at home. Strays would be impounded.

Walking on Thin Ice

Merchants refused to let kids warm up in their shops, unless we bought soft drinks and chips or played the pinball machines. Older boys typically hung out in Legault's store. They smoked and spent their newspaper money on Pepsi, Chips, Mae West cakes and pinball. We younger kids didn't stamp snow off our boots before entering so we left puddles on the floor. Without money, we were ushered out. "*Va jouer dehors.*" Go play outside.

Naomi and I had been locked out of the house. Not a problem for her, she had friends whose mothers didn't mind teen chatter. Cold and miserable, I walked down to my friend Ian Knight's house. His father was our scoutmaster and one of the few adults I knew would care enough to listen. There was no one home and nowhere else to go. Blinded with tears, I walked to the church. But it was locked.

I was so cold my feet hurt as I wandered out on the ice of Lac St. Louis. Maybe somebody would see me and come for me. Mad thoughts thrashed around in my freezing brain. The river ran under thin ice just past the lighthouse. I could fall through and all would be over. Maybe then somebody would care.

I might have prayed but the only God I knew was of shame and the fear of hell. The Crucifix was a picture of cruelty. I didn't know or understand the concept of Christ offering Himself out of love for us, let alone for me. Not having experienced love except in my earliest childhood, I found little meaning in the word. Like Oliver Twist, I wondered where love was or if I'd ever find it. Nevertheless, without words, I begged God to love me.

I hadn't seen him approach so I don't know where he came from. An old man put his hand on my shoulder and walked with me back to the shore. Blinded by tears, I hardly looked at him. I vaguely remember a ragged brown robe. And sandals. I was too filled with my own misery to wonder if his feet were cold. I do remember his warm, soothing voice.

We sat on a snow-covered bench and talked. While my feet and hands warmed, I talked out my troubles to the gentle listener.

Then, he was gone.

I didn't see him leave. I stood and looked around for him. I looked back to the bench where we had sat together. The sun, slanted low across the ice, fell on just one set of footprints. Mine.

I looked all around. I looked up at the sky. The scalloped moon floated cirrus-white, in the deep blue of the frigid expanse. On the bank up to the road, chattering squirrels searched the snow for scraps of food and found little.

After a while, I walked home. Warm, happy, and light of foot.

I told no one of my experience. It was too incredible.

Today, my rational mind tells me this didn't really happen. Yet, for all these years the vision remains, and I've held on by blind faith. This was a turning point in my life.

I wanted to live. I was worth saving.

In the midst of unhappiness, here was love. The stranger radiated the kind of love my aunties had provided when we first came to Canada. It was the kind of love I knew as a small child. It wasn't something I felt entitled to, now.

Give me a psychological explanation for my "invisible friend" if you like. I believe in miracles. I believe in a spiritual world. What happened was real for me. It saved me from suicide.

Six

BELL-BOTTOM TROUSERS

1950 – 1953

To Be Repaid In Full

Mother went out and left money on a ledge by the front door to pay for a delivery. One of Naomi's boyfriends came to the house, took off his shoes and even emptied his pockets – to be comfortable. Then he sat with my sister on the stairs. When he left, he picked up his belongings from the same ledge by the door. I did not know about the delivery money.

When Mother returned home, all hell broke loose. The delivery person had not arrived, but the money was gone. Naomi went up to her room and closed the door. I tried to explain what I thought must have happened. Mother pushed me down the cellar stairs and told me to stay there until I could think of a better story. I spent the night in the cellar.

Papa François' solution was for me to get a job. He didn't accuse me of stealing but held me responsible.

The school year wasn't finished. My stepfather took me to a farmer on the outskirts of Montreal West. I went to work hoeing between rows of spring vegetables.

The farmer was foul-mouthed and cruel. I hated him as much as he appeared to hate me. Since I never saw a penny of pay, I walked off and got a job at a sign-painting shop in Montreal painting telephone signs on glass with spray paint over stencils. Then, I cleaned up the edges around the letters as each sign dried – a job almost as tedious as weeding vegetables.

I must have painted hundreds of sheets of glass in the company of a Jehovah's Witness who harangued me on the evils of Catholicism. I fared poorly in religious argumentation.

My parents didn't mind that I quit the job on the farm, as long as I brought my pay envelope home each week. Now that I no longer attended school, I was required to pay room and board as well as repay the money stolen.

Royal Canadian Navy

On June 25th 1950, the North Koreans invaded South Korea. The resulting "police action" was to provide my rescue. In July, about a month after my seventeenth birthday, I visited the Royal Canadian Navy Recruiting Station at HMCS *Donnacona* in Montreal.

For recruits under eighteen years of age, the Navy required signed permission from a parent or guardian. I marched home, forms in hand. Papa François gladly signed. Mother insisted that, since I couldn't be trusted with money, the bulk of my salary be deducted at source and sent home by allotment. While waiting for my call-up, I scrubbed pots in the kitchen at the Grove Hill Golf Club.

The weeks dragged by until September 1st when I was to report to *Donnacona*. My prospective shipmates and I boarded the River Class Frigate HMCS *La Hulloise* and were issued hammocks for our first cruise down the St. Lawrence to Halifax.

We were "salts" already – boisterous and loud. Several recruits had served during the war; the rest of us were pimply-faced teenagers.

After docking at HMC Shipyards in Halifax, we were bussed to Cornwallis, for basic training. Upon arrival, we stripped to the waist. Nurses stabbed us with a series of needles. Then a medical officer made us lower our drawers for "short arm inspection".

A medical orderly "tiffy" ordered me to open my mouth. Before I could utter a single smart-ass remark, he ushered me to a dental surgeon. No waiting required. The "fang farrier" jabbed me twice with a blunt needle. Then, forceps in hand, went about the excruciating business of plucking a protruding canine and a couple of molars from my overcrowded mouth.

The rest of the preliminaries included a "bean shave", stacks of supplies, including Canada flashes and colour flashes to sew on coats and uniforms. We were to stencil our numbers (8921H) with black ink onto every bit of equipment provided. Our RPO, *Regulating Petty Officer,* ordered us to polish boots until we could see our faces in their mirror-like toes and heels.

Recruits, who had gone through the ropes before, taught us the secret of "bulling" our boots. With elbow grease, we smoothed the leather grain on the toes and heels with a spoon handle preheated in candle flame. After we made the leather sufficiently smooth, we applied a thick layer of boot polish – the "spit and polish" method.

"Spit and polish" worked like this. We took a piece of cloth over our forefingers and dipped it into black polish. Kiwi polish was considered best. Next, we spat on the polish and worked it into the boot with small, circular motions. We repeated this procedure until the whole area had a smooth coating of polish, which we then brought to high gloss with water and a strip of silk scarf. Those who had come prepared sold a ready supply of old spoons and strips of black silk.

We did all kit preparation during spare time known as "make and mend". All the while, our petty officer, "Frenchy", shouted orders "on the double". He let us know we were the sorriest bunch of mothers' babies he'd ever had the displeasure of seeing washed ashore.

Since we were happy to have escaped home, school, and parental discipline, we were a cocky bunch. Little did we know we were to be seized forcibly out of boyhood and dumped helter-skelter into a state, which was neither man nor boy. Old enough to die for our country. Too young to vote.

Much too early on the second morning, our Division Petty Officer introduced us to our first brutal awakening, to be repeated every day for months to come. While still dark, reveille sounded from a bugle. Then came a mad dash for the "heads" (washrooms) as the Division Petty Officer marched through the block shouting "Wakey, wakey, rise and shine; the sun is up, the morning's fine."

To make life more interesting, he employed endless variations such as "Wakey wakey, hands off snakey," or "Let go yer cocks 'n' on wif yer socks!" Slackers caught stealing a few extra winks had their blanket yanked off. When this didn't work, their buddies upended their bunks.

The first morning was the worst. After a mere twenty minutes, we assembled, a full division of raw, shivering recruits, on the parade square. All suffered sore arms from needle jabs. Some of us had sore jaws. None of this mattered.

The muscular P.E. instructor glared at us. "If you miss your mommies, please let me know. When we're done with you, you won't need your poor mothers to wipe your tears or blow your noses. We'll have you beaten into shape and you'll be ready to give your all for George (*King George*)."

There were some who preferred to keep their individuality throughout. One fellow in our division we nicknamed "Radar" for reasons unkind. From the start, he refused to conform. A likeable fellow, he ended his life on the west coast as a human helicopter. Fuelled by infusions of ditto fluid, he took off from the roof of one of the navy's administration buildings.

Several of my fellow recruits were braggarts and bullies, ready to fight at the slightest provocation. For the most part, their language consisted of short, colourless phrases, punctuated with profanity. However, like most of my shipmates, I was happy, despite the roughness.

In the following weeks, floors became "decks", ceilings "deck-heads", and walls "bulkheads". And the biffy became the "heads". (Sailors shouted "heads!" when they relieved themselves over the sides of ships in the days when ships were ships and men were men.)

Everything in Cornwallis was on the double. Some cracked within days. Listed AWOL, they were quickly caught and put on punishment detail – to make them wish they'd never been born.

On the third day, we were introduced to the gymnasium. "I want two volunteers for the boxing ring; you and YOU!" One was a big black fellow from Montreal and the other was the skinny bloke with the French name. Me! "Close your eyes; you're going for a ride," said my adversary.

I went for a ride. To the hospital!

Later, I figured, Commander Budge had received instructions from a certain ex-major of the Canadian Army that his stepson – me again! – was to be transformed, by some unexplained miracle, into a man.

Incidentally, Joe, the black recruit who had knocked me out, would become one of my best friends.

After a couple of days in the hospital, I returned to my division, only to encounter the fate of many new recruits: I was charged with a minor infraction – "insubordination". Seven days "number eleven" involved extra drills, complete with heavy packs and many hours of K. P.

K. P. (kitchen patrol), as with all assignments of cleanup duty, involved scrubbing and polishing miles and miles of wooden decks, cement pathways, stone steps, and, of course, greasy pots and pans.

Possibly the most bizarre eccentricity of scraping, scrubbing, and polishing in basic training concerned the "fire point" just inside the entrance to every building. This was a red-painted wooden stand, on which stood two or four red buckets, bearing the legend "FIRE" in black paint. One or two of these contained sand and the other one or two contained water. Before inspection, water in the buckets had to be changed to remove dust. Sand was to be raked to a clean and smooth surface.

One morning, running around the parade square with heavy pack and holding my rifle at arms length above my head, I tripped over my own feet and fell face down. I got up – only to fall again. Several others from the detail stopped beside me. In a spirit of support, they urged me to stay down. But I was angry and stubborn and got up anyway. This time I lost consciousness and ended up back in the hospital.

Following several days of bed rest, I was transferred to Fraser Division where I remained until graduation five months later. Happy in Fraser Division, I sent regular letters and postcards home, sure my parents would at last be proud of me. I sent snapshots taken in a booth in Digby with cap placed jauntily above my curly blond forelock. Looking at the photos in later years, I would have passed for a fourteen or fifteen year-old sea cadet.

On a chilly morning in November, we assembled at the outdoor pool for our basic swimming test. Wearing white ducks – heavy cotton summer uniforms – we had to tread water for five minutes. Then we removed our pants and tied the bottoms, filled the legs with air, and used them as water wings for several more minutes. The weather was blustery. I shuddered at the thought of spending the last moments of my life fighting to survive in North Atlantic waters. Five and a half years after that voyage on the RMV *Rangitata*, I felt the same panic. How relieved I was when we finally made the mad dash for hot showers and steaming cocoa.

On another cold day in December, we ran the assault course in pouring rain, crawling through pipes and under barbed wire in freezing mud, while live ammunition – we were told – was fired just above our heads. The tougher the training, the prouder we became as a division.

Shenanigans and hazing occurred, too. One of the rituals was to shave a recruit's pubic hair, then apply shoe polish. I didn't yet have pubic hair and did my best to hide my privates in the communal showers. Eventually, I got "blackballed". That was one of the roughest times for me in basic training. It was like being discovered – found out.

Every Sunday we lined up for church parade. Jews and atheists had to choose one or the other service: Protestant or Dogan. Church of England was officiated by our Commanding Officer with the Protestant chaplain. Sunday,

December 24th, 1950, Midnight Mass was celebrated for all the "Micks" (Irish – R.C.).

The following morning, we arose to a white Christmas. Since we'd already attended service, we Catholics were issued snow shovels and spent two hours clearing the parade square and various pathways. We grumbled, but I enjoyed the fresh air amidst crystal sparkles, while carols floated from the Anglican service. The sounds and feelings of the morning brought back Christmases in Finchingfield.

Highway Christmas

Almost everyone was given leave for the holidays. Many had already left by bus or train to spend Christmas and New Year's with family and friends. Christmas afternoon, I packed my small bag and set out to hitchhike home to Strathmore, a naïve and stupid thing to do in the middle of winter. But I had no money for train or bus fare.

A series of short rides took me to Truro and on to Moncton, New Brunswick. Then, on the far side of Moncton, I stood in the freezing rain as car after car sped past. Rowdies threw bottles; others even tried running me off the road.

Men and women in uniform were unpopular in the Maritimes in those early years following the Second World War. V.E.Day celebrations in Halifax had turned into a riot of looting and destruction when thousands of military personnel retaliated against the establishments that had treated them unfairly throughout the war. The showdown came when the city closed all liquor stores and taverns for V.E. Day so that hundreds of civilian workers as well as 25,000 servicemen on leave – who wanted to celebrate the victory – had nothing to do and nothing to drink. The brewery and liquor stores and many businesses in the Halifax downtown district were looted and smashed. The riot continued for two days.

In the wee hours of the morning, feet soaked through and icy cold, I flagged a car heading back towards Moncton. A series of short rides took me to a house party in Windsor, Nova Scotia where I fell asleep curled up in a chair in a back room. At first light, I awoke stiff and sore to a house in shambles. A strong wind whipped sleet against the window.

Later that morning, a young lady drove me to the Stadacona naval base in Halifax where I was given a bunk, a hot meal, and a ride for the next day. On Wednesday, I was back at Cornwallis to spend the remainder of my holiday reading on my bunk, feeling angry and cheated by my parents who obviously didn't give a damn. Not even a Christmas card, I was broke, lonely and miserable.

Hitchhiking Over Christmas

I stood, lonely,

shivering, a solo leaf about to fall.

Night swatted away the sun,

sewing up the last rays of evening.

A great white silence

cracked cheeks and eardrums.

Winter wind with razor teeth

flayed my flesh and split my lips.

Snow and ice crawled through my veins.

Tears froze to my cheeks.

I heard the uncanny yowls

of wolves at the forest edge.

I moved stamping,

silky squeak of snow underfoot.

Nearby, a stream yattered, a forsaken gossip,

a guard dog muttered disheartened warnings.

In the distance, children chanted carols.

At home, women would be stuffing turkeys

baking tortière in cozy kitchens,

stockings hanging by the fire.

Shaping Up

Before periods of leave, we were given lectures and shown movies warning of venereal disease and other dangers. Young salts were handed packages of condoms and antibacterial creams. Many made the bus ride to Digby and the beautiful Annapolis Valley, dreaming of sexual conquests. Too young to drink and too scared and out-of-pocket to take part in lustful activities, I nevertheless followed everyone into town and played the role of sightseer.

At a dance in Digby, many sailors had mickeys, purchased from the local bootlegger. They passed brown paper bags around outside the dance hall. Girls joined them, then took off, young salts in tow. One girl asked me if I "poontang".

Not knowing what the word meant, I said, "No."

"Hey! Slim doesn't poontang. He doesn't have a poon-tanger."

Boasting about sex was almost the only subject of conversation for many, as virile experts compared seduction techniques.

Digby had a tattoo parlour. Here the "real" men had their "pigs" (girl friends) inscribed on hearts or anchors. Some even had sailing ships tattooed on their backs and were covered in scabs for weeks. Others had a pig tattooed on one knee and a rooster on the other. If a girl put her hand on the left knee, or better still, sat there, he could say, "You're on my cock". If proof were needed, the sailor rolled up his bell-bottom and showed the tattoo. By the end of five months, some sailors became walking art galleries.

Despite the frantic rush of navy life, I made new friends and felt part of something greater than I ever had imagined. We marched and ran with heavy packs and daily became stronger. Learning seamanship, Morse code, semaphore, and a new vocabulary made us members of an elite group.

The night before our graduation parade at *Cornwallis,* a group of the more daring from our division carried out a fire-hose raid on the petty officer who had been more zealous than most. With pillowcases over their heads, they knocked at his door in the early hours. The very sleepy PO was greeted with a torrent of icy water. Before he managed to recover, we were all "sound asleep" in our bunks. The PO aroused us from our "slumber" with bright lights and blowing whistles and ordered us to stand barefoot in front of the Division hut until the culprits stepped forward. Though we stood for what seemed like hours, no one confessed.

Our commanding officer was Commander Patrick David Budge. I served under him when he was Captain of the cruiser Quebec. He was later promoted to Admiral of the Pacific Fleet. Having risen through the ranks from boy seaman in the Royal Navy, he knew his "spit and polish". His residence at Cornwallis was "Seamanlike Manor". Budge was reported to have declared, "This navy has been going to the dogs ever since they began letting civilians in."

One of my favourite stories of Commander Budge was of him crossing the parade square at *Cornwallis* to address a brand new sub-lieutenant – a "snotty" – who was being saluted over and over again by a much older chief petty officer.

"What's going on here?" Commander Budge asked.

"This rating passed without saluting, sir."

"Very well. Carry on!"

After several more salutes, Commander Budge inquired of the sub-lieutenant, "Do you not return a salute when you receive one?"

"Oh! Yes sir."

"Very well, begin again, one hundred times. And let me see each salute smartly returned."

Wet Behind the Ears

February 1951, I arrived home in Strathmore, for my first thirty days' leave, before moving on to courses at HMCS Naden, in Esquimalt, British Columbia. I was a man at last, ready to face the enemy in Korea. I marched home smartly, kit bag and high expectations at the ready.

The major did not return my salute. He ran his finger behind my ear, looked at Mother and shook his head. "Still wet!"

"It's salt water, sir", I retorted.

"Smart ass!" He smiled.

The four girls were happy to see me. Naomi looked at me with envy. I was free at last.

Following an ordinary supper (did I not expect a hero's banquet?) I was ready to show myself off to whomever I could find.

But home was back to normal. Dishes had to be washed. Naomi was not happy at school or at home. We talked little. Time had widened the gap.

The next day I marched over to L'Ecole St. Louis and proudly presented myself to the Brothers. But the boys who I thought would now look up to me, didn't. In the schoolyard, someone grabbed the sailor hat from my head. The hat flew from one to another through snow and slush. I retrieved it without the tally and its carefully tied bow, retreated home and changed into civvies.

With almost no spending money and former friends tied up with school, I soon regretted being home. I sat sullenly and read. Papa François wanted to see my "spit and polish" and handed me three pairs of shoes. Mother gave me the children's shoes. I sat at the bottom of the cellar stairs – Cinderfella – polishing polishing, polishing. Louise and Nicole had started school so I looked after the youngest of my little sisters, taking Jackie on endless toboggan rides. Then I skied alone on the Grove Hill Golf Course.

Fed up, I decided to hitchhike to Quebec City and visit my aunts and uncles. Although I arrived unannounced in Limoilou close to midnight, my aunts and uncles welcomed me warmly. The next day, Patricia and Madeleine took me to their favourite restaurant for dinner – complete with wine.

We reminisced about my family's arrival in Quebec and about how excited Naomi and I were to be in Canada. Now, here I was "*bien grandi, mais toujours le petit Benoît*" (all grown-up but still little Benoît). I spent time in *Lingerie Bertrand* – Aunties' shop. I was introduced proudly to customers and friends. And I explored parts of the old city I'd never seen before. Everywhere I went, people smiled at *le jeune matelot* (the young sailor). I felt proud and happy.

Much too soon, it was time to return to spend a few last days at home before taking the train to the Pacific coast. Aunts and uncles all wanted to make sure I had spending money before they put me on a bus back to Montreal. They refused to let me hitchhike. I was glad. The weather had turned bitterly cold.

Back home, when I tried to talk about having control over my own money. Mother made it clear the topic was not open to debate. Frustrated but afraid to let my anger show, I said my goodbyes, walked with my heavy pack to the Strathmore railway station, and took the train to Central Station in Montreal.

Cards, Booze and Railroad Tracks

The railway car westward was filled with Army, Navy, and Air Force personnel. Bottles in brown bags made the rounds. Cards were shuffled and dealt; greenbacks and silver coins changed hands. The air hung thick with smoke. Meals, first class railway style, were served in exchange for meal tickets issued before we left *Cornwallis*.

At night, the porters transformed the day cars into bunked sleeping quarters. Throughout the long nights, I was frequently awakened to the sounds of stumbling and cursing as some inebriate staggered back to his berth or tried climbing into the wrong compartment. The washrooms smelled of liquor and vomit. Now and then drunken fights broke out. Fortunately, these ceased as soon as they began. Accusations of cheating at cards caused most of the fights I witnessed. The few military police accompanying us spent their time in an adjacent car, accompanied by females they'd met on the train.

When we moved onto the prairies, sailors disembarked at the water stops for the mad dash to the nearest bootlegger then returned out of breath, carrying armfuls of fresh supplies. I had neither the desire nor the funds for booze. I did join in when singsongs got underway.

Ship ahoy, sailor boy, don't you get so springy.

The admiral's daughter is down by the water,

Waiting to grab you by the dinghy.

He's got the cutest little dinghy in the navy;

> *Heave Ho! Heave Ho!*
>
> *He's got the cutest little dinghy in the navy*
>
> *And you aught'a see the little bugger go.*
>
> *It isn't very long, it isn't very short,*
>
> *But it's the thing that gets him in and out of every port.*
>
> *He's got the cutest little dinghy in the navy;*
>
> *Heave Ho! Heave Ho!*

And, of course, there were rousing choruses of The North Atlantic Squadron:

> *Away, away with fife and drum,*
>
> *Here we come, full of rum ...*

After days of snow-covered forests, frozen lakes, and endless prairie, we came to our first view of the Rocky Mountains. I had never seen anything so majestic! From then on, even from my bunk at night, I gazed transfixed through the window. As the train wound its way through tunnels and along stretches overlooking vast ravines, I forgot the commotion around me. Throughout the train, all hands settled down.

When we left our boots out, we found them shiny clean in the morning. The porters were wonderful. Always smiling and polite to the rudest amongst us, they kept the cars clean, too.

At last, we passed through the portals of Paradise. The descent from snowy peaks into lush green valleys made me wonder if we'd entered a different country. It was only when we made our final dash through the Fraser Valley that we were ordered to get our kits together. Next stop: Vancouver and the Canadian Pacific Railway ferry, Princess Marguerite, to Victoria.

Zoot Suits, Rabbits and Narrow Minds

From the Supply School in Esquimalt, near Victoria, we ran miles every morning before breakfast. Though our route varied, it always led over moss-covered rocks and along trails bordered by the ubiquitous arbutus of the Pacific Coast. The roughness of basic training was gone. I felt at peace.

Zoot suiters (post war youth gangs) wore a long, loose coat with wide, padded shoulders, tapered pants with wide legs and tight ankle cuffs, worn very high above the waist, an oversized bow-tie, sometimes a wide-brimmed hat, and a long, hanging watch chain.

Throughout the Second World War, there had been many battles between zoot suiters and members of the armed forces. The law was almost always on the side of the servicemen even when innocent youths were attacked.

After the outbreak of the Korean War, turmoil resurfaced as swarms of randy servicemen invaded dance halls and attracted local girls.

One Friday evening, a troop of zoot-suiters came over from Vancouver to Victoria. Fights broke out, and several naval ratings landed in hospital. We were rounded up by the Shore Patrol, from locations in downtown Victoria, and loaded into trucks. Mustered on the parade square, we were informed by the Commanding Officer that all further leave would be canceled if one zoot-suiter remained on the Island by Saturday midnight. "Dismissed."

There's courage in numbers. Though not physically involved, I was a member of the company which reported that, by the time the Princess boat left Victoria Harbour for Vancouver, not one pair of strides remained on city streets. They all hung from the telephone wires of downtown Victoria. As for the "invaders", they were ushered into paddy wagons by the Victoria Police and returned by special boat to Vancouver wrapped in naval issue blankets. The blankets would be exchanged for pants following a weekend lock-up.

Since there was nothing to do in Victoria on Sunday, we removed the offending garments to be shipped back to Vancouver. The Monday was proclaimed "make and mend" until midnight. Everyone on the Island side was happy.

A tradition with a number of households in Victoria was to invite sailors to their homes for Christmas and Thanksgiving dinners. Personnel who could not be with their own families were selected at random and sent out in pairs. Joe, my boxing friend from *Cornwallis,* and I were assigned for Thanksgiving dinner at a residence in Oak Bay.

When we arrived, the lady appeared shocked and told us a mistake had been made. She only had room for one; I was welcome but not the other "boy". As usual, the sidewalks of Victoria were "rolled up" for the holiday, so we both reported back to Naden, too late for Thanksgiving dinner. Joe had a buddy in Cooking School. His friend served us a fantastic meal, complete with a bottle of officers' wine and extra Plum Duff.

Navy cooks were able to dig up goodies no one else could obtain. Pilfered items were called "rabbits". That term originated when a cook at HMCS *Naden,* who lived off base, decided to take a bunny home for his daughter. (Rabbits ran wild on the base.) He was stopped at the main gate and ordered to show what he had in the bucket. When he lifted the lid, the bunny jumped out and hopped away. The next day, the same thing happened again. On the third day, the cook passed through the main gate, unchecked, with his *rabbit*. The custom spread as other ratings began taking *rabbits* home.

Somebody "rabbited" some clothes-washing soap from the Supply School. Clothes-washing in the Navy was called "dhobieing". The rabbited "dhobey dust" turned out to be extra strength detergent for sails and other canvas. The culprit and his buddies limped bowlegged to sick bay with a severe case of dhobie itch.

One day, a fellow at Supply School suggested a movie double date with his girl's sister; I agreed. We met at the theatre and my date was very attractive. I paid for her and for myself and my buddy bought his two tickets, then we took our seats, popcorn in hand, to enjoy the show. I was elated. A third fellow came and sat on the other side of the girl I was with. We were a five-some. She held our popcorn and he began to help himself. Then I noticed the two holding hands. After the movie, I returned to base alone. I'd been had.

In general, I was shy in the company of girls and couldn't afford expensive dates. So I spent much of my spare time reading and working as assistant cubmaster, "Balloo", for the First Fairfield Cub Pack. I was unaware of the reputation this gave me. After several months, my parents succumbed to my repeated requests and sent my Scout uniform. The Cub Parents' Committee complemented that with a neckerchief and a few badges. At first, I carried the uniform with me and changed at the Cubs and Scouts Hall. But soon, feeling proud of my contribution to the community, I began to wear my uniform on Cub nights, both leaving and returning to base.

One nippy night, when I returned to base, a group of inebriated bullies surrounded me. "A Boy Scout on naval property. Well, well." Push came to shove and someone head-butted me on the nose while another kneed me in the groin. They stripped me and stomped me all over. Then, they stuffed me naked, head first into a garbage can. Once more, I ended up in Naval Hospital.

Hitchhiking — California

On November 9th, 1951, I graduated from Supply School as an Administrative Writer, with instructions to report to HMCS *Stadacona* in Halifax. En route, I had thirty days leave plus two weekends. There was no way I'd spend another period of leave at home. This time, I intended to travel, to see as much as I could in the time allotted. To solve the problem of lack of funds, I sold my travel voucher and embarked on a hitchhiking holiday.

The overnight ferry ride from Victoria to Vancouver was with a group of progressively drunken sailors, travelling with one female companion and all sharing a single-bunk cabin. I enthusiastically took part in some of the singsongs, but turned down the brown-bag bottles. I had no desire to visit the overnight cabin, certain the woman would turn me down, anyway.

After depositing my kit bag at the railway station on West Hastings in Vancouver, to be shipped to *Stadacona*, I took a trolley to the Pacific Highway and headed towards New Westminster, the Pattullo Bridge, and the Peace Arch Crossing into the United States.

Intermittent lifts took me past Seattle, Tacoma, Portland, Oregon, and a very snowy Grant's Pass. Then I caught a ride in a logging truck. As the sun rose between the ridges and peaks of mountains to the East, I sat high in the cab and observed, with awe, the giant redwoods surrounding us, until we came to the Pacific Ocean at Crescent City, California.

The coast was shrouded in fog. We stopped at a café where loggers sat drinking coffee black and consuming huge plates of flapjacks and eggs. My driver, a small man compared to the other men in the café, pointed to intermittent flashes of light that came from a lighthouse, way off the coast. He told me it was built on the site where more than two hundred had drowned when their ship hit a reef in a fog such as this, almost one hundred years before. Despite his own short stature, this trucker was proud of his fellow countrymen. "Some of these men will soon be cutting into trees that have stood along this coast since long before Columbus came to America. This here's Paul Bunyan country."

I looked around at the lumberjacks, some standing tall with arms the size of tree limbs. These men were giants. Their conversation and laughter matched their stature.

I managed to polish off a breakfast of flapjacks, sausage and eggs, offered free of charge to the young Canadian sailor. Then, my host driver and I continued towards his destination, Eureka. We drove on narrow Route 1, hugging the Pacific Coast. Here and there wide enough for only one-way traffic, the road perilously embraced cliffs above needlepoint rocks. At some points in the road, the loudest horn got the right-of-way and yielding traffic had to tuck itself into wayside pull-offs. Every bend took my breath until Eureka where the rotten-egg smell of pulp mills blew in with the ocean breeze. The houses, all built of redwood were pretty and the people loud and cheery. I was treated to a delicious crab supper and part of a pitcher of beer. Once again, for the sailor from way up north, the meal was on the house.

Following lunch, I headed back to the highway, with wishes for a safe and happy journey ringing in my ears. Before long, a travelling salesman picked me up. In spite of his boozy breath, I failed to realize the man was drunk. When I finally did pay attention, I was unable to muster the courage to ask him to stop and let me out. Worse, since I didn't know how to drive, I couldn't offer to take the wheel. I just held on tight to the side handle and felt sick.

At last! We stopped for coffee. He grabbed the travel bag from my hand and threw it onto the back seat. Then he locked the door and lurched into the café. I followed.

A U.S. Marine sat at the café counter. He told me he had a couple of pals in the Canadian Navy stationed in Halifax and that he was thumbing his way south to Ft. Bragg. When I suggested he ride with us and take over the driving, he jumped at the offer. While the marine drove, the car owner snored in the back seat.

At Fort Bragg, an American sailor returning from furlough offered a ride to San Francisco. I felt overjoyed and secure. The sailor regaled me with anecdotes about a trip to Hawaii and a journey up the Amazon with missionary friends.

We crossed the Golden Gate Bridge well past midnight. I wondered where I'd find a place to sleep at such a late hour. Since leaving Victoria, I had only dozed in an upright position. I was exhausted.

As my driver did not have to report to his ship until the following day, he took me to an "excellent place" where we could spend the night. I paid for my lodging, was handed a towel and a key and taken by an attendant down a long corridor to a small, cubicle-like room. I noticed many admiring glances. In this land so proud of its servicemen, I must have looked dashing and heroic in my naval uniform. Then, a heavyset man groped my behind. Another came up to me, told me I was cute, and asked about my friend.

I had paid to spend the night at a gay steam bath. In one room, a sweaty mass of naked bodies writhed like snakes in a pit. I fled to the front desk. The clerk, laughing but kind, returned my money and told me how to get to a USO that was open all night. Despite the late hour, they would be able to direct me to reasonable lodgings.

That night, I slept in a San Francisco USO/YMCA. By noon the next day, I was back on Route 1, headed to Los Angeles, anxious to distance myself from some unspeakable shame. I had lost all interest in San Francisco.

As palm trees appeared in greater abundance, I saw beautiful sandy beaches and my excitement grew. Then I discovered Santa Barbara, swam in the ocean, and visited the old Franciscan Mission Church.

In 1951, there wasn't the pollution and bumper-to-bumper traffic in Los Angeles we know today. There was no Disneyland. Hollywood and Vine was still the centre of the movie world.

At the USO, I was given a pass to a Meet the Stars party. I checked in at the YMCA and decided to take a nap before going out. I didn't wake up until the next day, thus missing the party. I did, however, meet several greying film stars at the Brown Derby and got their autographs "for my sister". But I went on no tours of the studios; entrance wasn't permitted without prearranged permission. Before long, I headed south once more.

In San Diego, I stayed at the naval base and was invited to another cocktail party. Edgar Bergen was there. His puppets, Charley McCarthy and Mortimer Snerd made rude remarks about various guests, especially the ladies. Charley asked me what I had in my pants pocket. The audience laughed. I patted my pockets and shrugged. More laughter.

The next day, I walked in sunshine in the second best climate in the world. (#1 was the Canary Islands.) I thought San Diego was one of the most inviting towns I had ever visited. Mexican fan palms, giant cacti, ficus trees, and monarch butterflies informed me that I was finally in the tropics. I saw adobe houses, some of the oldest buildings in California, as well as Spanish Colonial buildings. I regret to this day I didn't visit the zoo, famous throughout the world.

On November 19th, I decided to visit Tijuana, simply because I wanted to be able to say I had been to Mexico. Fortunately, I left my travel bag at the base. In warning me to be careful, people told me it was easy to get into trouble south of the border. Since I intended only to see the sights, I was sure I'd be safe.

In the Tijuana bars, everyone drank and talked to the señoritas. One of the fellows – or was it one of the bar girls? – persuaded me to try a small glass of tequila. "If you haven't tasted tequila, you haven't been to Mexico".

In a matter of minutes, all became a blur. The room spun about. I couldn't hold myself steady. I began vomiting on my way to the washroom.

Vaguely, I recall a dirty sink in a filthy bathroom. I managed to remove my shoes and uniform, wash my shorts, and clean myself up as well as I could – before passing out.

The U.S. Naval Shore Patrol picked me up, sans uniform, sans wallet, sans camera. I was much luckier than I ever imagined at the time. I'm sure the Shore Patrol brought me back to San Diego with the usual assortment of rowdies and drunks. Where I spent the night I can only imagine. The hours between passing out in Tijuana and being handed a towel and shown to a shower on the Naval base are a total loss. How I got away without being charged I'll never know. Not only was I treated with the utmost kindness by the Naval authorities, a Good Samaritan at the San Diego Naval Base had helped me out even further. My uniform was returned to me clean; even my shoes had been freshly polished.

When, some weeks later, I described my misadventure to a group of navy buddies, they told me of sailors who had spent time with murderers, thieves, drug addicts and child molesters in the old Tijuana jail.

Those who had spent time locked up in Mexico and other Central and South American towns never forgot the overpowering stench of urine and vomit, fighting for space on a dirt or cement floor, and being shaken down for cigarettes and money to pay for water and food. Sometimes it could take days for Naval shore patrol to locate them and pay their bail. Then they'd be brought back to face charges, not only for drunken and disorderly conduct but also for being AWOL.

Though base officials had told me, "Don't ever travel on your own", I stubbornly held to the belief that my only error in Tijuana was that I drank with people I didn't know. Why was I so well treated when I really deserved some sort of military punishment? Probably because both the Yanks and Canucks knew they were fighting the same "police action" in Korea. Or maybe I was just a kid who'd stepped into a situation way out of his depth.

The Americans made contact with the Royal Canadian Navy in Esquimalt. I was issued temporary I.D. and a flight by Naval Air Force to San Francisco, then to Tacoma, Washington and bussed to Vancouver. At HMCS *Discovery*, I was issued a new rail pass to Halifax.

All this came out of my pay, of course. Both parents were furious when I told them of my misadventure but especially when my pay allotment arrived short.

First Assignment — Montreal

I arrived at HMCS *Stadacona* in Halifax looking forward to my first ship and to excursions to exotic lands. But on the 18th of December 1951, I was sent back to Montreal to work in the Recruiting Office at HMCS *Donnacona*.

With a living allowance, I took a permanent room in the YMCA nearby. Everything was conveniently located on Drummond Street: *Donnacona*, the Y and Sir George Williams University. Wow! I'll take courses in my spare time, I thought. The Pay Writer working with me was studying at Sir George Williams, to qualify for Officer Training. Why shouldn't I? So I applied for the spring semester but was informed that, at eighteen years and far from qualifying as a mature student, I needed to complete high school first. Since my work at *Donnacona* also included evening watches, I'd have to study by correspondence. I began a course in Matriculation English.

Mother and Papa François were upset with me for deciding to live at the "Y", rather than use my living allowance to board at home. But I enjoyed my new freedom and needed to distance myself from my parents and the struggle to win their approval.

On July 27th, 1952, I was transferred back to *Stadacona*, where I was to remain until October 15th. Halifax provided good friends, summer weekend camping, sailing, and short hitchhiking trips. I visited Prince Edward Island and Sydney, Nova Scotia.

The Maggie

In October I joined the aircraft carrier *Magnificent* – The Maggie. She had been given to Canada by the British government and was undergoing refit at HMC Dockyard, Halifax.

Since I desperately wanted to fit in, I joined several of my new messmates for a skirmish ashore. Though I knew I needn't (and didn't dare) get drunk as they did, I foolishly accompanied one of the fellows I respected the most – a three-badge, able-bodied seaman, twelve years a salt-water sailor – Battle of the Atlantic and all that – who fully intended to drink himself silly.

We entered through a restaurant into a noisy, smoky private club. My friend sauntered over to join a group of sailors, none of whom I knew. Exhibiting more courage than I really felt, I followed. This elicited swift reactions from the strangers: "Hello sweetie. What brings your little cherub face in here? Looking for your daddy?"

"Buzz off, junior. Sea cadet night's been canceled."

"Run home, sonny. Your mother's looking for you. Time to change your shitty diapers."

"Hey! You heard the man. Fuck off before I come and break your face."

Shaking in my boots, embarrassed and betrayed, I beat a speedy retreat to the Seagull Club – a licenced dance hall for Canadian Naval ratings on Barrington Street. There I met a couple of my previous messmates from the Naden Supply School.

Halifax provided the opportunity to learn to drive on the hilly streets of the old city. While I was taking the road test, a drunk ran out from a tavern and hit the side of the car. He shouted that he wouldn't lay charges if I paid him instead. A policeman arrived and I thought I'd be in trouble. For sure, I'd fail my driving test. But the drunk overdid his act; he argued so loudly with the policeman that he was escorted to the hoosegow.

The driving examiner had sat in the passenger seat and observed the whole incident without comment. Perhaps he was watching to see how I'd react under stress. He drove the car back to the licensing office and told me to take a seat. A few minutes later he came out of the inner office with a smile on his face and my licence.

There were so many people coming and going on the Maggie that I had little opportunity to make permanent friends. The ship swarmed with rats (the animal kind) however, and they were friendly enough. They ran from hammock to hammock while we tried to sleep at night.

Every now and then, we sailed out past the Harbour so the flyers could practice takeoff and landing. Then we returned to the Dockyard so that refitting could continue.

In the ship's office, I got into trouble with a midshipman. Midshipmen (lowest ranking officers) were sent to the Royal Navy for part of their training. As sub-lieutenants, some of them returned to Canada sounding more British than the British.

I answered the telephone. A voice asked, "Are you theah?" – "Just a moment, sir, I'll go and see." I thought this was a great joke until I was brought up on charges for "gross disrespect and insubordination to a senior officer". To make matters worse, when I stood before the captain, I couldn't hold back a fit of giggles. The manner in which the young officer read out my offence in his phoney accent was just too funny.

I got seven days "# 11". This meant extra work details and curtailment of leave. As I got off lightly, I was relieved. I suspect the captain saw the humour.

Hitchhiking –

The Deep South

November 7th, my second leave. This time, I had a few dollars put aside, a gift from my aunts and uncles in Quebec City. Once more, I planned to hitchhike south of the border to explore the sunny and much warmer East Coast USA.

In the dark of night, my last ride parked in New York and shook me awake. We were pulled up outside a smoky tavern as a drunk whirled in front of the car, banging on the hood with a flabby fist and bellowing curses at no one in particular. My host driver reached to the back seat and handed me my coat and duffle bag. "New York City; end of the line, sailor. Nice talking to you; enjoy your travels."

I stood groggy, somewhat east of law and order, dazed in a bedlam of gabbling voices and taxi horns. With no idea of the scope of the city, I walked toward what I hoped would be the bright lights of Broadway. Strands of indecipherable music coalesced with laughter, shouts, and curses, all afloat on a nighttime sea of writhing sidewalks. Drunks sat in doorways clasping brown paper bags; some sprawled comatose across steamy grates. Hustlers, bag ladies, whores and urchins brushed past, reeking of armpits, garlic, stale cigarette smoke, cheap perfume, aftershave and urine. From dusty shop windows, lacy undergarments and sex toys, in myriad shades of pink and black, assaulted virgin eyes beneath a thousand neon veins. This was not the New York I'd come to see. I was in the wrong part of town.

Two U.S. Navy types pointed me toward a USO/YMCA. "They'll put you up for one night free. Tell them you lost your wallet. Happens all the time."

I fled past Washington, the Nation's Capitol, barely stopping to glance at the White House, not knowing what a tourist should look for. I wanted to see the world but only palm trees would signal my arrival.

Compulsively, I needed to keep moving. I'd been bitten in San Francisco and in Tijuana. I was anxious for adventure but terrified at the same time and my budget was extremely limited.

November 14th, I found a bed at the YMCA/USO in Norfolk, Virginia. Counting destinations on my personal score card, I wrote speedy postcards home but seldom stopped long enough to absorb culture and surroundings. I was running as fast and as far as I could, spending sparingly on junk food and postcards. "Look, Mom and Dad. I'm travelling the world."

Sometimes, state troopers picked me up and gave me rides to neighbouring counties where hitchhiking was not against the law. I was a serviceman from a strange country. "Canada? What state's that in?"

The further south I travelled, the shorter the rides. At a rickety country store, I stopped to buy a bottle of soda. The scene was bucolic, picturesque. In a large rocking chair on the porch, legs spread akimbo, a good ol' boy sat snoring, mouth open. A fly skittered into his mouth. Without awakening, he snorted and spat onto the dust, right beside a thirteen or fourteen year-old girl who sat on the porch step rocking back and forth.

With a voice as low and dark as weathered oak, soft as a feather pillow, the girl hummed a pretty tune while she repeatedly brushed back a wisp of blond hair hanging across her right eye. Her lips were full, sensuous, inviting. I muttered a low "Hi!" Her little brown-button eyes flashed alarm. Then I saw beneath her cheap blue dress, the roundness of a baby.

A cat padded across the road. For a moment, it stopped to investigate the stranger, then jumped onto the steps and sat beside the young, pregnant beauty. At that moment, a rough man in dirty, slung-over jeans came out of the store. He glared at me, then at the girl.

He spat out a stream of tobacco juice and pointed a filthy index finger. "What y'all gawkin' at?"

I shrugged and moved on. For days afterwards, the girl's face lingered in my mind.

In the South, I began to absorb my surroundings and some of what I saw made a lasting impression. "Whites only" and "coloured" signs were posted everywhere. In one town, curiosity got the better of me and I took a look inside a "coloured" washroom – just a hole in the ground. The stench was overpowering. The only time I saw a coloured person in a white washroom was the lady with a bucket and mop, cleaning up after sloppy white folks.

Near Savannah, Georgia, I stopped to contemplate the Savannah River – so wide, so smooth. Where had she been? Where was she going? What secrets did she hide? Would I were Tom Sawyer, innocent and free to sail my craft, fight off pirates and search for hidden treasure.

I removed my shoes and socks; dangled my feet in the water, and watched bits of wood drift by. The current caressed my calves. Soothed me.

Lazily, I glanced upstream and brutish reality invaded. A small stream plopped its cargo into the muddy river: the corpse of an orange cat, caught in a tree branch and half submerged. Then I saw a giant pipe dribbling yellow effluent onto the muddy shore. The heavy drone wasn't traffic in the distance but bluebottle flies gorging on the sewage. I whipped my feet out of the water and struggled quickly to the top of the bank, anxious to put distance between that floating death and myself. The spell was broken.

November 16th. Florida was warm and foggy. A big sign at the border begged, "Help keep Florida green. Bring money". I arrived for my free glass of orange juice.

By November 18th, I was in Miami. Apart from the beaches, many marked "private property" or "whites only", there was little to see. So I took off up the west coast of the peninsula. In the Everglades, Seminoles lived and cooked on raised platforms above the swamp and sold souvenirs made of alligator hide. They raised baby alligators in big muddy pits and charged visitors admission to see them. They owned almost nothing except a few pots and pans – and the alligators.

Past Tallahassee, I picked up a lift with a preacher screeching gospel songs and regaling me with a fundamentalism unlike any I had ever heard before. As the spirit moved him, he refreshed his vocal cords from a bottle tucked beside his seat.

After navigating through swamps and over long, single-lane bridges, we arrived in New Orleans. My host invited me to a gospel meeting where he was summoned to spread the good word. The congregation, entirely "po' white trash", brought the roof down with their "singin', 'n' stompin', n' praisin' Jeeeesus!"

I loved it!

Following the "meetin'", I booked a room at the Y and went from there, by invitation, to attend a New Orleans funeral. Members of the marching band started off slowly and solemnly then got livelier and livelier as they moved away from the cemetery.

In "N'Orleans" caskets were placed in rows, in above-ground vaults, stacked one upon t'other. I was told that when the rent didn't get paid, bones would be placed in a common vault. Then on Resurrection Day, people would be calling out, "Who got my arm?" and "Where's my leg?" and "Can't find my hipbone."

On Sunday, I attended Mass at the Catholic cathedral. During the service, Blacks knelt at the back of the church and did not come to the railing for communion. Did a Black priest bring them communion where they were? I failed to notice.

I was running again. A series of rides took me through Baton Rouge, Lafayette, and on toward Houston. Without stopping, I travelled south until a trucker, who had picked me up an hour or two earlier, slowed by a desolate strip of sandy beach. My bladder was at the bursting point. I begged to stop.

"Enjoy the view. Watch out for water moccasins!" Spitting tobacco juice from the window, the truck driver stopped his rig and dropped me off. Then, with a friendly wave and loudly protesting gears, he disappeared.

After relieving myself, I sat on a grassy bank and gazed at the salty foam tumbling odds and sods of material back and forth, back and forth. I wondered how long it would take to wear the pebbles and shells down into smooth sand. I was one of those bits of flotsam, tumbling back and forth, back and forth in the sea. A glittering wave – the wake from an oil tanker – crashed loudly on the sand, and retreated to leave bits of shells, polished glass, driftwood, and bone. Would I survive long enough to become as smooth as all those shiny little objects?

I walked along the white sand beach. The moving water beckoned me: "Remove your shoes and socks; cool your aching feet." Only ankle deep in white foam, golden flecks danced on the surface while silver minnows tickled my toes. The experience was sensual, almost orgasmic.

I looked about. Not a soul in sight. I stripped, tossed my Navy jumper, shirt, pants, and shorts onto the shore and plunged into the sea and sun.

This was about as far from anywhere as I had ever been in my life. Here I could have stayed forever. Nobody would ever have found me. One full hour passed in a moment.

Way off in the distance, I heard a truck. Hurriedly, I donned my clothes, grabbed my shoes and socks and hat and bag, and stuck my thumb out.

Just in time. The trucker who had dropped me off was on his return leg to Freeport. In Freeport, he knew a "feller" who had to drive to Houston. He'd arrange a lift for me.

By December 1st, I was in Northern California, exhausted and down to a handful of dollars and some loose change. Routes north of Sacramento were snowed in and too cold and dangerous for hitchhiking. As a stranded Canadian sailor, I cadged a long flight from McClellan Air Force Base to Amarillo, Texas, followed by a shorter jump to Albuquerque, New Mexico, where I hoped to get a flight northeast. But as everything was snowed in, nothing was moving.

December 4th, I inched my way towards Montreal. Outside Saint Louis, I left Route 66 with a trucker bound for Pittsburgh, Pennsylvania. Poor company for the trucker, I slept my way to the far side of Pittsburgh where he dropped me off.

Long past a frigid midnight, I stood in car-whipped slush outside a greasy spoon until I could bear no more. The door squealed my entrance. I cleared my throat. In stained apron, buttoned cardigan, and hair in curlers, she oozed up to the counter from behind a shabby green curtain.

"Hello. I'd like a cup of coffee, please."

She pulled the cardigan tight around her throat, reached for the near-empty pot on the two-ring burner, and poured me a cup. As she pushed it across the counter, some of the brown fluid sloshed onto the saucer.

"Do you have any cream?"

She dragged her slippered feet to the far end of the counter, grabbed a small pitcher, and slammed it down.

"Thanks for the warm welcome."

"That'll be ten cents. Jar's fer tips." With that she returned to the back room.

Nursing the lukewarm cup, I kept an eye out for approaching traffic – any approaching traffic. Nothing. As soon as I felt warm enough, I headed back out to stand my vigil once more. The café – actually it looked like an abandoned school bus – sat at a crossroads.

At the highway, I'd lost my sense of direction. Both roads looked the same. I had jumped around so much trying to keep warm that I couldn't remember the direction I had come from. My brain was numb with cold.

I slogged back to the café. The waitress reemerged, narrowing her beady little eyes.

"I'm sorry to bother you. But which direction is northeast?"

She shook her head. She had a real loser on her hands. Wordlessly, she pointed.

"Thank you."

Fingers crossed, I returned to the highway. Minutes felt like hours. The wind rose, cold and menacing, threatening snow. I looked at the stark silver sky and full frigid moon peeping through clouds and smelled wood smoke – alder, maple, and fir. Occasionally cars whizzed by. Nobody pulled in to the greasy spoon. Nobody stopped on the road.

The sun finally rose bright and cold, with the sounds of a new day. A train-whistle wailed, long and low. In the distance, someone chopped wood. Someone else revved up a chain saw. A dog sent his message down the line: an intruder had entered his domain. Another dog, with a deeper voice, recounted his night adventures. Still others boasted of various pursuits: a rabbit maybe, a cat on a fence.

A train howled nearby, warning chickens, foxes and sleepy farmers away from the tracks. Half an hour later, an egg salesman gave me a lift. In the warm cab, I soon nodded off and awoke to early morning light on the outskirts of New York City.

I headed into town for a YMCA-USO to catch some sleep before the last stretch to Montreal. At breakfast, three fellows introduced themselves as NHL hockey players and offered me a ride all the way to Montreal. Their names meant nothing to me as I knew absolutely nothing about hockey but I enjoyed the ride. At Montreal Station, I'd finished running for a while, I boarded the train to Strathmore.

My Sister Leaves Home and I'm to Blame

After hitchhiking through snowy weather, I was home at last. But I could stay only for one day to be told by my mother that, thanks to my influence, Naomi had run away from home.

I was blamed and guilty. I also felt a terrible sadness for my sister. As I had done before her, she had fled.

I remembered a conversation Mother had with me during my previous leave home. She told me how unmanageable Naomi had become and wondered, seriously, if she were "possessed by the devil".

The problem was, since an overwhelming speechlessness had arisen between us, I couldn't talk to Naomi, so pre-occupied was I with my own overpowering conflicts.

For her part, obviously, the increased number of household chores, compounded by Mother's railing outbursts and her lack of empathy and appreciation likely made Naomi's life unbearable. Alone, she would have had to do all the baby-sitting and so many of the chores we had previously shared.

Now, I mustered only shame and self-pity. Since I held myself responsible for "abandoning" my sister, I held myself accountable for her running away too. Naomi's pain became my own.

If only I could have turned back the clock. In our early years, Naomi and I had been so close. Then we were pulled apart – separate schools, separate friends. Most damaging of all, we came to vie for Mother's scant love.

In the end, neither of us won it. Ever.

Using her birth name, Naomi had joined the WRENS – the women's branch of the Royal Canadian Navy. I don't know how she enlisted without our parents' knowledge. Being underage, she would have required a parent's signature to join up. Maybe our parents did know how she signed up, but decided not to tell me. Maybe they signed for her. I don't know.

Because she joined as Milne and I was Bertrand, nobody in the Navy would have connected the two of us. We were destined not to see each other again for many years. It never occurred to me to look for the name Milne. My father was dead.

The next morning early, confused and angry and more alone than ever, I made my way through Montreal and got a ride all the way to Quebec City. My aunts and uncles greeted me warmly, as always. I told them I had to leave as soon as possible or I'd arrive AWOL and be in deep trouble. They served me a good dinner and insisted I stay the night. The next day, Uncle Emilien paid for a ticket and put me on a train for Halifax. I got back just under the gun.

HMCS *Quebec*

From December 17th, 1952 until January 6th, 1953, I was stationed as a replacement Admin Writer at HMCS *Shearwater*, Naval Air Station, Dartmouth, Nova Scotia, across the bay from Halifax. While others took Christmas and New Year's leave, I sat on duty at a desk in a draughty office at the back of one of the hangars. The base was all but deserted. I had little to do except read and look forward to my next posting.

January 7th, I was transferred to the Cruiser HMCS *Quebec* (another gift or purchase from the Royal Navy). The "Old Man" was Mr. Seamanlike Manner himself – Captain Budge. On the Maggie, I had been disappointed at not having visited foreign ports. This posting promised travel at last.

My messmates were all supply ratings – writers and stores personnel. We slung our hammocks crisscross above the mess table. Soon we became the best of buddies in the cramped quarters. In the evenings we drank hot cocoa and dined on toast with peanut butter or jam.

Ships at sea carried movies, which were exchanged in port. Sometimes we saw the same movie several times. We whooped and whistled during love scenes or when an actor or actress said a phrase that could be given a double meaning. Mostly we read pocket novels – Erskine Caldwell was popular with three or four copies of *God's Little Acre* and *Tobacco Road* in circulation at any given moment. Others played cribbage at every opportunity or solitaire when they found themselves alone.

For our meals we took trays up the gangway and along the ship's railing to the galley, then returned to the mess as quickly as possible. In calm weather this was easy. In rough weather, food got soaked with salt spray or even washed from our trays.

I was happy onboard the *Quebec*, especially when we were at sea and despite the occasional seasickness. Although I didn't play cards or roll dice, I was one of the boys. There were no bullies among the supply ratings.

In February, we put to sea on a Caribbean Cruise: Bermuda, Tortola in the Virgin Islands and, finally, Trinidad and shore leave.

Some Trinidad taxi drivers had a reputation. They drove unwary passengers by a circuitous route and charged a much higher than normal fare. Our driver turned out to be one such crook. Having previously visited Port of Spain, a member of our group knew what to do. At first, he said nothing. Then, when we drew close to town, he announced, "Stop, quick! I'm going to be sick." As soon as the driver stopped, we all bailed out to "help" the poor fellow.

"One, two, three!" We ran like hell, leaving the taxi driver cursing the fate he so richly deserved.

In Port of Spain, shopkeepers vied for attention. One called out, "Dirty postcards. You want dirty picture, Johnny? You like?" (The moniker "Johnny" came from the wartime comic strip – Johnny Canuck.)

I tried to ignore the little man in the long yellow shirt and orange turban. But he persisted, grabbing at my sleeve with his grubby hands.

"No, Johnny? You no want? I give them to you cheap. Look! Look!" He shoved the cards into my face.

I glanced at the black and white photographs – very explicit. I shook my head. "No, thank you."

One of my Navy buddies helped me out. "Fuck off. He's not interested."

Another in our group haggled with the man. When he sensed he'd gotten a bargain, he bought the pack. The triumphant vendor melted into the crowd of hawkers. Persistence pays off. In the safety of a quiet corner, we all crowded round to view the purchase. The first five photos were what we'd seen; the other nineteen were just ordinary postcards.

Wherever we walked on the streets, young boys of eight or nine ran up to us, tugged at our Navy whites, and peered up at us with big, appealing eyes and earnest faces. "You want girl? You want fuck my sister?"

Our refusals didn't stop them. "Johnny, you want my mother, my brother? You give me money."

Through all of this, I didn't realize a group of my messmates had taken up a collection to help rid me of my virginity. When they treated me to a rum and coke at a rough wooden table outside a motley collection of straw huts, I should have suspected this was where my "rite of initiation" was to be conducted.

After we laughed and chattered a while, a black girl, maybe sixteen years old, sat down to drink with us. Her thin cotton dress exposed her small, firm breasts; the hemline passed just below her aureola.

My breath shortened. Extraordinarily, to me at least, she snuggled up, held my hand, and gazed right into my eyes. I felt flattered – and horny.

Meanwhile, one of the guys paid "the man". "Go get her, tiger!"

Mesmerized, I followed the girl's swaying bottom and bare feet. Inside a dirt floor hut, I saw a room with several curtained-off sections. My companion took me behind one of the curtains and whispered into my ear, "Take off your shoes." Shaking like an overeager puppy, I obeyed. She undid my pants buttons, removed my bell-bottoms and shorts, and gently washed my privates with a warm solution. My knees nearly buckled.

All the while she gazed into my eyes. Oh, what love!

At last, she removed her dress and stood before me, stark naked. Never before had I seen a female body in such magnificence. This was beyond my wildest dreams.

She led me to the nearby cot, lay down, and pulled me on top of her. Suddenly, horror of horrors, my equipment shrank to the size of a raisin. No matter what this gorgeous creature did to arouse me, "wee Willie" would not cooperate. She placed my hand on her wet fur and writhed, groaning in my ear. Nothing! I wanted the dirt floor to split open and swallow me up.

In the face of utter failure, I turned into a whimpering child. "It … it must be the rum."

Eventually, the girl's pimp grew impatient; other customers were waiting. "No more time. No more time. You get dressed Johnny."

When I exited the hut, I sensed the whole world stared at me, this sailor with the pea-sized penis. I raced back to the ship in a taxi on my own.

Though I scrubbed and scrubbed in a long, long shower, I couldn't get clean. Deep down, I was terrified I'd come down with some horrible venereal disease. Maybe this was why I had been unable to perform. Sex with a prostitute had nothing to do with love. My teenage fantasies had been shattered. Another phase of my life had passed.

Navy life certainly had its cruel turns. One day, one of the supply ratings was accused of stealing from a messmate's locker. A group of men held him down and stomped the fingers on both his hands to a pulp. He told the ship's doctor a hatch had crushed his fingers. No longer able to write, he was handed a medical discharge.

Another time, three stokers decided to take a side trip to Venezuela. Several months later, they were brought back to Halifax where they were sentenced to six months in the army detention barracks. There, the Army Provost Corps used every method imaginable to break the spirits of unruly soldiers, sailors, and airmen.

Some inmates even broke their own arms to escape time in detention. First, new arrivals had their heads shaved. After that, things got worse. Punishments were exquisite. Scrubbing decks with toothbrushes. Spending hot days running up hills carrying packs loaded with rocks. In icy weather, digging deep holes then filling them in, and digging new holes elsewhere.

Those who did time in detention seldom behaved the same after their release. Depending upon the original charge or charges, dishonourable discharge usually followed. Some poor souls had their sentences lengthened for attempting to escape. Detention was reserved mainly for striking an officer, theft, desertion, and sleeping on duty.

On duty watch, talking to the seagulls for hours and hours, I sometimes found myself dozing off. It is a dreadful feeling to fight drowsiness on pain of major punishment. I heard about one seaman who stood watch during the wee hours of the morning. He had just dozed off in a standing position when he looked up to see the officer of the watch standing before him, the padre at his side.

"Sleeping on watch, my good man?"

"Just saying a short prayer, sir."

"God bless you, son."

Following further exercises at sea, we sailed from the Gulf of Mexico into the muddy waters of the Mississippi and docked at New Orleans, quite a way inland.

I went ashore on my own. While I looked at art hanging in a small gallery, an artist offered to pay me if I would permit him to paint me in uniform. The portrait would hang in the window of his art shop. Thrilled by the thought of being an artist's model, I said, "Sure!"

The man painted a remarkably quick portrait. Then he suggested we relax for a while. At this point, I realized he had other intentions. I refused his advances and asked for the money he promised to pay me; instead, he threw me out and threatened to call the police. I fled the scene.

Before returning to the ship, I bought a small set of oil paints, turpentine, a couple of brushes, and three small canvas boards. The next day I remained on board ship and tried my hand at painting.

I spent the afternoon covering a canvas with a beginner's impression of the New Orleans dock. When several shipmates returned onboard after having spent the day in local bars, one of them remarked favourably on my painting. Another ran his hand across the wet canvas and wiped the paint on my shirt. Someone yelled, "Hit him, Slim!" Quickly a group of spectators assembled.

Everyone yelled, "Fight! Fight! Fight!"

I stood, shaking. A rating in the shouting circle calmly urged, "Count to ten, Slim, then hit him!" Another sneered, "Ah! He's too yellow."

I could no longer lose face. These were the messmates with whom I lived day after day. Anything to avoid a fight? Laugh off the ruined painting and the paint on my shirt? No! Not this time. It was time to take a stand.

Suddenly I felt the excitement of the moment. I counted. "One. Two. Three. ..." Before I reached ten, I drew back and swung with all my strength – and connected.

Displaying a look of utter amazement, the fellow reeled, dropped to his knees, tottered, and fell forward, oh-so-slowly. Everyone cheered. Though I shook like the last petal on a dead tulip, I felt elated, dangerously heroic. Messmates slapped me on the back and gave me three rousing cheers. A few seconds later, my knuckles and wrist began to hurt like hell.

Slowly, menacingly, the inebriate hoisted himself from the deck and tried to get back at me. Luckily for me, someone held him back.

Attracted by the commotion, the officer of the watch appeared and demanded an explanation. Fighting on board ship was a serious offence. There would be no excuse for what I'd done.

Next day I was brought up on charge. Captain Budge asked the customary "Do you have anything to say for yourself, son?"

"No, sir!"

"Fourteen days number eleven. And ... congratulations!"

Was I now a man? If so, my stepfather's mandate had been met. No matter, I had gained acceptance by the crew, and several of my messmates approached me to voice support. Even the fourteen days punishment involved only light duties, a mere formality. Best of all, the fellow I hit came to shake my hand. We didn't become the best of friends but I had gained his respect. At last, I fitted in.

Exercise Mainbrace

On our return to Halifax, I was transferred back to *Stadacona*. The *Quebec* prepared to sail to Portsmouth for the "Spithead Review", where ships from all parts of the British Empire would sail by in honour of the newly crowned Queen Elizabeth II. Though George VI had died early in 1952, the coronation of the new Queen wasn't held until June 2, 1953. I was bitterly disappointed not to be going.

At this point, disheartened with the Navy, disappointed with my parents, and angry with God, I did something I later came to regret. With strong encouragement from the Presbyterian padre, I officially renounced my Catholicism before his congregation in Halifax and was received warmly as a newfound "Christian". That was my last visit to any church for several years.

I made my statement all right. But I paid a penalty for it: I lost many of my closest friends. As I thrashed about, lonely and confused, I applied for a discharge from the Royal Canadian Navy. I wanted to return to school and make something of myself, far from constant disappointments, far from the bullying, the threats, and the stench of drunken messmates. I was getting ready to run again.

When the *Quebec* returned to Canada in September, I was reposted to her. Almost right away, we sailed through a hurricane to take part in Exercise Mainbrace, where we played war games with ships and submarines of the American, British, and other Commonwealth navies. I had reached my twentieth birthday that June, and was now eligible for the daily tot. Without that daily rum ration – a drink so strong that the first gulp almost pulverized me – I would not have survived the seasickness that attacked many of us from the moment we left our hammocks. The Navy rum mixed with Coca Cola gave us the appetite we needed to eat a hearty lunch. This, in turn, set our stomachs straight for the remainder of the day.

Sometimes, when the weather was especially rough – as it was during that hurricane – many of us not on watch unrolled our hammocks and slung them from iron hooks. Set into the cross members of the deck-head, the hooks were spaced far enough apart to permit each man a regulation eighteen inches. Swinging gently as the ship rolled at sea, the hammocks provided a fair amount of comfort.

Each morning we rolled our hammocks into tight, cylindrical shapes, secured them with rope lashings, and stowed them for the day. On stormy days, following morning inspections, many of us re-slung our hammocks and left them that way for the remainder of the day.

Following a rough crossing, we anchored off Greenock, Scotland. Glad to touch solid ground, every one of us who wasn't on duty boarded the train for Glasgow. A number of us ended up at a dance crowded with sailors from several national navies. When a fight broke out between Australian and American sailors, I escaped with my dance partner, Molly.

Molly invited me to spend a weekend at Milngavie – ("Moguy") – in her parents' home. We walked along the glen, talked, and held hands. When we kissed, her mouth tasted like honey. I was in heaven. Unhappily, when we attended a movie and stage show in Glasgow on Saturday night, I sat in a nest of fleas. I made frantic trips to the theatre washroom, even removed my pants, turned them inside out, and shook them thoroughly. Nothing could rid me of the annoying itch.

Molly's parents cooked a beautiful dinner, then left us to spend a romantic evening alone. Apparently they not only liked me, they trusted me with their daughter. And I respected that trust. I had never before spent such an intimate time with anyone.

When I boarded the train back to Greenock, clutching the apple Molly gave me with her last kiss, I swore I would love her forever and one day come back to Milngavie and my true love.

Forever ended, all too soon. My true love never answered my love letters. I'm sure I was the butt of Molly's parents' condemnation, when they discovered pesky insects in the bedroom where "that wretched Canadian sailor" had slept.

Not long after my return to Halifax, I was again transferred to *Stadacona*. My discharge was granted, effective November 22nd, 1953. I had thirty-two days to wait.

Those final days in the Navy proved to be the unhappiest and most confused of my life. I was full of regret. I could have remained in the RCN, I thought, and retired after twenty years – after all, I only had a small taste of world travel. Instead, I ended my first career in failure, without friends and without any reasonable prospects.

Seven

Sparks and Sputters

1953 – 1955

Hitchhiking

New Brunswick

I was paid out, with advance funds included for annual leave. I sent my kit bag by train to Montreal and headed for the highway, in civilian clothes, to hitchhike west.

My intention was to leave my navy gear at my parents' home and travel to Victoria, where I would find a job and attend night school classes. Foreseeing no difficulties, I brimmed with idealistic plans. I had worked with Cubs and taught swimming at the "Y", and enjoyed both. I set my sights on becoming a teacher. My future lay ahead. I was free to make my own choices and ready to set the world on fire.

With more money on my person than I ever had in my life, I divided the larger bills and placed them flat in both shoes for safekeeping. Though this felt uncomfortable, I welcomed the sense of security it gave me. Then with my light carrying case and Navy Burberry (light raincoat), I headed for the highway. It was late afternoon before I got my first ride. My hands and feet were frozen. But the cab of the transport truck soon warmed me. And the driver was equally warm.

As I didn't want to spend money on motels, I decided to keep on travelling. The trucker dropped me off near the far side of Moncton, New Brunswick. Following a lengthy walk to a suitable lift site, I got a short ride with a group of partying college students. They left me on a lonely stretch of highway, before taking off up a gravel side road.

Occasionally a car splashed by. The night grew dark and windy; gradually I turned into an icicle. I was alone in Siberia. Confidence seeped from me as minutes turned into hours. The wind caterwauled with whistles and shrieks.

Then, silence, until the moon peeped out from behind a heavy snow cloud and bathed the trees in ghostly light. A crow flew down from a pine top, cawing and flapping over the glistening roadway. Birds and other creatures of the night joined in the chorus.

The moon hid her face once more. With the renewed blackness, silence returned, punctuated only by the periodic hooting of an unseen owl. A nearby river reinforced my fear. As though pursued by wolves, it gushed out of the forest and tumbled helter-skelter over rocks and tree limbs.

I stood, stamped my feet, ran on the spot, sang into the dark – anything but walk away. I couldn't walk away; the encircling forest would swallow me up. Toes, fingers, ears throbbed with cold.

In the small hours of the morning, a logger and his girlfriend picked me up and took me as far as the Greyhound bus station in Fredericton.

After a hot cup of coffee, I inquired about bus fares, then went into the washroom and took out enough money for a ticket to Quebec City via Rivière du Loup.

Quebec to Kitchener

Three pleasant days in Quebec with aunts and uncles provided the breathing space I needed before facing my parents. As the weather in Quebec was exceedingly cold, I paid for a train ride to Montreal, trusting my funds would hold out until I got to Victoria. I picked up my kit bag at the Montreal Windsor Station and purchased another ticket for the short train ride to Dorval. During the previous October, the family had moved to a new home on Claude Avenue. Since I had no idea where that was, I splurged on a taxi. This was something I would not repeat for many years.

When I informed my parents of my intention to travel west and eventually return to school, both were skeptical. They were especially unhelpful when I said I wanted to study to become a teacher: "It requires character to be a teacher! Why don't you apprentice for a trade? You'd make a good carpenter".

After my brief visit, I left navy gear and other belongings in my mother's care, picked up an extra jersey, a heavier coat, and an old pair of brown shoes – all of which were too tight and would soon have to be discarded. Then I gave Mother most of my money for safekeeping and set out to hitchhike to the Pacific Coast. I wanted to leave the cold climate – my parents and the Canadian winter both.

Instead of travelling north of the Great Lakes, I decided to head for Windsor and take the southern route through the United States. But I was no longer in uniform; hitchhiking was next to impossible.

On the outskirts of Oshawa, a travelling salesman invited me to share a motel room. It was late and well below freezing. Not a good time to try for another ride. He registered as a single so the stay would cost me nothing. However, there was only one bed, a wooden chair and a bedside table. Where would I sleep? I resolved to remain dressed.

The salesman took a bottle out of his travel bag and poured each of us a drink, neat. Soon we crawled into bed in our shorts. Hesitatingly at first, then with increased aggression, he tried putting his hand inside my underwear pants.

I got up quickly, put my feet on the cold floor, and lit one of his cigarettes. Trembling from the cold and from the feelings of revulsion and anger that churned in the pit of my stomach, I hurriedly dressed without saying a word, grabbed my belongings, left the cigarette to smoulder on the salesman's jacket, which he had tossed across the chair, and departed. During all that time, the salesman glared at me. He did not move, even to extinguish the smouldering cigarette. I left the door open, hurriedly backtracked through the cold drizzle, and waited for a fresh lift.

Kitchener, Ontario was as far as I got. That friendly town would become my home until the following spring. Hitchhiking in winter was too much.

Stretchers and Microphones

November 23rd, 1953, I began work as a medical attendant on ambulance service with the Kitchener-Waterloo Hospital at thirty-five dollars per week. Mine was the morning shift – 7:00 AM to 3:00 PM. I was to pack a bag lunch to eat en route. I found room and board with a German-speaking family on Louisa Street.

My first ambulance trip, I helped bag the remains of a person cut to pieces by a train. A policeman on the scene became violently ill. While he vomited, I picked up body pieces and carried them to a plastic sheet. Although latex gloves were used in hospitals, at that time they were not available on that ambulance. This experience didn't bother me until weeks later, when nightmares returned. The hand I'd picked up from the railway track became the hand of a sailor reaching up to me from the frigid North Atlantic almost nine years earlier.

On one call, I sat beside a Mennonite and read to him from his *Bible*. He died before reaching hospital. On still another trip – some déjà vu here – I helped deliver a baby while stranded in a zero-visibility snowstorm, en route to hospital.

Between calls, I worked as an orderly in the wards. I emptied bedpans, changed catheters, and administered enemas. This was a messy job. Once in a while, I got splattered or had a major cleanup. I needed tact and a sense of humour without which I risked overlooking human dignity.

Over the weeks and months, I befriended musicians, conductors, teachers, farmers, doctors, and paupers. It never failed that the dying were anxious to tell their life stories. Every day, I found inspiration in a milieu where all walks of life are levelled.

I was told I had a gentle touch. I shaved patients for operations or for the pleasure of helping an elderly soul. I read to people, held their hands, prayed with the dying, and took the deceased to the hospital morgue. With the elderly, I was frequently the only "relative" present. One patient urinated on my hand and died as I took his rectal temperature.

My favourite part of the hospital was the children's ward. I read stories and sang comical songs from my own childhood. But when a child died, I was devastated for days.

When I left the Navy, I had developed an annoying stutter. Since I wanted to get rid of this, I decided to emulate Demosthenes. I placed marbles in my mouth and practiced speaking clearly in front of a mirror. The Greek had used pebbles. Close enough. This seemed to be working for me until I swallowed a marble.

Public speaking of a kind soon followed self-improvement. A friend introduced me to James Mitchell, manager of the Kitchener-Waterloo Broadcasting Company. Mr. Mitchell offered to try me out as part-time announcer and disk jockey. Soon I was leaving the hospital at 3 pm then working the afternoon shift at CKCR, doing newscasts and being "Mr. Musical Sunshine" from four until *God Save the Queen* at midnight.

My salary at the radio station was thirty-five dollars per week, no matter how many extra hours I worked, no matter that I worked on weekends and holidays or not, and no matter that I filled in for other announcers. I was happy. On air I was someone special and Kitchener was my home.

The weather for the day had to be located on a huge vinyl disc with many grooves. Among those grooves, winter snow was situated close to summer heat waves. Most commercial jingles were prerecorded on audiotape. Everything had to be cued to the exact spot and turned on at the right moment. All this got aired in the intervals between popular songs. *Oh Mein*

Papa or *How Much is that Doggie in the Window?* Popular requests of the day were all preselected by each announcer for his own airtime.

We also delivered live commercials and chatted happily with an unseen audience. Some people loved me and phoned in to tell me so. Others couldn't stand my English accent. When I got a terrible cold, several listeners suggested I keep my new voice. It was the deep huskiness they liked.

Excellent rapport existed among the staff. Occasionally, when a special guest came to town, we threw a late night party at the Press Club. On Sunday mornings, I often got called in to broadcast live church programs, including "Maxwell House Coffee Presents Everybody's Favourite Gospel Singer, ... ".

One night, just before closing, I was alone in the station when an ex-employee turned up high as a kite. He begged me to let him do the traditional station closing. "This is CKCR, AM and FM, broadcasting from the Waterloo Trust Arcade Building in downtown Kitchener. We are on the air from ... etc. Ladies and Gentlemen, the Queen."

I was crazy to let him at the controls. Instead of playing the preset recording, he stayed on the microphone and, in a high pitched voice, intoned: "Hello, Canada. So glad to be heah!" I prayed no one heard. Sure enough, the company received several indignant phone calls. Following my contrite explanation, I was warned to keep the door locked when working alone.

Actually, nearly every announcer made bloopers:

"Everybody's Favourite Gospel Slinger, Sinner, er... Singer"

"Where's that damned tape? Oops!"

Though I was happy with both my jobs, I exhausted myself with long hours and lack of sleep. It all caught up with me. I fainted pushing a cadaver down a hospital corridor on a gurney. Corpse and gurney went crashing against swinging doors. One of the hospital administrators told me I could not keep up two jobs. I would have to make a choice. I chose to stick to radio.

On February 21st, 1954, I bid farewell to all the nurses, doctors, fellow orderlies, and hospital staff, and went to prepare for my afternoon programming at CKCR.

Not long after that, on my way to work, I passed a group of people standing near an apartment building. Smoke drifted from an open window. Someone had heard a baby crying. Slim and light, I volunteered to be hoisted through an open window several feet above ground.

Once inside, I saw smoke pouring from a pot on the stove. I put the pot in the sink and turned on the tap. Then I turned off the element and unlocked the apartment door. (There was no baby.)

Firemen and policemen entered with an inebriated owner, who promptly ordered me arrested for breaking and entering. I was not charged. However, a story in the local newspaper the following day reported, "Local announcer held in break and entry". My fellow workers found the event amusing – a certain amount of rivalry always existed amongst members of the media – and I laughed with them. Trouble was, my only suit stank of smoke.

After filling in for fellow workers on several occasions, I had a few days off owed to me. I also had loaned another announcer one hundred dollars. On the Friday, I was due to take my leave I was let go without notice. Though I never got my money back, I was given a letter of recommendation, signed by Mr. Mitchell, recommending me as "an able operator".

In those days, employees had no recourse. Jobs were scarce; competition was keen. Bosses and owners were all-powerful. A more experienced disk jockey left the station at the same time as I and went to a radio station in Toronto.

Down But Not Out –

West Coast

Despite the fact I had done fairly well as an announcer, I had to work hard to find a job. I went to Montreal and applied at CFCF. Then I took a CBC bilingual audition and was told to call back in a few days for the results. Finally, I went to CJAD in Montreal, where I was given a job as technical operator on a trial basis. I moved back into the YMCA. My life seemed to be back together.

One day a message came for me at the front desk of the "Y". I was to contact the CBC. Vancouver had an opening for a bilingual announcer at the new television station. The people at CJAD congratulated me and I left immediately for Vancouver.

It was now spring. As always, I was short of money. My parents "could not afford" to lend me the fare, let alone give me the money they were holding "in safe keeping" for me. So I hitchhiked west, and arrived in Vancouver about a week late. The job at the CBC was already filled; besides, my level of education was "far below par". "Come back when you have a university degree".

I traveled all over the west coast, applying at numerous radio stations. I had run into a brick wall.

Back in Vancouver, with just twenty-five dollars in my wallet, a policeman handed me a twenty-five dollar ticket for jaywalking, payable on the spot.

Crooked police and a gullible victim. This would not happen in Vancouver today.

Now I had no money. And no job! And no place to stay!

That first night, I slept in Stanley Park. Starting at dawn the next morning, I combed the streets looking for work.

Desperately hungry, I entered a restaurant and ordered pasta with meat sauce. Worrying so much about not being able to pay the tab, I developed a stomachache before finishing. I checked out the bathroom and the surrounding area and found no back door, except through the kitchen. Instead, vowing to return and pay my bill as soon as I could, I walked straight out the front door without glancing back.

I felt like a criminal. Not a vagrant, though. I was too well dressed for that.

In desperation, I entered a phone booth and tried a reverse-charge call to Dorval, to beg for temporary funds. Mother hung up. Following a second night in Stanley Park, I saw a help wanted sign at a car wash. I was ready to do anything.

I vacuumed and cleaned inside cars. When I found loose change on the floor or in the ashtray, I considered the money a tip. Before long, someone complained, and I was let go without getting paid. "Go! Or I'll call the police". I left.

With no more than small change, I returned to the restaurant where I had taken the free meal. Introducing myself to the manager, I explained my situation and offered to pay the skipped bill. The manager was impressed and gave me a job as a dishwasher with all I could eat. Soon I had enough money to find a decent place to sleep.

I hated the work; the waitresses and busboys held me in low esteem. But I decided to stick it out until I'd enough saved for the ferry to Victoria.

Vancouver was unfriendly compared to the Victoria I had known. I got into an argument with one of the busboys over a tip supposedly left under one of the plates I was washing. He accused me of taking money I hadn't even seen. The threat of physical violence encouraged me once more to move on. When I received my next pay, I thanked the restaurant manager and resigned. I said nothing about my altercation with the bus boy. Naval training had taught me to keep my mouth shut.

Also, I had never learned to stand up for my rights.

In Victoria, I took a room at the YMCA and found a job selling yard goods at Eaton's. That June, the "Y" was preparing for summer camp at Camp Thunderbird, in the Sooke Hills. As I had been a volunteer swim instructor, I was offered the summer position of camp waterfront director. I quit my job at Eaton's and was driven to camp to prepare for the season. My job was to repair the docks and get the canoes, swim float, and all other waterfront equipment into running shape. A couple of canoes required patching. And the swim area had to be raked and cleared of winter debris.

Camp Thunderbird was established on property that once had belonged to a Japanese fruit farmer. At the start of the war, a vigilante group stormed over from Vancouver and hanged the old man from one of his apple trees. Or so the story went. It was a good one for late at night stories around a campfire. Of course, the man's ghost could often be seen at night – sitting near the dock or strolling down the road with a swinging lamp! Every summer camp must have its ghost. It's obligatory.

The hill on the camp property boasted a long stairway, at the top of which was a chapel for Sunday services. Usually the camp director, Clayton Cameron, conducted the service. But occasionally the duty fell to me. I enjoyed the honour of being chaplain for the day. As I led the campers up the steps, we sang "We Are Climbing Jacob's Ladder." I pointed out the wonders of God's creation to all the restless campers and dreamt of becoming a missionary.

When camp was over in August 1954, I got my job back selling yard goods at Eaton's and took a room with the Cameron family. I taught swimming and diving at the "Y" and became "Akela" – Cub leader, for the 1st Fairfield Cub Pack. The following Christmas, I didn't think of going home. For the time being, my ambition to return to school was set aside.

Shortly after the winter snows and cold weather, the Cameron family moved to Calgary. I moved back to the YMCA, where I learned of an opening on James Island packing explosives. The pay would be better than what I was making at Eaton's, so I took the job, commuting back and forth with a fellow worker in his yellow Cadillac convertible.

Working with dynamite produced terrible headaches and nausea; I was told this would pass as I accustomed myself to the fumes. My coworkers took Copenhagen snuff to help them deal with this. They tucked the powder behind their lower lips and spat out the juice. I tried but swallowed some of the juice and became even sicker. Headaches and nausea persisted.

The William J. Stewart

March 19th, 1955, I got a break. After returning with my pay from James Island, I saw an ad posted on a bulletin board in Victoria harbour. The *William J. Stewart*, a hydrographical survey ship, required a steward. I walked on board and signed up. As the boat was scheduled to sail within a couple of hours, I had to run. I picked up my few belongings at the "Y" and signed out. Then I left a hasty message for the Fairfield Scout Group Committee, regarding my resignation from the Cub pack. I made it back to the ship just before the gangplank was hoisted up.

The first few weeks were great. My duties were light. I cleaned the captain's cabin, made up his bunk, and served meals in the officer's mess. As I could type, I helped out with correspondence and other paper work. In my considerable spare time, I read, fished, and admired the spectacular scenery. With a large hook and a strip of bacon rind, I caught a huge halibut. Several hands helped haul the fish on board, and the cook immediately went to work cutting it up. We caught many red snappers too. But as bottom fish, they were considered garbage – much too bony. So they were thrown back, to float away on the surface. The surveyors often returned with clams and oysters and the occasional abalone, a shellfish that was beaten with a meat mallet and fried. We ate very well indeed.

We stopped at Namu, Bella Coola, and Bella Bella, and charted the inlets of the Queen Charlottes. The other steward – with whom I shared a cabin – told me he planned to disembark at Prince Rupert and make his way north to where "the big money" could be made.

He nearly convinced me to join him – before he showed his sadistic side. In excruciating detail, he described how he tortured his wife by beating her, urinating on her in the bathtub, and pouring cold water on her while she was sleeping. When he asked if I "did special favours for the captain", (implying I was gay), I feared he might want to beat me up.

This short, wiry man could have been handsome if he had taken care of his body and mind. As it was, with his acne scarred cheeks, cigarette stained teeth, long, dandruff-flaked black hair, and malevolent eyes, he repulsed and terrified me. He hated himself nearly as much as he grew to hate me. This meant that, since we had set out to sea, I had to stay out of his way as best I could.

Why did the man come to hate me so? Did my looks rub him the wrong way? Or was it my manner of speech? Maybe he noted my distaste for loud, smelly men with greasy faces, huddled in the boiler room, brandishing wrenches. Maybe he took this as an affront.

Then again, bullies recognize victims. Maybe he had no particular reason at all to dislike me. Hatred sustains itself exceedingly well without benefit of cause.

It wasn't long before I realized that he wanted to kill me.

He was jealous. His job was heavier than mine. He had to wait on the surveyors, their helpers, and other ship's crew. He really wanted my job.

One day, he turned on me and put the boots to me. While I delivered a tray from the galley to the officer's mess, he knocked the tray from my hands and tossed it and its contents overboard. Then he knocked me to the deck and kicked me savagely. I woke up in sickbay with the captain applying ice to my bruised and bleeding face.

I didn't say a word. Instead, when we returned to Victoria, on June 5th, I signed off and ran from another job I had loved.

I had worked at Eaton's for only two short periods. Since I hadn't built up a suitably lengthy employment record, the store wasn't interested in rehiring me. I looked in vain for another job. A new waterfront director had been hired for Camp Thunderbird and all other staffing positions were filled. Someone advised me I would have better luck in Calgary; jobs were opening up throughout Alberta. I traveled with another fellow in the same position as I and shared driving and gas costs.

Thanks to a recommendation from Clay Cameron, my former landlord and camp director from Camp Thunderbird, the Calgary "Y" hired me as a group counsellor for Camp Chief Hector Crawler, located on Bow Lake in the Foothills.

Unfortunately, I had to wait for two or three weeks before starting. A crew had already been signed to do all the required preparation work, such as setting up teepees, preparing the waterfront and main lodges, and cleaning the grounds.

Eight

BED SHEETS AND MATCHES

1955

INTRODUCTION TO CIVIL RIGHTS

June 1955, while waiting for camp, I volunteered to help out in the YMCA youth office. I typed, filed, and provided general assistance in exchange for room and board.

One of the staff introduced me to a well-spoken black fellow, a Quaker – member of the Society of Friends.

Winston was in need of a volunteer to assist with correspondence and to accompany him on a brief visit to the Tenth Anniversary Commemoration Celebration of the United Nations in San Francisco, from the 20th to the 26th June 1955. His involvement came through the National Association for the Advancement of Coloured People. Winston explained there would be no payment involved. But I would be welcome to live comfortably in his home, where I would be well cared for. And the experience would provide me with an opportunity to help my fellow man. Winston handled the arrangements with the "Y" for me. I would work at Camp Chief Hector Crawler for the six weeks of camp, during July and part of August. But first, I would attend the San Francisco Conference. Without second thought, I jumped at the opportunity.

Winston's house in Calgary was in a well-kept neighbourhood. I thought I'd be very comfortable. There was just one problem. Winston invited me to sleep with him. In response, I asked to sleep on a chesterfield or in one of his spare rooms. Immediately, I was shown to a private bedroom. But that didn't stop me from planning my quiet departure. I had made a terrible mistake.

I waited fully dressed until I thought my host would be asleep. Carefully, I opened the bedroom door and headed for the front entrance. I had to pass through the living room. To my dismay, Winston sat at his desk, going over papers.

He spoke in a soft, steady voice, without looking up. "There's no need to sneak off like a thief in the night! Come and sit down."

I shook uncontrollably, almost in tears.

"What is it about me that frightens you?"

I couldn't answer. I just stood there, confused and dazed, and looked at my hands, my bag on the floor in front of me. I thought I'd throw up.

Winston swivelled around to face me. He spoke in an even tone. "I promise you that who I am and how I live has no bearing on what I do or the cause I work for. You told me you want to fight prejudice. Do you really know what prejudice is?"

He paused for an answer. I couldn't speak.

"You judge me by people you've known before. Maybe they've hurt you. Well, I'm not them. I'm me. So accept me as I am. Since I respect you for who you are, I'd expect no less from you."

Knees buckling, I felt an absolute fool. I struggled to fight back tears.

Winston continued. "If you still wish, you may leave, but allow me to drive you to the Y. You'd probably get lost from here."

Stammering, "I'm really sorry." I took a deep breath and shook my head. I tried to still the quaking in my knees. "I made a hasty judgment. I'd like to stay. I really am sorry."

Finally, I sat down, feeling sick and dizzy.

I felt humiliated and vulnerable and terribly, terribly wrong. Winston offered his hand. I took it. "I'll get you a cup of coffee. I think we need to have a good talk."

At about three in the morning, Winston and I made our way to our separate bedrooms. For the first time in years, I felt a sense of purpose. What an introduction! I had so much to learn. I even felt a sense of excitement: "Yes, Mother. I'll be a hero yet."

The next morning the sun beamed through the curtains. I heard a knock at my door. "Are you going to sleep all day? Come have some breakfast; we've got work to do."

Before long I was busy taking dictation and typing letters.

Visitors – and there were many – always knew, without a word being said, that I was "straight". Winston had many friends, both men and women. Most were dark skinned. Since everyone was kind and considerate, I felt increasingly comfortable working and learning. But there were times when I wondered if people at the Calgary YMCA "knew" – and misunderstood – about Winston and me. I had a terrible fear of being labelled "homosexual".

I enjoyed Sunday afternoon barbecues and relaxed with Winston's guests in the warm sun. One very dark woman told me why people of African descent cover up with big hats, long sleeves, even gloves. "We burn in the sun just as white folk do. Our dark skin attracts the burning rays. Light colours reflect the sunlight and keep us cool."

I learned many lessons in the short period of time I was involved with the Friends and the civil rights movement. The Quakers had founded the American Friends Service Committee in 1917 to assist black servicemen during World War I; in 1947, the committee won the Nobel Peace Prize. I learned also that the Friends served in many countries worldwide as doctors, nurses, and teachers, during the Second World War and during later civil wars, long before *Medecins Sans Frontiers* (Doctors Without Borders), the American Peace Corps, and United Nations Services were formed.

I had already seen some of the conditions that "people of colour" had to suffer, not only in the South, but also in parts of Canada – such as near Halifax where I had black friends during my days at Stadacona and Shearwater. Although, during my travels through the United States, I never stopped long enough to really observe what was going on, I heard stories of how non-whites were insulted openly as "black cows" and "black apes". I was told how Blacks were forced to pay their bus fares, then get off the bus to enter by the back door, and that sometimes drivers, with their fare in the box, were encouraged to drive off without them.

In some states, there were separate theatres for "negroes". Their films were always a couple of years or more behind what the whites had already seen. I had seen the separate toilets and drinking fountains and knew that only whites were permitted to eat in good restaurants or stay in decent hotels or swim at public beaches. I had felt very uncomfortable when Blacks stepped off the sidewalk to allow a white person to pass by.

I had also witnessed the racial intolerance that existed in Canada. Blacks had difficulty registering at hotels in Montreal. The situation in Halifax was even worse where blacks were not permitted in many restaurants and where they were segregated in theatres. Friends cautioned me while others openly called me "nigger lover" for befriending a black family in Africville while stationed at Stadacona.

During the 60s, the City of Halifax amalgamated Africville and relocated the residents to make room for a bridge.

Somewhere around 15th June 1955, Winston and I left for San Francisco. First, we drove west to Vancouver. I didn't realize at the time that, had we traveled the more direct route over better highways through Montana and Idaho, we would have experienced the difficulties posed for mixed races travelling together.

While at the Commemoration which opened June 20th at the San Francisco Opera House, I had the privilege of being introduced to Paul Robeson. The famous bass singer was active in Civil Rights for much of his life. When I was small, he had also been a good friend of my mother and father in Finchingfield. Mother's oil portrait of him hung in our home for many years.

Robeson remembered my parents and repeated what Mother had once told me – that when I was born, a witch doctor foretold I would one-day work for his people. Again I entertained visions of travelling to Africa. This man's influence was primary in convincing me to commit to the struggle for justice for African Americans.

Camp Hector Crawler

After San Francisco, I attended the Calgary YMCA Camp as a section counsellor. Not having gone through orientation with the younger counsellors and having replaced a more popular fellow who had been "let go", I found myself unwelcome.

The counsellors at Camp Hector Crawler were rougher than their counterparts in Victoria. Campers who wet the bed were dumped into the lake. I protested, and the practice was not repeated in my section. Although the Camp Director was likely unaware of the way some counsellors treated their young charges, I was told by my fellow staff members not to try to change traditions or interfere in areas that were none of my business.

I suggested the ceremonial campfire lighting we had used at Camp Thunderbird, where we placed a piece of magnesium on a tin plate and covered it with fine kindling. Then we buried a rubber hose up an incline to a spot behind a tree. Water poured into a funnel ignited the magnesium. the fire that was started by the "sacred words of the Camp Chief".

Because, by age-old tradition, the campfire at Camp Hector Crawler featured a flaming arrow shot by a senior counsellor from outside the ring, my suggestion fell on deaf ears.

The YMCA had a contract with some local First Nations to provide ponies at the camp. Most of the horses were mild and even-tempered. Only a few were frisky and shied at the slightest provocation. Campers and counsellors went riding bareback along narrow trails in the steep foothills. My first time out, someone flicked my mount with a branch he was using as a whip. My horse took off at breakneck speed. I held on to its neck as long as I could, but got thrown onto a rocky path. I returned to camp on foot. My pony grazed dispassionately in the paddock.

The next time we went riding, the pony crew assigned me an ancient nag, separated from her skeleton by just a few pounds of meat. When I urged her to get moving, she broke wind and wafted me with the aroma of her impending death. I ended up so far behind even the most timid camper that I turned old Bessie around, returned to camp, and passed up the entire excursion. Though I felt a little guilty – the group for which I was responsible was off in the mountains somewhere without its "fearless leader" – I enjoyed a day without responsibilities.

A few nights later, a group of hooded counsellors yanked me out of bed and tossed me into the freezing waters of Bow Lake. This was an embarrassing situation. I was supposed to be in a position of authority, but had lost all respect. What was I doing at that camp? At Camp Thunderbird – the Victoria Y camp – I had been effective as a youth leader. Here, in this violently macho atmosphere, I was lost.

I was happy when the season ended. I didn't remain for cleanup.

Training on the Reserve

Back at the "Y", Winston suggested I try my hand at helping with native children not attending regular or band schools. I would live with one of the band families, as it would be too far to travel back and forth each day. Flattered, I jumped at the opportunity. Of course, I knew absolutely nothing about teaching. Winston was unaware that I hadn't even finished high school. He hadn't asked and I wasn't about to tell him. Since this was to be a short-term volunteer position, I didn't think it mattered.

So, every day for about three weeks I sat with two or three of the youngest children and helped them stumble their way through a primary reader. "Lessons" never lasted longer than fifteen or twenty minutes before my charges ran off with a whoop. Sometimes, insistent mothers would bring several such groups to me in succession. I felt very useful and important.

Many of these people lived in squalor. On weekends, beer, whiskey, cheap wine, and lemon and vanilla extract turned up and fights broke out.

Some, perhaps many, of those Native Canadians, who had served in the Canadian Army in Europe, had learned to drink with their comrades. There they had become accustomed to being treated like everyone else. Back home in Canada, however, they broke the law. The RCMP routinely raided and seized whatever they could find.

One Friday afternoon, I was asked to drive a fellow who had lost his licence to Calgary. En route, a truckload of screaming youths harassed us and tried to drive us off the road. The only thing we could do was keep going at a steady rate, being careful not to break speed limits.

I had mixed feelings when Winston and another Friend drove up and some members of the band came out to bid me farewell and presented me with doeskin pants, top, and moccasins. I was thrilled I had passed the test. My work with the Alberta Friends was complete. It was time to move on to another assignment.

Bed Sheets and Matches

I had been preparing for this a long time. My "missionary" zeal was soon to be tested to the extreme. I was to be driven by various people to New York City, where I would work with one of the Friends in Harlem.

When we arrived, we climbed several flights of stairs in a noisy tenement. A knock at the door provoked loud barking and "Down, boy!" We identified ourselves and a grey-haired matriarch in a wheelchair opened the door. She had no dog. She did her own barking.

For the next several weeks, I typed letters, delivered messages, and ran for groceries. I soon learned why I lived with such a vicious guard dog. In that neighbourhood, muggings and break-ins were an everyday occurrence. At night, I lay awake, listening to the sounds of poverty. Babies cried endlessly, sirens wailed, unhappy voices screamed at one another. But not all was sadness.

On Sundays, we went to the Baptist Church where the singing and preaching and "amens" and "Praise Jesuses" were sweeter than I had ever heard in my life. In Harlem, I felt a love and acceptance from everyone I met, at the church meetings as well as at various private gatherings in people's homes. I never did get to attend a Quaker meeting either in Calgary or Harlem.

Apart from what I wore, I had scant belongings. I had an electric razor – which I still used only twice a week at most – and a toothbrush and comb. Everything fitted into my well-worn Navy carry bag. In my wallet I kept my old Navy I.D. and British Columbia driver's licence. There were no credit cards and S.I.N. numbers in those days. At the most, I had a few U.S. dollars I had been given for emergencies, and some small change. When a well-spoken white fellow, about my age, called for me, I was ready to go.

We drove through Philadelphia and Baltimore. In Washington, we switched to a car with southern licence plates, joining two other volunteers, one white, one black, about our age. My companions were college students who had taken a year off to work for Civil Rights. Not all volunteers were members of the Quaker Church. Many had no religious affiliation whatsoever. All were idealists.

Now and then we stopped at safe houses to freshen up and eat. The term "safe houses" made me think of the safe houses in Harriet Beecher Stowe's story of the Underground Railroad in *Uncle Tom's Cabin*.

Every now and then, a fifty-miles-per-hour speed limit suddenly turned to fifteen miles per hour and a police car would be waiting behind a billboard. Fines were paid on the spot, or with room and board added before a local judge the following day.

While we drove, I learned a lot more about the Movement. My companions talked of Gandhi and nonviolent resistance:

"Evil can only be overcome by love."

"It is better to be the recipient of violence than one who inflicts violence."

"Communism resulted as a protest against hardships and injustices suffered by the underprivileged in many countries."

No, my driving companions were not Communists.

We drove through Lynchburg, Virginia. What a name!

Instead of taking a southwesterly route through mountainous territory, we headed directly south. We took turns driving, sleeping, and looking out for speed traps. We crept through Charlotte, North Carolina, and turned southwest toward Atlanta, Georgia, "Gateway to the South".

Late in the day, a heavy rainstorm forced us to pull over and stop in a rambling community of tumbledown shacks.

Everywhere, rain dripped like tears from leaning gutters. In front of one shack, a mother sat on a porch step under a yellow tarp and dandled her baby. Two toddlers, wearing only ragged t-shirts, floated sticks in a puddle at her feet. When we stopped, she got up and called her children inside. The screen door slammed behind her.

We sat in our car and waited out the storm.

Occasionally, we passed chain gangs cutting ditch grass with scythes. For what I was about to do, I wondered if I might end up on a chain gang.

We stopped to eat at a restaurant in Birmingham. It seemed all eyes were fixed upon us. Not one of us said a word. Our volunteer guide, who had come from the south, ordered for us all.

Later, as we drove southwest towards Tuscaloosa, I learned about Montgomery even further south. It was in Montgomery, the Alabama state capitol and "Cradle of the Confederacy" that Jefferson Davis, the first and only president of the Confederate States of America, raised the rebel flag that now flew in such abundance in every town and hamlet.

Martin Luther King Jr. had, that August, become the pastor of the Dexter Avenue Baptist Church, located just across the street from the state capitol – cradle of American apartheid.

Early in the morning, we left the main road and drove over dusty back roads to a small community that, at first sight, looked abandoned.

Here, well off the beaten track, I saw maybe one hundred and fifty metres of battered shacks. Five cement steps led up to the front door of a sad, red brick bank with a clock in the wall above a big, dusty window. Next to the bank sat a general store with a sloping front porch; in front, a Pepsi sign hung teetering on one rusty chain. At the end of the road, I spotted an unpainted wooden church with a single wooden spire topped with a plain wooden cross. Behind it, a grove of dwarf spruce spread their branches through a white picket fence. Amazingly, the fence appeared freshly painted. Not far from the church

I saw a handful of grave markers. They all looked so dreary – yet, in a strange sort of way – picturesque. Many lay flat, smothered now by thistles and nettles. Behind the graveyard, a turd-brown river slithered along under a rickety wooden bridge.

The entire village seemed deserted.

Caught up by the depressing nature of this place, we hurriedly whispered our goodbyes. One of the fellows grabbed his scant belongings and sped out on foot to follow a path from the church graveyard, across the rickety bridge, and into the woods. He knew where he was going.

I was glad this wasn't going be my assignment.

My own rickety bridges and torpid rivers were to come later.

From Tuscaloosa, we travelled northwest and crossed the state line into Mississippi. Before long, we drove off the main road and into a small community of clapboard houses. Everything was neat and clean. The porches were un-littered and the gardens well cared for. Many of the homes looked freshly painted.

We got out of the car before a plain-looking wooden church. Heat baked the tops of our heads. A black man walked by and lifted his wool cap. "Sho is hot enough. Aint it?" A white cat padded down the street carrying a mewling kitten in her mouth. She placed it on the dusty ground by the church steps and preceded to wash it.

The minister came out of the house next to the church, introduced himself, and invited us inside to meet the handful of people who had turned up to welcome us. The place looked pleasantly comfortable.

We sat on straight-back chairs and sipped ice-cold lemonade. The minister was thin, tall, and shiny bald, with a forehead furrowed like the grooves on a pine fence. While he spoke, a big red Labrador walked in and planted himself at his master's feet.

The Reverend chatted away but, exhausted from the long drive and distracted by the dog, I missed what he said. The dog bit at his fleas, scratched an ear with his hind leg, got up and shook himself, and circled back down into a doze. A large orange cat then walked in, rubbed herself against the Reverend's leg, and curled up beside the dog.

The barefoot minister extended his toe to scratch the scrawny feline under the chin. Just as he made contact, the beast got up, stretched, jumped onto the back of a large easy chair, and tore at her fur with a sandpaper tongue. A flea appeared and crawled across the dog's nose. The dog flicked his head and pounced on the annoying insect.

After introductions were made all 'round, we all got up to depart. I left with the woman in whose home I had been invited to stay. My travel companions drove on to their assignments in Louisiana. I'd never see any of them again.

Apart from whisking me to and from church on Sundays, my hostess expressly warned me to remain indoors throughout my entire stay.

My job was to teach reading and writing on a one-on-one basis, to men and women who had worked in the fields since childhood.

It was a tough job. However, I had patience and a will to succeed. But, in a milieu of fear, I could smell my own fear, and it made me ashamed. I struggled to be heroic.

The neighbourhood had remained peaceful – on the white man's terms, that is – for years. These people certainly didn't want to be labelled "troublemakers". Even if they passed the "literacy test", many of them knew they wouldn't be allowed to vote.

Despite the danger, some were eager to learn. Others, who couldn't overcome their fears, told me, "Why can't you white folks just leave us be? Things was peaceful before you come along."

Some evenings, four or five showed up for lessons. Other evenings, only one or two dared come.

One day I asked my host why he and his wife didn't teach friends and neighbours themselves. He told me he and others like him were teaching many in the community, but that it took a great deal of persuasion for some members to accept help. Without "qualified teachers" – students from northern universities, for example – no one could persuade frightened men and women to attempt to change the status quo.

"Qualified teachers." Why had I allowed everyone to think I was educated? No one had ever asked me for a résumé. So I just stepped in deeper and deeper. What if my students or the Society of Friends discovered that I had not even completed high school? What if they found out that there could be no comparison between me, and those young heroes with whom I had driven to Mississippi?

I was a phoney. Worse, I jeopardized the lives of those I was attempting to help. When I fretted about this – which I did often – a sense of doom overcame me.

I had lived in the Old South only a few weeks when, late one night, a rock crashed through the front window. With much whooping and laughter, a truck screeched off into the dark.

"Don't you worry none," my hostess told me, although I could tell she was shaken. "This just goes to prove you're doing a good job, and some people are taking notice."

I wasn't so sure I wanted them to be taking notice of me. That night, I lay awake listening to the moaning and wailing of the wind. Whipping the tree branches against the cracked windowpane, it played a wild fugue, sometimes dropping to pianissimo, sometimes rising to frenetic crescendo. Occasionally the porch door slammed, screeched, then slammed again.

The next evening, no one showed up for instruction.

Since I was probably the reason for this fear tactic, I knew I had to move! Nobody else wanted to put me up. The people were afraid that their church would be burned down if I stayed where I was. But how could I get away without someone to pick me up and drive me to another location? Despite the fact that I had remained in hiding, the white hierarchy had found me out. Now I was terrified and so, I believed, were my hosts.

A few nights later, I was awakened as several men broke into the house and smashed their way through each room. I hid under my bed. They found me, pulled me out, and wrapped me up in a rough blanket. Sticks, boots and fists flew at me from all directions. I smelled smoke.

My attackers threw me into the back of a pickup truck. With a screech of tires, we sped off. Laughter and more blows from boots and sticks followed. The shouting and violence went on and on. I lost track of it only when I lost consciousness.

The rest is a strange nightmare.

Somewhere in the black of night I heard laughter, bright as polished brass. Then I saw them. Little black boys and girls emerged naked from the woods and danced in a circle around me. They held out their hands to me and called in high, tinkling voices. Then another materialized out of the forest. This boy wore a long, loose-fitting white shirt. He took my hand and led me into the dance, his face oddly familiar.

"Dance, dance," he called, in singsong fashion.

"I can't," I replied. My legs were moored in oozing mud.

"You used to dance with us ... used to dance ... used to dance ... used to dance." As the children retreated into the trees, his voice trailed off. The trees glowed as if on fire.

"Please, don't go." The more I struggled the more my legs sank deeper into the mud. I thought I would be swallowed up.

Shrill laughter echoed from the flaming forest. The children reemerged, now albino white, shrouded in white robes. They attacked me with clacking, sharp teeth and pulled at me with hands that morphed into animal claws. I screamed, loud and long.

Suddenly, the little people vanished. The forest melted. I sat up alone, naked and cold, shivering violently. I tried to open my eyes. But they were glued shut.

I must have passed out again.

When I came to – minutes later? Hours later? – I vomited, alone, in the blackness. After a while, through eyes puffed almost shut, I saw stars in the sky. I groped around and found my pyjama bottoms. When I stood up to put them on, I felt dizzy and blacked out again. Much later, I awoke to a grey dawn, shivering cold and racked with pain. I expected to see signs of the burnt crosses I had heard so much about. Instead, I saw that I was in a garbage dump.

With difficulty, I walked to a dirt road. When I passed a shack, I thought I heard voices. So I knocked on the door. Nobody answered. I walked on, shivering and crying in pain and fear.

Eventually, a police car drove up and stopped.

Much of this is recalled only in nightmares. The rest remains blank. I can only imagine the kind of treatment I must have received at the hands of local law enforcement and judges. How I escaped being sentenced to a prison farm with long days on a chain gang, I'll never know. I vaguely recall somebody driving me to Windsor, Ontario, then to Toronto. From Toronto, somebody else drove me to Dorval. I don't remember if I was driven by Canadian policemen or by people from "The Society of Friends". But I do remember being reminded constantly that I should thank God for being alive.

Rejected – Disowned

I arrived at my parents' home somewhere around the ninth or tenth of December, without money, without having brushed my teeth for days. I wore ragged clothes and desperately needed a bath. My head and face were badly bruised. I needed shoes, socks, underwear, pants, shirts, and, above all, a coat.

I was greeted with disgust and few words. I made my way to the basement where I'd left my belongings stored in boxes. Most of my clothing was gone. I climbed back upstairs and asked Mother where my things were. She told me she'd thrown out my Navy gear a long time ago. And since my doeskin outfit, which I'd mailed home before leaving Calgary, stank of wood smoke and stale sweat, she got rid of that too.

All I could do was return to the basement and scrounge around. I found a pair of grubby Navy boots and brushed them off. I tipped out the rag box and found a couple of Papa's old shirts. I also found a pair of better fitting pants of my own as well as some underwear. Then I spied, hanging on a nail inside a spider web, my Navy flight jacket from Shearwater. Since I found no socks, I screwed up my courage and asked Mother for them. She dug out a pair from the laundry hamper, walked to the top of the cellar stairs, and threw them at me. Not to me.

No money, though. "Sorry! As a matter of fact, Benoît, you can consider yourself disowned."

I felt too ill to argue. I managed only to whisper, "When have I ever **not** been disowned?"

Until now, my stepfather had stayed out of the whole thing. He walked to the top of the cellar stairs and looked down to where I stood, two steps down.

At this point, I hoped Mother would just shove me down the stairs. Then I could hold her responsible for all my troubles. But this didn't happen. I actually stayed just out of her reach. Otherwise, I believe she would have shoved me.

Papa François stood to one side and pointed toward the front door. He looked furious. Never a loud man, he uttered just two words: "Leave, now!"

I stared at him, open mouthed, not daring even to walk past him.

Then he shouted: "Out!"

Mother had opened the front door. I darted to it and slammed it shut – from the inside. Now I, too, was angry. I'd face the Dragon Lady even if it killed me.

At the top of my lungs, I shouted, "Fuck you!" Then I burst into tears. Luckily, since they were in school, my little sisters were spared the rancour. Mother wasn't done with me yet. While I stood at the door trembling, angry and fearful, she gave me the biggest dressing down I ever got from her. As she did so, my stepfather returned to his newspaper; as far as he was concerned, this was strictly between Mother and me.

This time, she didn't shout. I felt all her frustration and venom. Now she stood between the front door and me. I had no choice but to stand there and take it.

"What the hell did you think you were doing, interfering like that in a situation you know absolutely nothing about? You go into somebody else's country with some asinine idea in your head that you can convert the world to your way of thinking. You know absolutely nothing about the people. You have no understanding of the situation. You interfere and create havoc and do nothing but upset everyone. All this so you can be some kind of hero. Well, you might think you can set the world on fire, but don't you dare – don't you dare – come running to us for more matches. You've gotten yourself into this situation. Now you're bloody well going to have to get yourself out of it. Furthermore, when you break the law, you bring shame not only on yourself but on your family, too. We're not going to let you shame us any further. Now, take your belongings and go cry somewhere else."

She stepped aside. I couldn't even look at her. In my anger and humiliation, I shook all over. If I were by a highway or a railway line, I gladly would have thrown myself before an oncoming locomotive. I felt like a stick of dynamite with a lit fuse. I dashed out of the house without knowing which direction to take.

My tears blinded me. Safely out of hearing distance, I threw my bag of clothes to the ground and screamed, at the top of my voice, "Bitch! Bitch! Bitch! Fucking, fucking bitch!"

Yet – as always – not one decibel of sound passed my silent lips. Even at a safe distance, I had no safe distance. My silent scream begged for an audience. My chest ached; I could barely breathe. The world spun about like a kaleidoscope. I took deep breaths; gradually, I regained my composure sufficiently to pick up my things and head for the highway.

Now I felt resolve. Clearly, suicide wasn't the answer. I'd show them. I'd bloody well show them. I'd gone this far. I can go all the way.

I walked the frozen miles to Montreal; it must have taken me several hours. My toes were numb with cold. I don't remember even arriving. I don't remember where I got to. I don't remember where I stayed.

Someone must have taken me in. Perhaps the Salvation Army sheltered me. I only know I ended up, after several days and nights, at H.M.C.S. *Donnacona* on Drummond Street looking for work. I'd come to the right place.

Rising From the Ashes

On December 13th, 1955, wearing an ill-fitting uniform, I again found myself as a Reserve at *Donnacona*, filling in as a Leading Seaman Admin Writer in the recruiting office, while one of the regular staff went on thirty days leave. Luckily for me, there was a shortage of staff over the holiday season. The recruiting officer was able to push through my papers without delay. And the pay officer gave me a small advance on my future earnings, so I could get a room at the YMCA on Drummond Street.

Until Christmas noon, the holiday season had been the loneliest and unhappiest of my life. Christmas dinner turned out to be a hamburger at a fast food joint. That's when everything began to change within me. I felt a desperate need to survive.

While I sat in a plastic booth at a greasy hamburger grill, the Christmas spirit yanked me forcibly from the doldrums. I felt suddenly delirious. I took a sprig of plastic holly from the decoration on the counter and crowned my hamburger "turkey". Then I placed salt-and-pepper shakers as candles at each side of my regal platter. I even splurged on a glass of Pepsi-Cola. Better wine I never tasted.

Tucking a paper serviette under my chin, I took a knife and fork and skillfully carved. After watching me for a while, the waitress sat across the counter from me. Maybe she doubted my sanity. No more than I. Or maybe she thought I was drunk. Well, maybe I was.

"Happy, happy Christmas," I said and toasted her with my first sip of magic wine. She smiled, got up, and walked into the kitchen. I savoured my first bite of festive bird and mashed potato bun. Delicious!

The waitress returned with a slice of lemon meringue pie and placed it before me, with a ceremonious curtsy. "Christmas pudding. Compliments of the house." She smiled and raised her eyebrows, as if to say, "I understand."

Yes, it was Christmas. I had much to be thankful for, although I hadn't figured out just what or where my good fortune lay. I felt deliriously happy. Before returning to my room at the "Y", I strolled St. Catherine Street and took in the joyful sounds of the season – Christmas concert, courtesy of the merchants of Montreal.

I slept well that night.

On January 14th, when the regular Admin Writer returned, I was dispatched to *Stadacona* in Halifax for a fortnight. Since I saw nobody familiar, I felt uncomfortable. The regular ratings seemed to be laughing at me, the reserve replacement, so out of place. A nonresident in a scratchy, ill-fitting uniform, I was forever "moving on" or "hanging about", in corridors, empty offices, even the lavatory.

I felt like a homeless tramp in a large railway station. I had one consolation only: I had managed to pocket a few dollars to help me get started when I returned to Montreal.

I applied to reenter the regular force at *Stadacona*. But, since I had left before completing my original five-year stint, I was turned down. Also, since the Korean conflict had ended, there no longer was the same need for personnel as in 1950.

In mid February, I returned to Montreal, went onto the Emergency Call-up List, found a job at Eaton's selling men's shirts, and took a room in Snowdon, the Jewish section of Montreal.

Nine

SEARCHING FOR THE FOUNTAIN OF LIFE

1956 – 1968

NEW LIFE

In early March 1956, I began night classes at D'Arcy McGee High School in Montreal. The De La Salle Brothers of the Christian Schools taught the classes. I had not seen the inside of a Catholic church since I turned away in protest three years earlier. But the Brothers were kind men and I enjoyed learning under them.

I sped ahead and completed my secondary English and French the following June. I was informed at exam time, however, that since I had not attended the full year of studies, I was not permitted to write the final exams.

Defeated again, I stormed into a nearby church. Then I knelt, sobbing before a statue of Mary. I must have been there a long time. An old priest put his hand on my shoulder. I sat down with him and, like a river breaking through its dam, I sobbed out my failures, my shame, my anger, and my inability to please. I don't recall the old priest's words, only his sense of peace and love. As I sat with him, I felt quietness and peace enveloping me. I wanted to touch God. Through this gentle priest, God reached out and touched me.

I knew my life was going to change. I could succeed. I could prove myself. But I needed help to do it. I don't recall when the old priest left. A caretaker came to where I was sitting. "*Monsieur, c'est tard. Il faut barrer les portes pour la nuit.*" (Sir, it's late. I must lock up for the night.) The church was empty. Before returning to the "Y", I walked deserted streets until I could walk no more.

One of the Brothers had loaned me a copy of Thomas Merton's *Seven-Storey Mountain*. As I began to read Merton's story of conversion to Catholicism and of his journey to the Trappist monastery, I saw parallels in my own running from, and search for, God. That book, more than any other, had a profound effect on me.

Recalling the words of the African witch doctor, Paul Robeson had confided to me in San Francisco, "One day you will return to help my people", I went to see the Missionaries of Africa known as the White Fathers. I was invited to speak to a priest in charge of admissions and told him I'd like to study to become a missionary priest.

The kind Father listened attentively as I poured out my life story. However, I did not mention difficulties I'd had at home. When I was finished, he took my hand and told me that first, I'd have to complete high school before even being considered for the seminary. I'd also need letters of reference and my birth certificate. He suggested I talk first to my parents and to my parish priest and invited me to return to see him once I had a plan of action in mind.

I knew I'd have to consult my mother about my latest ambition, and the prospect terrified me. At one time, she had mentioned the witch doctor's prophecy. This was at about the time I was considering the Navy. I think I was still trying subconsciously to gain her approval. Maybe I could make the prophecy come true, and she would love me as she did when I was a little boy. Maybe even Papa would be happy that I had, at last, found my vocation.

A short visit home brought me more pain. "You, a priest? Benoît, you do not have the character to be a priest. We've given you every opportunity, and you have squandered your life. What have you ever done to show any appreciation for all that we have given you? Be thankful we brought you to Canada. You and Naomi were brought here out of love and kindness, yet you have never tried to belong! You ran off to the Navy, but couldn't even make a go of that. Because of your influence, Naomi ran away, and we have no idea where she is. We've given you everything and you have only given us heartache in return."

Blinded by tears, I fled the house and walked for many hours. Finally, I went back to the White Fathers. This time I kept nothing back including the circumstances of my birth. The Father informed me as gently as he could that, unjust as it might seem, under Canon Law illegitimacy remained a permanent impediment for ordination to the priesthood. Even if I were able to return to school and complete university requirements, the order would not be able to accept me.

Later, a new Code of Canon Law, effective in 1983, declared that being born out of wedlock would no longer bar an applicant from any position or office in the Church.

I prayed. I offered my life to God. But God did not answer my prayers. He didn't want me. I was Catholic enough to accept the miracles God sent my way, but not enough to accept divine plans that contradicted my own.

A Brother who taught night school was the only person I could confide in. I told him how I wanted to be a missionary and how I had struggled to prove myself over the years. I even told him of my visit to my mother and stepfather. He asked, "Do you really want to dedicate your life to God?"

My answer was quick in coming. "Yes, I'll do anything."

The Brother took out a sheet of paper and began taking notes while asking me specific questions such as place and date of birth, Baptism, First Communion, Confirmation. I did not know the dates for the last three. But how could I face my parents again? Surely, I could just sign up and not have to face my mother again until I'd proven myself. No! I had no choice but face more skepticism and further rejection.

I was due for a shock.

For the first time in many years, this new direction – to be a Christian Brother – got my mother's warm approval.

Mother's Secrets

Mother confided in me. She told me I was not the first to be born illegitimate and that it was nothing to be ashamed of. I still don't know whether or not she too was illegitimate, but she did tell me that her grandmother, my great grandmother, and others before her, came from fascinating liaisons.

Mother also told me how her mother refused to acknowledge her as a daughter, passing her off instead as a niece. That was why she had been born in London rather than in Denmark. Mother told me she got revenge by getting into all sorts of mischief.

To keep her out of trouble, her older sister, Ruth, looked after her until she could be sent off to boarding school, and out of her mother's hair. In Mother's words, "Ruth was more a mother to me than my own mother. She looked after me and introduced me to art. Still, I got into all sorts of shenanigans. While boarding at a convent, I took a dare from some classmates and crawled under the bench in chapel to see what the nuns wore under their habits."

Mother told me her father, Oluf Andersen, died when she was just nine. He was not only a ship's captain, he was Mayor of Svendborg in Denmark and was a very popular and jovial man, and a doting father. Mother was devastated when he died, especially when, not long after his death, her mother remarried.

For the first time since early childhood, I felt close to my mother. I clasped her hand and put it to my lips.

Training for Religious Life

My life had taken a major turn. How far I had come from that unhappy day, eons ago, when I formally renounced my Catholic faith in Halifax. After making a full General Confession – privately, with a Catholic priest – I now was back in "a state of grace".

On June 2nd, 1956, just prior to my twenty-third birthday, I was accepted as a Postulant in the Brothers of the Christian Schools and driven to the Noviciate in Scarborough, east of Toronto. I was entering a holy order, devoted to the education of poor boys. This was what I longed for. At last, I could become a teacher.

The Christian Brothers' Mother House was a huge brick building with a bell tower at its centre. It was built on land donated by Senator O'Connor, the founder of Laura Secord Candies. Since the Senator's hobby had been breeding racehorses in the farmland suburb of Scarborough, the property was sizeable.

Boys who indicated a desire to become Brothers were provided high school education as well as room and board. Enrolment in the Junior Noviciate peaked in

1956 –57, with over one hundred boys, some as young as thirteen and fourteen. At age seventeen, these boys entered the Postulancy, where they prepared for acceptance into the Noviciate. The Postulancy lasted for three months, at the end of which candidates became Novices.

Noviciate lasted one full year. After taking First Vows of Poverty, Chastity, and Obedience – "Novices" then became "Scholastics" and studied Dogma, Moral, Worship, Church and Bible History, and the History of the De La Salle

Brothers. Also, they were permitted to continue their higher education, either at Teacher's College or University.

Apart from myself, just two other Postulants had not come directly from the Junior Noviciate. One had worked in comedy with the CBC in Toronto; he left a few weeks into the Postulancy. The other was a fellow from P.E.I. whom the Novices nicknamed "Spud". He and I became very good friends during my time at Scarborough. All the other Postulants were in their teens.

The day began at 5 A.M. with a loud clanging bell and "Live Jesus in Our Hearts" to which we were to respond "Forever!" Another bell rang about fifteen minutes later to call us to chapel for prayer and meditation. After a short break, Mass was at 7 followed by a silent breakfast.

During meals, every Novice and Postulant was invited in turn to stand at a podium and read. When I read, my pronunciation was often corrected. I was sure my version was correct, still I had to repeat the correction as an exercise in obedience and humility.

Reprimands were frequent in those early days. "You were heard singing in the shower!" "There will be no singing!" "The Brother's eyes are to be cast downward at all times." "There is to be no laughter." "Only the devil grins. A serious look must replace that hideous smile."

The Director reminded me that I had come to the Brothers with several strikes against me. I had been a Navy seaman and a radio announcer. These occupations were not in my favour. And the accident of my birth was another point he would "not be sufficiently uncharitable to mention in public."

The day was filled with conferences (sermons), prayer and manual labour. I scrubbed washrooms and ran a heavy polisher over miles of ceramic hallways. On sunny afternoons in late summer, heavy black robes hitched up to our waists, we all trekked to the fields to bring in truckloads of baled hay.

After lunch we had a short siesta, then recreation. Sometimes we teamed up for baseball. One sunny afternoon I connected bat to ball. This was such a surprise to everyone in the game that I managed a home run. All were shouting directions at me: "You missed a base." "Go back!" On another occasion, while we played football, I caught a pass and ran for a touchdown – to the wrong end.

Sometimes I felt as adequate as an umbrella in a swimming pool. But I was not alone. Before the year ended, one of the Novices thought he was John the Baptist and was taken to the mental hospital at Penetanguishine.

I also had fun moments on the sports field. Once, when I was up to bat, the pitcher teased me – as pitchers are wont to do. "You hit it and I'll catch it."

"If you do, don't swallow it," I replied. It scored a point and everyone laughed, even the pitcher.

Though we learned a lot about religion, only a few developed any degree of piety.

Every Sunday, we were permitted to write one letter to our parents or, with approval, to a close relative. The only close relatives I had, apart from parents, were my aunts in Quebec City. I liked writing to my aunts and wanted to impress them.

And every week I wrote a duty letter home. In these letters, I spouted prayers for my lost sister and praise for my God-fearing parents. My correspondence was terribly sanctimonious, especially after my "salty" navy letters. Despite the fact that they never found time to answer my letters, both Mother and Papa came to Scarborough for the Noviciate admission ceremony – "taking of the habit".

Every prospective Novice had to select a saint's name from a list. I selected St. Francis, my favourite saint. However, the name Francis was already taken. Without a second immediate choice, I was assigned the name Tatwin. Brother Tatwin? That sounded like a bad joke. A secondary name was tacked on, that of Saint Bonaventure. In the story of Saint Francis, when the young Francis of Assisi called out for followers, one man heeded the call and Francis was reputed to have exclaimed "Benvenuta" (*Welcome*), and the first follower became Brother Bonaventure (good luck). Of course, I preferred to be called Bonaventure. Friends called me Bonnie.

Here is a stroke of irony. Was it this little known Saint Tatwin, an Anglo-Saxon poet, who influenced my disposition to write poetry?

On the day we Postulants received the monk's habit and became Novices, the Novices who had just completed their year of Noviciate made their first vows and became Scholastics. They would get to study for a year to prepare for Teacher's College and/or university degrees. We Novices were not to have any communication with the Scholastics until the end of our own year of Noviciate. Our year of preparation would be one of total isolation from outside influences. The Scholastics, in turn, would look down on us "mere mortals".

While my parents were leaving following the reception, Papa remarked that the Christian Brothers' House of Formation was on the Maryvale Stud Farm. He called out a cheery "Keep your pecker up, son!" (The term "pecker" in Canada has a different connotation from the English "Keep your chin up.") An innocent enough remark, but the Director was not amused. He made sure to mention the irreverent remark during his next Conference.

Before leaving, Mother gave me a copy of Thomas A Kempis, *The Imitation of Christ*, "As a source of inspiration for meditation and personal prayer."

I thought I would be permitted to keep the one gift and token of approval I had received from my parents in many years. However, *The Imitation of Christ* remained at the Mother House when I moved on.

We were each given one good habit for chapel and meals, and another for manual labour. Because our robes were seldom laundered, they soon began to smell like dead skunks. For manual labour and sports, we hitched the bottom around our waist, no matter how hot the sun. We also wore a little skullcap called a calotte.

On Fridays, we stood for breakfast and, later in the day, we each knelt before our confrères, arms extended, and begged them in charity to point out our faults. I didn't consider it charity when a fellow Novice blurted, "It seems to me, my very dear Brother, that you sometimes look over the divider when another Brother is in the washroom."

I squirmed in silence. Brother Director intoned, "You will thank your Brother for his kindness."

I remained silent. I felt angry and embarrassed. Of course, the accusation was untrue.

"You **will** thank your Brother for his kindness."

"I thank you, my very good Brother, for having had the ... kindness ... " Increasingly, I found myself alone in the chapel, frustrated and tearful. Some mornings I was so exhausted that I slipped a note under my door. "I'm sick". As the year wore on, I sent out more and more of these notes. I was not the only one.

In chapel, I wrote poetry. It just came to me, as though dictated. Some poems were amazing. When the Brother Director discovered what I was doing, he ordered me to burn what I had written and resist the "temptations of pride." We were to resist "the World, the Flesh and the Devil." Though I nodded "yes," I continued writing in secret. I hid what I wrote, and my collection grew.

Poetry was my only disobedience apart from the occasional cigarette. Cigarettes were not hard to come by. Many of the retired Brothers smoked. One old Brother smoked cigars. When he died, Novices had to clean out his room. The smell of cigar smoke was sickening. Our director of Novices smoked a pipe; eventually he died of cancer of the mouth. One day, someone tattled on Spud and me for smoking while out for a meditative stroll. Brother Maurice, breath reeking of pipe tobacco, told us it was a downright sin to smoke when we should be praying. I asked if it would be all right to pray while smoking. That humour was not appreciated. I don't recall the resulting penance, but Spud and I chuckled over that one for days.

Apart from tobacco, the only other worldly pleasure apparent was alcohol. We had wine on feast days. On weekends, the Director of Novices and other Brothers smelled of more than wine. One Novice wore after-shave and covered his facial blemishes with a medication that his aunt brought to the Mother House on her monthly visits (the limit allowed). Such frills were at least frowned on if not forbidden.

Several Novices left during the year. We were told how shameful it was to throw this sacred vocation back in the face of God. I could never leave at such peril to my immortal soul. We were told St. Paul had said that we were to "knock the dust from our sandals and forget those who had walked away." (What Saint Paul really said was, *"And if any one will not receive you or listen to your words, shake off the dust from your feet as you leave that house or town."* Matthew 10:7-15)

Sometime later, I met Harold White, music specialist for the Montreal English Catholic School Commission. We became good friends. But White was unwelcome at the Brothers' residence. He had been Sub-Director of Novices, but left and married – **a woman**.

>"The word 'woman' comes from Woe to man."

>"Eve brought God's curse upon human flesh."

>"The worst sins are of the flesh."

>"Never look a woman in the eye."

When we showered, we were to wash down as far as ... And up as far as... We were to leave "as far as" alone and to permit only cold water to fall on those unmentionables.

Every morning, before Mass, a line of sleep-eyed Novices queued up at the confessional at the back of the chapel to unburden themselves of steaming sins.

"Bless me Father for I have sinned. I accuse myself of lack of prayer, feeling angry towards my Brothers … and … I've sinned against purity."

"Alone or was there someone…?"

"Just me, Father."

Personal friends were forbidden. Relationships could lead to temptations.

I wanted to say, "I only touched it, and it exploded." No matter how I struggled against my youthful sexuality, it got the better of me. Needless to say, I soon got seriously terrified of "failing the test".

For me, nothing less than perfection would suffice.

"My son, the devil is a sly one who comes when we let our guard down. You must pray, pray, pray to remain steadfast in the struggle against evil. Now, for your penance, say five Our Fathers and five Hail Marys. And make a good Act of Contrition."

"Oh, my God, I am heartily sorry…"

In the daily director's Conferences, we were told of the lives of those saints who gladly inflicted their bodies with scourging and hair shirts. These were men and women who died in the "Odour of Sanctity". My robe had the odour of sanctity.

In the Royal Canadian Navy, recruits were told, in a paraphrasing of Alfred Tennyson's *The Charge of the Light Brigade*:

> *Yours is not to reason why.*
>
> *Yours is but to do and die.*

In the Noviciate the wording was different but the message was the same: "*Dei sacrificium intellectus*" – sacrifice intellect to God. But was the Director of Novices God? He told us, "I am the voice of God." So we obeyed. In contrast, before joining the Christian Brothers, my motto would have been: "*Omnibus disputandum*" – question everything.

With no one in whom to confide, I had to face my doubts and confusion in frightening solitude.

Our district sent Brothers to mission schools in Nigeria. Brother Maurice thought this a waste of time. According to him, "Satan mated with a gorilla and produced the black savage." Near the end of the Noviciate year, we received a very black Postulant from Nigeria. He was a short fellow who often came to chapel barefoot. Brother Anselm Uba earned a university degree and was posted to St. Michael's College of Education in Malta. Brother Maurice actually treated the young Postulant kindly.

Finally, we went into an eight-day closed retreat. The silence and intense prayer – broken only by the peal of bells – were intended to prepare us for our first vows.

These days I can live with silence. But then, I was different.

Following graduation from the Noviciate we would truly be Brothers and Scholastics. Some Scholastics would go to Teachers' College or to University. Some would obtain their master's degrees and even doctorates before becoming teachers. Others would remain at the Mother House and complete senior matriculation. Some would remain to work on the farm and look after the retired Brothers.

First, we all travelled to Brothers' Island on Lake Simcoe, near Orillia. Our Director of Novices had planned a week of well-earned holiday. During the week, I discovered snapping and painted turtles, frogs the size of my hand, and slithering garter snakes. Dragonflies skimmed the water amongst black flies and bothersome mosquitoes. Swallows swooped and darted. With beaks full of insects, they returned to their nests in the eaves of the main cabin.

One day, we Novices sat on the dock and hoped for a turn on our one pair of water skis. Brother Harold finally returned to the dock, steering the motorboat back for gas.

"No more skiing today. Maybe tomorrow. Anyway, Rosary's in twenty minutes." he said.

"Shit! It's not bloody fair."

Novices don't swear. So no one heard that.

Brother Director offered solace. "The Basilians have their island close by. They have more water skis and a boat with gas in the tank. Tomorrow we'll pay them a visit."

As promised, we visited the Basilian Fathers. But we didn't water ski.

One day, we left the island to attend a funeral at Saint John's Training School, a "reform" school in Uxbridge. One of the young Brothers had drowned in a small lake nearby. Following the funeral, we were treated to wine, sandwiches, cake and other goodies. Then we were given a tour of the school.

I remember the "blue room" where boys were sent to cool down after running away or for certain other infractions. Though the paddle and strap were used, the dedication and love the Brothers showed for the unfortunate boys, was obvious.

Today, any form of corporal punishment is out of place. Thank God, we are living in a totally different age. However, St. John's was without fences, and I do not recall locks on the doors. Many of the boys were from abusive homes or had been deemed incorrigible by teachers and parents. Given the opportunity, they would run off in a staff car or terrorize residents in neighbouring communities while they were on the run. They required a mixture of discipline and love, which the Brothers appeared ready and able to supply.

Years later, I read with shock and dismay about children being physically and sexually abused in the Catholic and other religious schools. I knew some of those charged and felt disbelief and horror that I too might be accused as I remembered the countless boys and girls to whom I had shown affection but I was always clear about the limits to any physical display. Yet, in my nightmares, I waited for that phone call or for the RCMP visit and the accusations that might follow.

During our final evening on the island, we had a ceremony in which we were to write our worst faults on slips of paper. These would then be bunched up and thrown into the campfire. What a wonderful idea. The Novice Director had a special surprise for me. He produced a stack of my poetry he'd taken from my cell before we left. I'd had it stashed under my mattress. He handed me the bundle to cast on the fire and obediently I did so. However, to my knowledge alone, I'd copied out completed poems and had them folded at the back of my Missal. The pile I burned was working copies. I easily convinced myself that, since I didn't always understand what I had written or where the poetry came from, it was a gift and should not be destroyed.

During the Scholasticate year that followed, I completed my final year of secondary school as well as religious studies. Our time was well scheduled, and we had very little to distract us.

Sometimes during that year we went to see school plays or such suitable movies as *The Robe* or *Bernadette of Lourdes* or *Court Jester* with Danny Kaye. On such outings, we wore black suits with Roman collars. The older Brothers wore Roman collars on what were known as "dickies". (A clerical dickie is a front piece that ties around the waist and, under a jacket, looks like a full black shirt and Roman collar.) There's a story that on a busy Sunday in Toronto, a very holy old Brother saw that he'd closed a car door on his dickie. He yelled at the driver, "Stop the car. My dickie's caught! My dickie's caught!"

When we heard that a beer truck had run down the Bishop of Toronto, I blurted out, "the drinks were on him!" I was becoming the class clown. My jokes were never considered funny by the Brothers. That jest cost me a full day in chapel, kneeling in front on the cold tile floor.

One Saturday afternoon during the May / June period of final exams, we went to a matinee dress rehearsal of Gilbert and Sullivan's *Trial by Jury* at De La Salle Oaklands High School. During the performance, I fell ill with an allergy or food poisoning. My hands, feet, face, and throat swelled up, and I had difficulty breathing. In panic, I asked to see a doctor. The Brother director gave me two aspirin and sent me to bed. I recovered in time to write my Algebra exam the following Tuesday morning. Nothing lost but study time.

When the exam results came out, Brother Romuald, head of the Order in Canada, gave me permission to attend St. Joseph's Teachers' College in Montreal. First, though, he sent me to spend the summer as entertainment director at De La Salle Camp on Jackson's Point, Lake Simcoe.

De La Salle Camp served the sons of those who could afford the fees. Thus it provided a source of funds for the upkeep of the Mother House, among other projects. This annoyed me. I thought I had joined the Christian Brothers to teach poor boys, not the sons of the rich.

My judgmental attitude notwithstanding, I enjoyed a busy and productive summer. At last I felt useful. I helped the campers produce skits for entertainment nights. I organized campfires and led singsongs. During the day, I supervised activities such as moccasin and wallet making, the painting of plaques, finger painting, and nature study (about which I knew very little).

Hamsters, Guppies, and Knights of the Road

In the last week of August 1958, five shiny new Brothers drove from Scarborough to Montreal. We brought with us our meagre possessions and, on my part, an overflow of enthusiasm. I was introduced to Brother James, the Director and principal of St. Dominic's Elementary School. The Brothers' residence was attached to the school. This was convenient. Lessons could be prepared in the classrooms. I was to get ready to teach grade five and would not attend St. Joseph's Teachers' College. Brother James assured me the grace of God would be sufficient to teach. He reminded me I must be obedient without question to anything he, as my spiritual director, ordered. And so, I obeyed.

I loved my class and learned with my students as I taught. Never did I divulge my lack of training. When we fell behind in the curriculum, I made up for lost time by introducing extra-help sessions. Usually, all my boys attended.

My weakest subject was still Mathematics. Now I discovered shortcuts to replace learning by rote: Nine is ten minus one. Eleven is ten plus one. Eight – ten minus two. Five – half of ten. Multiplication and division made sense at last.

Teaching of religion called for memorized Catechism answers with very little explanation and less understanding. We used the standard Baltimore Catechism. All prayers were to be memorized in English and Latin. Those who attended mass before school received a gold star to paste to a chart at the front of the class. Money was collected for missions and children could buy black and oriental babies to paste on their mission charts. The sticky cutouts represented the souls of the "heathen" the school children were saving with nickels and dimes.

History, Geography and English became an adventure. Grammar was learn-as-you-go. Recalling my enjoyment of the weekly story at St. Pat's, I made sure to include a weekly reading of *Tom Sawyer, Treasure Island,* and poems such as *Evangeline* and my favourites from Robert Service.

I got to know the families of all my boys and visited their homes. I was sometimes invited to stay for dinner. Parents and teachers worked together to help the boys succeed. I seldom met parents who were not totally supportive.

St. Dominic's was a blue collar, immigrant school. I taught a Pasquale Pietrantonio, a Roberto Ricci, a Rizzuto, a Vincenzo, a Luis Delaporta. Some of my Sicilian students later filled the ranks of the Montreal Mafiosi. But they were good boys when I knew them. At lunchtime, they ate enormous sandwiches with sausage and cheese and drank green wine from Coca-Cola bottles. Very few brought milk to school.

In those days, Roman Catholics in North America were supposed to abstain from meat on Fridays in memory of Christ's passion and death. This is no longer the norm. Most of my students were freshly arrived from Italy, Sicily, and Hungary. People from Italy, Ireland, and a number of other countries ate fish regularly and were not subject, in their home countries, to meatless Fridays, except for Good Friday. Still, during lunch periods, big, redheaded Brother George examined all the sandwiches and made the boys throw their meat into garbage cans. Anybody who resisted earned a smack upside his head. I hated to see good food go to waste, so I permitted my boys to eat in the classroom, while I gave extra help where required. I did not examine sandwiches on Fridays. Nor did I confiscate the wine, which I recognized as part of the cultural upbringing in Montreal's "Little Italy". My students noticed

I did not go to the "residence" for lunch. So they quite often brought an extra sandwich and a bottle of vino for "the Bro".

Once I did appreciate Brother George's gruffness. This happened when he dealt with a cigarette company representative. After parking his company car by the gate, the man – no more than nineteen himself – walked onto the elementary school playground. Pockets jingling with coin, he struck up conversations and handed out free cigarettes to schoolboys who swarmed about him. Any boy who chanced to own a packet of the favoured brand "hit the jackpot": he received a free carton of cigarettes.

I'll never forget the scene. An angry Brother George, somehow bigger than I'd ever seen him before, stormed over to the fellow, seized him by the back of the neck, and literally booted him off the school property.

Secretly, I cheered.

Horace White, whom the Brothers called "Duck" White, came to see if all classes were being taught to sing. The prescribed curriculum included *God Save the Queen*, *Holy God We Praise Thy Name* and selections from well-worn songbooks. Other inspectors from the Montreal Catholic School Commission appeared without warning to ensure that our registers were up-to-date and that all boys had clean hands and nails. From time to time, a nurse also came by to check for head lice. The parish priest dropped in to question the boys on their Catechism.

At times like these, I often felt more nervous than the boys. The parish priest might ask, "What is Matrimony?" He received a memorized answer from the Baltimore Catechism. Sometimes the answer to "What is Matrimony?" could turn out to be the answer to "What is Purgatory?" "Matrimony is ... Matrimony is a state of temporary punishment..."

Except for some experience as a choirboy in grade school, I had absolutely no knowledge of music. It was logical, therefore, that the leadership of the parish boys' choir fell to me. If it weren't for Horace White, I couldn't have done the job. He helped me with basic conducting and taught me the rudiments of music theory.

To this day, I don't know how I did it. With a signal and slight wave of my hand, I launched the boat – and treble voices, now in motion, rose upon a crest, moving forward on waves of sound.

The boys sang like angels. I was in heaven. I organized the Christmas concert and teamed up with a Sister from the girls' school to put on *HMS Pinafore* in the spring. When Sir Joseph Porter came on stage, a proud papa cried out, "That's a my Tony. Bravo, Antonio!"

Science went well, too. I repaired an aquarium and, with the help of several parents, acquired plants, guppies, and paraphernalia. We obtained a cage of hamsters and a terrarium filled with baby turtles. When a local fish shop donated a huge aquarium to my class, we started breeding guppies and black mollies by the hundreds. The sale of baby hamsters provided pet food.

The classroom became my life. My boys did well in all tests administered by Brother James and the school board. When refugees arrived from Hungary following the 1956 revolt, many of them came to my class. I gave them the extra attention they needed. I had little time to spend with the other Brothers.

At the end of the school year, I applied to take music courses at St. Michael's Choir School in Toronto. Permission denied. My services would be more valuable as entertainment director at De La Salle Camp. The director at St. Dominic's made it clear that music courses were not "masculine endeavours".

In my second year, I was moved to a grade seven class. I had to leave all the equipment I had procured during the previous year, and start from scratch. I left a bright, well-decorated room for a classroom with a cracked blackboard and scant library books.

Brother George took over the choir which then fell apart – due, in the Brother's words, "To the boys' previous poor training." But he did say I might be called on to help with the spring production. That year, no spring production was held. And a lie was relayed to the parents: "Brother Bonaventure does not wish to continue with the choir." Under vow of obedience, I was forbidden to say anything. I was to mature in the self-denial of religious life.

I was also forbidden, as before, to waste my time writing poetry. When my poem *Poor Pagan World* was published in Saint Joseph's Oratory Magazine, I had to return the cheque with apologies.

Despite such irritations, I enjoyed teaching the more challenging grade seven students. Everyone passed the provincial examinations. Top provincial marks in religious knowledge went to a student of mine, a Jewish boy.

I made sure the boys understood what I taught. I insisted they pronounce every word clearly. As children frequently misinterpret and misspeak words, I simply accepted full responsibility. I had heard kids reciting the "Act of Contrition" – "O my God, I'm hardly (heartily) sorry for having offended you."…

When I was three or four years old, I asked for a blazer for my birthday. Clothing was the last item on my mind for a birthday present. Little boys like teddy bears, trains, and tricycles. When my birthday present turned out to be a blue jacket, I was terribly disappointed. I wanted a "blazer" to shave like my daddy.

Once more I set up an aquarium for fish and scrounged another aquarium for the care and breeding of hamsters. This time a public health nurse from the school board visited the class and told the Director (so he said) that hamsters posed a health hazard. Normally, I wouldn't have thought much about this. But Brother James explained children could be bitten while handling them.

Then my blackboard notes got erased after I had prepared special lessons over a weekend, I began to believe somebody didn't appreciate the extra work I put into my teaching.

A new boy, a refugee from Hungary, came to school during cold weather, with ragged shoes and no coat. I asked the Director if anything could be done for him. He replied, "Our job is to teach and pray." This wasn't good enough for me. I spoke to the pastor at our church. He told me to get in touch with the Saint Vincent de Paul Society. They in turn said the boy could turn to refugee agencies for help. "We already have provided these new families with lodging and food. Nothing more can be done at this time."

I became aware of many poor people in Montreal. Their situation was desperate. I knew, at least, I had to try to help this boy. After school a few days later, I walked him down to one of the clothing shops on the Rue St. Joseph and asked the store owner to fit my charge with boots, pants, sweater, coat, gloves, and toque. When the owner wrote out the bill, I said I didn't have any money but that, without proper clothing, I knew the lad would fall ill.

I didn't know any other way. My only hope was that, as it was getting close to Christmas and Hanukkah, someone might help with a little charity. I guess I believed in miracles. I said I was from St. Dominic's School, signed the bill, thanked the merchant, and left.

The next day, Brother James ordered me to take the boy back to the store and return the clothing. I told him I couldn't. Although I had now sinned against my vows of obedience and poverty, I was obstinate.

In the end, the storeowner allowed the boy to keep the clothing. He couldn't sell it to anyone else anyway. When I next passed the store, he looked at me with a smile and shook his head.

We "poor" Brothers each were given a carton of cigarettes every other week. The Molson's truck delivered beer to the residence on Fridays. The hypocrisy made me rebellious. Like my fellow Brothers, I had sworn a vow of poverty. Yet I had to ask, "What poverty?" because I felt we were well taken care of. I was reminded, "Jesus said, 'The poor we have always amongst us' (Matthew 26: 11)." I countered: "I was hungry and you did not give me to eat; naked and you did not clothe me. (Matthew 26: 11)." But I couldn't win the argument.

Saying, "Satan himself uses Holy Scripture to lure men into the sin of pride," the director ordered me to chapel to pray. "You are in very grave danger, Brother. Pride is the sin of Lucifer himself."

I was kneeling in the company of Saint Francis. I was happy.

My rebellion came to a head on Christmas morning. While the aroma of turkey wafted from the kitchen below, the Brothers knelt in the chapel. Someone insistently rang the front doorbell. Usually Brother George or the sub-director answered the door. But this time nobody moved. I got up and went to the door.

A "knight of the road" stood outside, shivering. The old man wore rubber boots, baggy pants, and a ragged coat fastened by two large safety pins. His white hair stuck out in strands from under a filthy Toronto Maple Leafs toque. His stubbly, frost flecked whiskers and rugged eyebrows framed the flinty eyes of an explorer, a survivor of life's Arctic blizzard. Brother George usually sent such beggars across the street to the rectory. In turn, the good pastor sent them back to the good Brothers.

This was a standing joke.

The poor fellow greeted me with a cheery "*Joyeux Noèl*" and asked "*s'il vous plaît, le charité, pour l'amour du bon Dieu.*" (Please, for the love of God, have charity.) Indicating the direction, I quietly asked him to go to the lower side door. Then I went to the kitchen entrance and invited him in. The turkey was ready. I prepared a plate with a bit of everything. Brother James came down, asked me what I thought I was doing. He told the beggar to leave. I wrapped the meal in wax paper and newsprint and gave it to the man who thanked me and left.

Brother James sent me to chapel for the rest of the day. I had given my Christmas dinner to the derelict. Stubborn as I was, I didn't mind the sound of tinkling glasses and laughter from the refectory. I did mind that I was not permitted to visit my parents. I wasn't even allowed to phone to wish them a happy Christmas. Even on Boxing Day I wasn't to visit. I was to say I had decided not to go. To make sure, the Brother Director monitored my telephone call.

A few mornings later, I arrived at chapel late for prayer. Brother James announced that the Brother who had "condescended" to join his dear brethren in prayer, kindly would repeat the morning offering for all to hear. I began, "Behold, O kind and most sweet, sweet, sweet Jesus, I cast myself upon my knees in thy sight, and thank you that I live with such holy and loving men..."

So, in this order of God-fearing Brothers, I was judged to be suffering from psychotic delusion. Right after the holidays, I was sent off to visit a psychiatrist in Montreal. Special permission was obtained from the Provincial, Brother Romuald.

The psychiatrist was a kindly Jewish doctor. I told him of my struggle with disillusionment. I said I got angry when the Molson's truck pulled up in front of the residence to deliver beer on Friday afternoons. I only wanted to work with children and help the poor. He asked me if I ever thought of leaving the order. I answered that such a thought was out of the question. I might have been confused but I loved teaching.

Having visited the psychiatrist several times, Brother James announced I was no longer to see him. The date for my next visit came up, I boarded the streetcar on Rue St. Joseph, even though I had no money. The driver let me on without paying. I arrived at the office a few minutes late. The doctor was on the telephone. He hung up, surprised to see me. Brother James had just told him I refused to continue seeing him. The doctor wanted to know why.

I discovered other lies. I had "refused" to attend teachers' college. I "disliked" teaching grade five. I "didn't wish" to teach music. My application for summer courses "was never sent". I had been a "constant troublemaker". I was "not well-suited" to the religious life.

The doctor recommended to the Provincial that I change my community. But I wanted to complete the year with my grade seven class. I promised to do my best to keep out of Brother George's way and Brother James' way.

I spent another summer at De La Salle Camp.

In September, after three years of elementary school teaching, I was transferred to Bishop Whelan High School in Lachine. I would teach French, English, Vocal Music, and Art from grades eight to twelve. Brother George also was transferred to Lachine, but now seemed friendly. Still, I avoided him.

I began teaching teens, having barely completed high school myself. I certainly had no teaching diploma. I faked it successfully, mainly because I loved my job and loved the kids. Nobody guessed I had not studied at some teachers' college or university.

My arrival in the Lachine community brought promises of a new life. Bishop Whelan was an all-boys school employing a dozen Brothers, complemented by lay teachers. (Similarly, Immaculate Conception Girls' School, near the parish church, had Sisters and lay teachers.)

At first, I taught French and directed the Glee Club. I also registered for my first evening course at Sir George Williams University. Several of us drove together once a week, to our various courses.

Yodelling Down the Mountain

Apart from assorted hockey sticks and pairs of skates, the Lachine community owned several pairs of skis, boots, mitts, and goggles. One day I joined a carload of Brothers for a skiing trip to Mount Orford in the Eastern Townships, approximately one hour's drive southeast of Montreal. Having mastered the slopes of the Grove Hill Golf Course as a teenager, I was enthusiastic.

Orford's vertical drop of 1,770 feet was accessible from top to bottom by a double chair lift. Though it included several expert runs, I elected to ski the long, winding roadway that descended gradually from the summit to the base of the mountain. As I gained confidence, I sped faster and faster down the windy trail, yodelling like a Swiss mountaineer. Through soft, fluffy powder, I flew over moguls. As I tore by, I waved at less daring novice skiers.

The afternoon wore on and the sky turned purple-pink. I saw fewer people on the slopes. The wise skiers packed it in for the day and headed to rendezvous points for the drive home. Just one last run, I thought.

At the summit, the chair lift was almost deserted. A cold wind bit through my parka. I paused to warm my fingers and to drink in the view. Below, lights twinkled in cottages. "The Brothers will be waiting. Better speed it up."

I traveled faster than I had dared on any previous descent. On a sharp turn, I miscalculated and barrelled into a shrubby bank.

"Crack!" I lay still. Something felt wrong. My ankle was on fire.

Spraying a cloud of snow, someone came to a halt beside me. "*Ca va? Es-tu blessé?*" (How are you? Are you hurt?)

Yes, I was hurt. I nodded weakly. "*Attends. Je vais chercher de l'aide.*" (Wait. I'll go get help.) The man pushed off down the hill.

Meanwhile, another skier stopped to keep me company. Then Brother Ralph found me. When I failed to turn up at the car at the designated time, he had returned to search for me.

Three ski patrol fellows pulled up beside me with a sled. They asked where I hurt. Pain tore all the way from my foot to my stomach. The young men packed my leg tightly between slats of wood and lifted me onto the sled. I remember nothing of the ride down the mountain and only briefly recall being loaded into an ambulance.

The hospital at Magog, five minutes from the ski hill, was run, with much bustling, by nuns. Prayers and announcements rattled over loudspeakers in French. I lay for a long time on a trolley in a hallway. Draped in a sheet and alternating between gas pains and explosive relief, I developed an uncontrollable fit of giggles. Close by, a sign pointed to "Maternité". With both hands, I raised the sheet over my stomach. Thank God my good friend, Brother Ralph, stayed with me and shared my strange sense of humour. Anybody else would have wondered what was so funny. At last, a nurse gave me a needle and put me to sleep.

The next morning, I was wheeled in to surgery. The doctor inserted a pin into my ankle to secure a broken bone. That pin was destined to become my persistent weather vane.

Following my operation, I spent six lonely days in that hospital. I was overjoyed to be transferred to Lachine General, where friends and students visited me, loaded down with books and magazines.

I wore a cast for a long time. For the rest of my days in the Christian Brothers, I never skied again. The equipment I used on that fateful trip had disappeared.

Music Training

The following July, I attended St. Michael's Choir School to learn Choral Techniques, Music Theory, Music History, and Vocal Training. In August 1962, I joined a group of the remaining Brothers who had been my confrères in the Noviciate. Together we made another thirty-day retreat before taking final, solemn vows, promising to dedicate the remainder of our lives to serving the poor as Christian Brothers. I returned to Lachine with added enthusiasm and love for my vocation.

During the summer of 1963, my music training continued with Music for Children at the University of Toronto. There, I studied Orff, Kodaly, Jacques Dalcrose, and more theory. I was happy to be back on track with part-time studies. I would not only complete a Music Specialist Diploma at the McGill Summer School of Music, but I would also advance towards a B.A. at the University of Windsor.

The music inspector from the Montreal Catholic School Commission, a one-time Christian Brother named Horace White, helped me compose and arrange music. In turn, I directed an all-female cast of *HMS Pinafore* with the St. Mary's School of Nursing and assisted with a baby-sitting course in Montreal. I also became a District Cub Leader for campfire singsongs and skits. My friend, Peter Dawson, played the banjo.

Peter had taken part as a senior student in my first production at Bishop Whelan. He eventually became a teacher and was my best friend for many years. Another student, Charles Baranowski, played Sir Joseph Porter in my second high school production, *Pinafore*. Chuck also became a teacher and lasting friend. Following that production and most likely at Peter Dawson's instigation, the cast gave me a guitar.

Flying With Angels

November 1962, I chose twelve boys from my eighty-five-member Glee Club, to sing in a local production of *The Man Who Came to Dinner*. These youngsters proved especially dedicated and continued to practice with me daily before school. By the end of that year, we had polished a small repertoire of French and English songs. With the active encouragement of Mayor Lois Joseph Gaston of Lachine, the group became known as "Les Petits Chanteurs de Lachine".

The following spring, Ralph England of the E.Z. Players of Dorval introduced me to Joe Hart, president of Hart Motors who agreed to be our sponsor and to supply the boys with their first set of uniforms – grey slacks, sky blue jackets with crests, white shirts, and blue and gold striped ties. We adopted the additional name "Hart Singers" and soon were performing in four-part harmony for charity performances, on radio, on television, and live. In the fall of 1963, the number of boys had grown to twenty-six.

In 1963, Immaculate Conception School became a coed elementary school and Bishop Whelan a coed High School. I was assigned to teach Music and French in both schools.

The children I taught were my great joy. Natural, happy, and sincere, they responded to me with trust un-shattered by trauma. With them, I rediscovered my own strength. It was a simple matter to build a bond with them, devoid of threat. I did not lose patience. When a child failed to understand, I just found another way to explain, to illustrate.

Most of all, I loved teaching Music. We sang. We played instruments. We danced. We not only sang songs created by adults for children, but also improvised songs to go with play. We made up silly songs too; after all, music is fun.

In my French lessons, I adopted the same technique. We sang our French conversations, creating simple melodies as we went. Soon we were writing words and music on the blackboard – but not until they were established in memory.

I wanted to use Karl Orff's Method of *Music for Children*, but I had no funds to buy instruments. So I began experimenting. We improvised our own instruments.

By June 1964, the Hart Singers, as "Les Petits Chanteurs de Lachine", performed a twenty-minute program, entirely in French, for the St. Jean Baptiste celebrations at Fletcher's Field in Montreal. Several thousand people heard "Les Petits Chanteurs".

Accompanied by Peter Dawson, Chuck Baranowski, and Brother Cyprian from the French Brothers, I began an annual one-week music camp at the French Brothers' "Camp de la Salle" at St. Alphonse de Joliette, on Lac Rouge in the Laurentians. By hiring the Brothers' camp crew, we acquired professional chefs and a qualified infirmarian. We also ran a Red Cross inspected waterfront.

The boys slept in heated cabins and participated in a wide range of activities: boating, water skiing, canoeing, bicycling, music instruction, and local performances. The Hart Singers attended this camp for thirty dollars, transportation included. Other boys were welcomed for ten dollars more. Youngsters whose parents couldn't afford the fee were given a free week, with tuck money thrown in.

Every school year, I taught guitar classes on Saturdays for one dollar per student per class and showed Walt Disney movies on Friday evenings. Although some of these proceeds went towards school sports, the bulk of the money paid camp costs, group travel, and additional uniforms. In short, I was able to subsidize my school music program.

Happily, I missed the rowdy sessions with the other Brothers as they watched hockey games. On one occasion, I returned early enough to find one bottle of beer left on the table. As I put the bottle to my mouth, Brother George claimed the beer as his and, when I resisted, punched me. I fled with a bleeding lip.

Fortunately, I had the Hart Singers and my work to keep me involved and away from the "community".

A parent, Rolly Leroux, served as business manager for the Hart Singers. All its banking and financial dealings were also scrutinized by the Brother Director. My life was full. At last, I had found success and acceptance. When some older girls asked to join the Hart Singers, we formed a second group known as "The Young Set". By that time, quite a few of our singers also played guitar.

When the Vienna Choir Boys came to perform at Place des Arts in Montreal, we were invited to join them during part of the program. The epitome of our group's success was reached when we performed several times during Expo '67. We sang in various languages and even belted out our own Expo song, which I composed in both English and French. That fall, we sang at the Parliament Buildings in Ottawa. During the winter, we spent a weekend in Quebec City. We also produced a long play recording.

Because I often sang the Gregorian Masses at the French church in Lachine, I was invited to join the Brothers from L'Académie Piché for breakfasts. The Brothers served huge breakfasts of sausage and steak and eggs and hash brown potatoes. I made many good friends at Piché.

I usually went straight from Piché to my morning classes at Immaculate Conception School. By that time, the Hart Singers practices had been changed to after school, three days a week, at Bishop Whelan.

I was happy teaching Music and French, enjoyed the Lachine community. However, dark clouds began to appear on the horizon.

At Bishop Whelan, Brother Barnabas taught mathematics. He was an alcoholic. But he loved the opera on Sunday afternoons.

Once he remarked to some First Nations students – from the Kahnawá:ke Reserve – that they had the brains of savages. Retaliation was not long coming. When he made an appearance in the schoolyard, several Mohawk girls pelted him with snowballs.

I always got along with the Mohawk kids and sometimes visited families on the reserve. I was present when the snowballing incident occurred, and I knew why. When the Director called me to his office and demanded a list of names, I said I didn't know. Brother Barnabas knew differently.

Changes and Dissension

The following September, a change of Directors brought changes in teaching assignments. I was no longer to teach music. Worse, my music room at Bishop Whelan became part of the school cafeteria. This meant that the Hart Singers' uniforms had to be hung elsewhere. We had to use a regular classroom for our practices. I was also told to become involved in other extracurricular activities besides music and drama. "Something "more manly".

One of my assignments was to lead a group of art students in building a snow and ice sculpture. Not only was this an entertaining project, our sculpture won a prize in the community. Though I taught more English, I still managed to retain some French classes, but at the expense of Music.

A favourite colleague of mine was Gordon Blickstead, a lay teacher at Immaculate Conception School. Gordon sang, helped with the Hart Singers, and provided an annual trophy for top performer in the group.

During Christmas holidays, 1967, Ron Garinther (at that time Brother Ralph) and his cousin, Gordon, invited me to join them on a trip to Florida. Ron asked for leave to visit his parents for the holidays. I asked to spend Christmas with my aunts in Quebec City. Both requests were granted. We drove to Florida and had a great time swimming and enjoying the nightlife. When we returned, people asked me where I got the suntan. When I said Florida, they knew I was lying. I had obviously used a sun lamp.

Gord took the rejected football tryouts from Immaculate Conception School and turned them into a winning team. He even purchased uniforms. However, his success inspired jealousy. The school coach and physical education teacher wished to recruit Gord's winning players, the principal announced that Gord's team uniforms were school property and that Mr. "B"'s team should be disbanded.

Gord spent a lot of time with extra coaching and with what he called the "STA Club". STA referred to the new mathematics program "Seeing Through Arithmetic". Gord's club was "Ships, Tanks, and Airplanes".

The privilege of belonging to the STA club had its price. Every member had to promise not to smoke or do drugs. When a couple of boys were caught smoking, they were suspended from the club and from the football team.

The disgruntled boys spoke to their friends. Somebody said, "Oh, Mr. B.'s a fag!" That got into the football team argument. When the principals of both schools questioned students about the comment, they made it clear that there was only one truth and anyone who lied would be severely punished.

It took months for the real truth to come out. Meanwhile, some insisted, "Where there's smoke, there's fire." I wished to speak on Mr. "B"'s behalf. But the Director would not permit me to get involved. He reminded me that since Gord and I had been close friends, I could easily be tarred with the same brush. With a feeling of terror, I withdrew my offer. In doing so, I knew I was being disloyal to an innocent colleague.

The entire community split over the issue. But, as such events go, the accusation alone turned out to be enough to damn my friend. He lost his job. His wife left him. And his house was vandalized. Even when every boy testified that the story had arisen from one careless remark, even when the school board ordered that the teacher be reinstated, the school principal was adamant. She would not believe the boys and refused to comply with the order. My friend left teaching.

While all this was going on, I retreated into countless hours with the Hart Singers.

During those years of happiness mixed with frustration, I came to know many of the students' families – as I had in Montreal. I developed strong relationships – enjoying family meals and some of the comforts of home life.

Those close moments with loving parents and happy kids helped me to persevere in my otherwise lonely vocation. Sometimes, however, I dreamt of having a family of my own with a loving wife and happy children.

One of the Hart Singers became despondent following the death of his father after a lengthy fight with cancer. The lad's mother invited me to supper to discuss her son and see if we could help him pull out of his lethargy. The evening progressed, and the boy went to bed. The mother and I sat up talking. She poured me another glass of wine.

Suddenly, she broke into sobs. I held her hands in an effort to comfort her. I told her I understood her loneliness. Unexpectedly, she kissed me. Not on the cheek but fully on my mouth. She took my hand and placed it on her breast, the nipple of which stood out hard through her soft sweater.

"Wait right here," she whispered in my ear. I stood shaking as she left the room.

Then I panicked. How did I get into this mess? Remembering my vow of chastity, I grabbed my coat and quietly opened the front door, slipping out into the cold night.

Oh, what a fool to have let myself into this situation. Oh what a fool not to stay and enjoy what I had only imagined so many times. "On my God, I'm heartily sorry." Oh, how my body ached! I hurried down the leaf-scattered street, praying that no one had seen me. As I escaped, imaginings of dire things to come spurred my feet forward toward the monastic discomfort of my icy bed.

The Lachine community remained divided over the Gordon Blickstead affair. Unhappily for the Hart Singers, administrative support for my music program quickly evaporated, and I was informed that the group would have to be disbanded. Lachine had gone sour. I requested a year of full-time study at the University of Windsor, and my application was approved.

Peter Dawson and I organized one last singing tour. We took the twelve most supportive singers to the Maritimes. I didn't ask permission to do this. It was enough that the parents got behind us. Several mothers sewed white sailor suits as a second uniform for every singer. We left as soon as school was out. Our plan was to camp out and to stay in motels only as need arose.

Somewhere in New Brunswick, the motel we planned to stay at turned out to be full. As we had faced rain for several days, the motel owner told us we could stay in his mother's house, a huge old structure up on a hill. We all had sleeping bags. Peter went upstairs with the younger boys. I slept on a couch in the living room.

Peter told the kids ghost stories. When he said the motel owner's mother had been murdered in "this very room", a ruckus ensued. I wrapped a sheet around myself and went upstairs to tell everyone to pipe down. We had a busy day ahead of us. I made a perfect ghost!

We sang at HMCS *Cornwallis,* drove through the Annapolis Valley, visited Green Gables and the beautiful sandy beaches of P.E.I., and entertained the officers in their mess at *Stadacona*. At the end of the trip, only uniforms and fond memories remained. Peter and I gave the uniforms to the boys, including extra pants and jackets.

The music fund had been well spent.

MacDonald College

From July 4th to August 4th, 1968, I was given permission to complete courses at MacDonald College while living at the Lachine community. But Brother Barnabas had been appointed Lachine community's summer director. He ordered me to stay where I was, to cook and look after the house. Though I didn't say "no" outright, I intended to disobey anyway. While I packed my bags, in preparation for taking the bus to Senneville, *Sunday Afternoon at the Opera* bellowed from the stereo in his room.

Finally, bags in hand, I stole quietly to the front door. Then, with a horrible sinking feeling, I remembered that I'd stuck my wallet beneath my mattress, for safekeeping. I had to return to my room. While I crept up the stairs, an uncooperative floorboard creaked.

"Have you got a minute?" Brother Barnabas, from his room.

I took a deep breath, opened the door and was assaulted by stale smoke, sweaty socks and a heavy contralto voice. In his brown leather easy chair, Barnabas sat in a haze of smoke, glass in hand, surrounded by piles of old magazines and newspapers. On a side table beside his unmade bed, a half-empty bottle of Bacardi rum, a quart bottle of milk, an open package of Export A cigarettes, a half-eaten sandwich on a saucer, two crumpled O Henry chocolate bar wrappers and an overflowing ashtray.

"Do you mind telling me where the hell you think you're sneaking off to?"

"I'll be back shortly," I lied and closed the door.

I just had to get out of there. I flew into my room, grabbed my wallet, and descended the stairs three at a time. Then I was gone.

From my parents' home in Senneville, I wrote to the Brother Visitor (Provincial) and told him that (a) I was terrified of Brother Barnabas, and (b) I already had his permission to complete my Music Certificate Program.

The Provincial responded by sending me funds for my courses and for room and board.

Murray Shaeffer, a well-known Canadian composer, wrote music for high schools. I appreciated his creativity, especially when our summer session music class paraded around the MacDonald College campus playing mezzo forte on invisible instruments in an imaginary marching band. We had so much fun we didn't concern ourselves that the other students on campus, including teachers on summer courses, questioned our sanity.

On one glorious excursion to the woods we played bells and listened to nature's response. Hundreds of songbirds joined in with their own music.

One of the most joyful experiences of my life has been flying just above the angelic voices of an all-boys choir while conducting sacred music. To control the ebb and flow of those clear tones is sublime. I have sailed with arms gently waving to the august strains of the *Avé Verum* and the *Panis Angelicus* and have been left breathless at the gift of angelic music. I have known the twofold bonus of praying with music while conducting the *Missa des Angelis* and have felt the elation of participating in Palestrina's polyphonic *Missa Papae Marcelli* while studying Choral Conducting at St. Michael's Choir School in Toronto.

In response to those who told me that singing is unmanly, I say, "I agree." Singing is not for men – or women, for that matter. It belongs to the angels. We humble humans are offered a mere part. Those who grasp this opportunity are blessed forever.

God gives all of us a voice to use as an instrument for good. To children, especially to boys between the ages of ten and fourteen, He gives a clear bell with which to ring His praises.

Call me unmanly. I have flown with the angels.

Tears in the Chapel

While I was in Lachine, my sister, Naomi, returned to Canada with her husband Don and small son Freddie. They had been in Lagos, Nigeria where Don worked for Canadian External Affairs. Naomi had developed inoperable melanoma and been flown to hospital in London, England. But too late. Doctors could do nothing for her. She and Don returned to Ottawa where Naomi got a job as a bank teller. When her cancer worsened, she quit work and went to live with Mother and Papa François in Senneville.

Don went to visit Naomi on weekends. One day, he invited me into the village of Ste. Anne de Bellevue for a couple of beers. I was happy for the chance to get to learn more about my sister's life since I had known her as a teen. But the beer turned my brother-in-law into a bully. He harangued me for being Catholic, insisting he knew more about popes and priests than I did. Finally, calling me "queer", he pushed me into a ditch on the way home. Sick with hurt, I didn't fight back.

Instead of showing sympathy upon my return home, Mother, Don, and Papa François reminded me that I had spent a lot of time with Sigvard . Apparently, he had died in Denmark, in their words, "surrounded by his little boys." I stood accused. Denying my Uncle Sigvard had ever touched me, I tearfully fled the house to the accompaniment of their laughter and my own sickening shame.

I could never reveal the terrible secret that would destroy me. The promise I had made to my uncle was now a promise to myself and had to be kept, no matter the cost. It didn't happen! It didn't happen! It didn't happen!

I did not return to Senneville for a very long time.

Naomi was admitted to Lachine General Hospital to spend her final days. One afternoon I went to visit her, but Mother had left orders that I could not see her unless she or other members of the family were there. Maybe she was afraid I might get preachy. Or so I thought at the time. Later, I surmised that Naomi had some things she wanted to tell me. Perhaps she had discovered what happened to our own Dad.

My mother also ordered that no clergy should be admitted to "bother" my sister. We had a little priest from Ireland, Father Bell, who assisted at Immaculate Conception Church. I spoke to him about Naomi, and, before long, he was visiting her regularly. Later, Mother called and told me I could visit my sister too. When I arrived, the entire family was present.

At last, I got a chance to say goodbye to Naomi, but with everyone there. She was in a cold sweat and having difficulty breathing. As Mother had ordered that her lungs should no longer be pumped out, I knew she wouldn't last long.

The next day, the Hart Singers performed at a mental hospital in Montreal. As we boarded the bus, I told Peter I wanted to visit my sister as soon as the concert was over and asked him to drive me. Naomi died at the same time I spoke to Peter on the bus. As for her son, Freddie, he was away visiting a paternal uncle in Ontario. He remained with his uncle until after the funeral. Either my mother or Don thought it better that Freddie, aged ten, not attend.

Naomi was just thirty-five years old.

When we were little, Naomi was my best friend in the world. We were constantly together sharing giggles and tickles and butterflies. Everything felt beautiful in the Garden of Eden.

Granted, like any small child, I knew love in simple terms only. Yet I know I loved Naomi. I would have done anything for her, including defend her.

Though Naomi and I grew apart, she never stopped representing for me a link to my lost joy. Frequently, I yearned for her company. Yet I couldn't tell her anything. Whenever we talked, we were defensive and guarded. She didn't tell me her secrets; I didn't tell her mine.

In boarding school, the teachers refused to allow me to talk to Naomi. We lived in different worlds. Whenever these collided, we landed in trouble. Naomi got caned because of me over the "Catholic Truth Society" booklets. Naturally, I had shared the books with my sister and so she also was caught with "stolen material" and punished.

Then, after Mother married our stepfather, we moved away from London and the worst of the bombing. In Sussex, we walked many miles to and from school. Every day proved to be an adventure. Once again, the two of us looked forward to a wonderfully mysterious future. I felt a lot of my old love - the companionship, closeness, and familiarity part of it - for my sister.

Then came Canada. And things got worse again, a lot worse. I vied with my sister for scarce moments of Mother's attention. At least, I vied for snippets of approval. This resulted in our finding ways to get each other into trouble. Mother only had time for one of us at a time, never two. Any motherly love went to the three Bertrand girls. Naomi became Cinderella. I was Cinderfella.

Despite this, we soon shared long bicycle rides. By this time, at the ages of between fourteen and sixteen, our personal agendas broadened to include sexual urges and adolescent exploration. The trouble was, whenever my imagination ran wild I felt terribly sinful. On this, I can't speak for Naomi. All I know is that, since she had her boyfriends and her own secrets, I feared she, too, would end up in the fires of hell. Instead of "going all the way" with any girl, I masturbated and lived in constant dread of dying in a state of mortal sin.

Later still, when Mother told me Naomi had run away from home, she implied that she did so because I had provided a bad example by leaving home myself when "things got tough".

During the period of my involvement with the Christian Brothers, Naomi eventually returned - but at a great distance from me. Naomi was dying from cancer. I wanted to see her. I wanted to save her soul. But I had it all wrong. My sister's soul didn't need saving. She just needed me to love her. I didn't really know how to love, though I thought I knew. The love I learned in the Brothers was superficial at best.

When Naomi died at the age of thirty-five, I regretted our lost moments. If only she and I had gotten closer during our lost years. If only I had behaved like other big brothers.

When Naomi joined the Navy a year after I did, she had the guts to reclaim our original surname. She must have missed her father as much as I did. Yet she never shared this burden of hers with me; we had grown too far apart.

My half-sister, Louise's younger twin Nicole "Nicky", joined the White Sisters of Africa to become a missionary nurse. I saw her when she was working with sick children in a West End Montreal hospital. She radiated joy. Still, she left the order before taking final vows. Had she become disillusioned with the religious life?

Before long, while working with a parish youth group in the same area of Montreal, she met and married another volunteer, Roger. Roger started seeing another woman, and the marriage ended on the rocks. Then Mother developed a friendship with Jean LeBegue, an automobile dealer from France who sold Peugeot sports cars in Pointe Claire. Nicky and Jean developed a relationship. However, he was supporting a wife in Bermuda and took unfair advantage of my little sister.

Ten years later, Nicky developed cancer but, remembering the grief Naomi's sickness and death had caused Mother, did not tell the family until it was too late. Nicole died alone in the parking lot of the Lachine General Hospital. The year was 1979. Like Naomi, she was thirty-five years of age. The sad epilogue to her life is that Jean ran off with all her assets, leaving many bills unpaid.

Was Nicky attracted to the White Sisters of Africa in the same way I wished to join the White Fathers of Africa? Did she have the same desire I had to do something special with her life? Was Nicky struggling as I had struggled to please her mother? Why did I feel so guilty when my little sister died so tragically?

The Making of a Martyr

Over the years, in my childhood and adulthood both, people in authority routinely mistreated me. It wasn't long after I was beaten to within an inch of my life in the American South, and subsequently made to feel, by my parents, that I brought this horror on myself, that I went "all the way" to another form of martyrdom in the Roman Catholic Church. Since no one thought to offer me professional counselling – indeed, counselling had not reached the degree of acceptability it has today – my unresolved feelings had to go somewhere. So I unknowingly and hopefully signed on for more mistreatment, in education and training both, in order to become a Christian Brother.

Why did I persevere when I perceived so much hypocrisy and cruelty in the Church? Why did I continue when so many were falling away from religious orders and the Church, like wasps from a burning nest? The answer was obvious to me at the time: It was I who had run away from God. Now God had welcomed me back. Since my faith was a simple one, I lacked the sophistication to question it. Besides, at the time where else was there for me to go? Also, I surely felt that my life was improving.

My two years at the Christian Brothers' Mother House provided me with opportunities for spiritual reading and meditation. I often went to chapel, suffering from terrible headaches. My vision blurred, I gazed at the ten-foot crucifix hanging before me. There He was, with nails in His hands and feet, a gaping wound in His side, and thorns piercing His head. How could I complain of a mere headache? Here were love, forgiveness – and healing – personified. Often I meditated on Christ's suffering and death by following the Stations of the Cross around the chapel's interior perimeter.

Faith brought me into the Church. Granted, I was still willing to suffer anything to gain approval and through suffering, I had to atone for the toxic shame I'd felt since early childhood.

SABBATICAL

I brimmed with new and exciting ideas for teaching music but the music program in Lachine was scrapped. I was definitely at a crossroads. My time with the Brothers had been a mixture of joy, sadness and betrayal. Still I held on, looking for the perfect existence. With much to sort out, I cast about for a fresh start.

I had been teaching for more than a decade without qualifications. I had neither teaching diploma nor university degree, despite summer courses and evening classes at Sir George Williams University. It was time for a sabbatical.

The Brother Provincial granted permission to complete my B.A. at the University of Windsor (previously known as Assumption College and still under the auspices of the Basilian Fathers). I packed my few belongings and said my goodbyes to the friends I had made during seven years in Lachine.

The parents of the Hart Singers presented me with a mandolin, which I was ordered to leave with the Brothers in the Lachine community. I was sure no-one would ever get to play the instrument. I did, however, take my guitar and two harmonicas, musical instruments that had come as gifts from parent groups during memorable years with the Hart Singers. These I had been permitted to keep. Though the vow of poverty was hard to swallow at times, I usually obeyed.

At Windsor, I joined sixteen other Brothers, many of them fresh out of Scarborough Scholasticate. Most were sent to live on campus at La Salle Hall. A handful of us went to live several miles from the university, at St. Joseph's, with Brother Symphorian as director. My good friend, Brother Charles, who had taught with me in Lachine, lived at the same residence. He now served as an elementary school principal.

Brother Symphorian did not approve of my course selections, including a Major in Drama and a Minor in Fine Arts. Instead, I was supposed to study "more useful" subjects such as History and Mathematics.

"Furthermore," he said, "I will approve no transportation to attend extracurricular activities, such as play rehearsals. Even if the Provincial does permit you to study Acting."

At this point, I decided I'd been bullied long enough. I registered for Painting, Print Making, and three classes in Theatre. However, I had no money to pay for art supplies. Then, by chance, I was invited to take part in some entertainment at a Friday and Saturday evening coffee house. There I made money to pay for canvases, paints, and engraving tools I had already purchased on "credit".

It was the age of Folk Music. We sang songs by Woody Guthrie – he died that year – and Pete Seeger, Oscar Brand, Burl Ives, the Clancy Brothers, and many great entertainers. Other regulars at the coffee house did some fancy guitar "picking".

We all had a good time. I made friends and went to parties. I sometimes played harmonica and sang with Pete Cowan's Dance Orchestra, a group that imitated the Harmonicats. I played harmonica for other folk singers, too. Without my black jacket and black tie, it was easy to forget I was still a member of a religious order.

Apart from the vow of chastity, I broke free of the intense control I'd been under for the past twelve years. I certainly broke the vows of poverty and obedience.

Having no paid transportation for my late returns, I hitchhiked, often arriving at St. Joseph's long after curfew. I rapped on Brother Charles' window to let me in. Sometimes, we shared a bottle of Crème de Cacao and sat up talking half the night.

Every weekend, one or two of the Brothers drove to Detroit to pick up duty-free liquor and cigarettes. As there was no question of staying the required forty-eight hours in the United States, they just slipped back into Canada without declaring what they'd bought. So far no one had been caught.

When it was my turn, I got cold feet. I drove across to Detroit. But, at the last minute, I couldn't enter the duty free shop. On the drive back, with a clean car, I was asked to pull into an inspection spot, and the car was searched with all the thoroughness of Canada Customs. When I returned empty handed, the Brothers were unsympathetic. Henceforth, since I was not a contributor, I was cut off from cigarettes, beer, or any form of leisure supplies.

Since I was seldom present for the Friday night parties and since I used my cigarettes as a form of barter – having given up smoking during Theatre courses – I didn't feel the loss much. With the one exception of Brother Charles, I didn't care about my colleagues. The Brothers returned the sentiment, having decided my Canada Customs story was a lie.

I was given the grandfather role in the university production of "Angels in Love" and started to grow my own beard and let my hair grow longer. The Brother Director asked me one Sunday morning what I had on my face.

"Where? Where?"

"Go and shave that abomination from your face and get Brother Roy to give you a haircut."

"I'm growing this for a play."

"You are not to be in a play; it's unheard of."

Tediously, he lectured me on the evils of the stage. "Don't you realize that Satan leads astray the hearts of men in notorious, lewd songs? The theatre is the home of intemperance, pomposity, and impurity, where flagrant characters are forever in pursuit of sexual conquests and other lusts. You imperil your soul.

"You do not have my permission to take part in such debauchery. I forbid it."

Enough was enough. I dashed to my room in frustration and drafted a letter to the Brother Provincial requesting a dispensation. I could no longer continue the battle to study and be involved in the arts without the support of my community. I could no longer observe the life-binding vows I had made of poverty, chastity, and obedience. My religious vocation had come to an impasse. Rome would have to release me from vows.

In my letter, I explained to my Provincial that I might have remained forever had I been permitted to continue teaching music.

I no longer could tolerate the idea that it was unmanly or ungodly to paint or sing or act. When I told Brother Symphorian my decision, he reminded me, "You're throwing your vocation in the face of God. God will not forgive you." That was the last time he ever spoke to me. But maybe that was because I avoided him.

I had to remain in the order until my dispensation came through at the end of the school semester, in April. But that was just as well. I still needed a roof over my head. I rode to the university with the Brothers in the morning. But was no longer given a bag lunch. Now my meals, indeed, my very survival depended on my own resources.

Threat of Deportation

After the final night of "Angels in Love", the cast was invited to a party in Detroit. On our way across the border, I was called into the U.S. Immigration office. Likely, this was because of my long hair and beard and traces of make-up. The officer asked me to provide identification. I produced my Quebec driver's licence. He took the card into another office then returned and asked for my birth certificate. I had been asked for a birth certificate previously, so I carried a folded photocopy. My birth certificate bore the name Patrick Milne, born in Tanganyka Territory. I showed a Canadian Citizenship card, also under the name Benoît Bertrand.

The officers told my fellow cast members to carry on without me. I was ushered into a small office and questioned by two officers in plain clothes. They asked about my affiliation with the Communist Party. I told them I was not and had never been a Communist. I was a member of the Christian Brothers studying at the University of Windsor.

One of the men asked, "Who are you trying to kid?" He looked at my birth certificate. "Maybe we should just deport you back to Tanganyka. Save us all a lot of trouble."

After a long time, I was given back my wallet and escorted back to Canada Customs at the Windsor end of the tunnel. American Customs kept my birth certificate copy and citizenship card.

I had to walk the entire way back to St. Joseph's. As always, Brother Charles let me in, freezing cold and this time in tears.

"What the hell happened to you?"

I told Chuck the entire story. While the two of us polished off what remained of one of our famous bottles of Crème de Cacao, I began to see the humour of the situation. The following morning I shaved. Later in the day, I asked Brother Cosmos to give me a haircut. For this service, he customarily demanded a package of cigarettes. As I didn't have one, he gave me a sloppy brush cut. My emotionally overloaded reaction to this was, "What the hell? Who cares?"

A couple of days later, on the advice of one of my professors, I made an appointment to see a lawyer. After some investigating, the lawyer discovered that, despite having been granted Canadian Citizenship in January 1961, I had never been legally adopted and would have to go to court to change my name from Patrick Milne to Benoît Bertrand. The fact that I had served in the Canadian Navy as Benoît Bertrand had no bearing. I would have to apply once again for a new document and required a "Declaration of Heredity" from Papa François to qualify for my Canadian Citizenship. As it stood, if ever I entered the United States again, they could deport me to Tanganyka on the strength of my birth certificate.

I was relieved when Papa François provided the necessary document in January 1969. After the customary advertisements appeared in newspapers in Montreal and Windsor, I appeared before a judge to legally become Benoît Bertrand in March of that year. My new Canadian Citizenship document was granted in May 1969. Still, the lawyer advised me not to try reentering the U.S. in the foreseeable future. I was on their list of "undesirables". Fortunately, as I no longer had the financial support of the De La Salle Brothers, the lawyer's services were offered pro bono.

A little more than a week prior to the end of classes, my dispensation came through. I was no longer bound by vows of poverty, chastity, and obedience. It was difficult for me to find a defining moment in this. I know of no one else who left a religious order without having been given some provision for transition to secular life. Yet I was provided with none.

Throughout most of the year, I found it necessary to support myself. Fortunately, I managed to save enough to make a down payment on a Volkswagen station wagon. I was not able to make the purchase myself, as I was still living at the Brothers' residence. I sent Mother the money, and she made the purchase for me and drove the car to Windsor.

With the help of my good friend Horace White, I was offered a teaching job in Dorval at L'Ecole Sécondaire Jean XXIII to teach English as a Second Language, covering for a teacher absent on medical leave. (She'd suffered a nervous breakdown.)

The only Brother to bid me farewell and good luck was my good friend Chuck.

Of Saints and Sinners

During my final year with the De La Salle Brothers, I reached the peak of rebellion. True, I found many grounds for disillusionment. On the other hand, I had lived and worked with countless dedicated and holy men.

I sought perfection in my confreres while I, all too often, broke my own vows of poverty and of obedience (if not in fact, at least in spirit). I judged my colleagues' actions to be inferior to mine. Though I was just as fallible as everyone around me, I didn't respect enough in them to learn this essential truth: the gifts of others are as valuable in their own way as mine.

Religious orders, like all organizations, are inhabited by saints and sinners both. Sometimes the good wins out. Sometimes the bad. I saw this "bad" so much in others, I tended to be harsh in my judgments. Most of all, I saw this in myself and was hardest on myself.

Since leaving religious life, especially, I have met many great and generous men and women who carry their goodness and leadership abilities into service of others. Thousands upon thousands of them serve in poverty, chastity and obedience. The reasons why one enters and departs from a religious community, even the priesthood, are as complex as life itself. God is the sole judge of our lives. So God alone knows the answer to this.

What prompted me to join a religious order? Was it an unselfish desire to serve God and fellow man by dedicating my life to teaching the children of the poor? If I could provide an unqualified "yes" to that, I'd be well on the path to sainthood. But I know I also had other, subconscious motives.

Here, out of the unmet needs of my childhood comes the answer. Like so many of my life's decisions, I surrendered to a pattern of attempts to please my mother and win her approval and her love. Later, I transferred this pattern to other meaningful people in my life. Even deeper than the lifelong search for love was the constant running, my attempt to escape the terrible, although misguided, guilt of childhood. To escape that shame, I was willing to risk my life and die as a martyr. Suicide by good works was my subconscious choice between the fires of hell and the eternal refuge of heaven.

All this did not remove the meaning from what I did. The hardships I faced helped me to develop a spirit of generosity. Sometimes I even reached a point where I could love without expecting return – Agapé.

In the process of my growth in love, I still had much to learn. But I have kept working at it. In fact, this has characterized my entire life.

I joined the Christian Brothers in an attempt to rescue and redeem myself from the shame I felt, day in and day out, since boyhood. This proved insufficient, of course, to sustain, for long, a truly religious and spiritual life. That's why I eventually left.

Two types of men stick it out in religious orders. First, there are those who truly are motivated towards sainthood. Second, there are those who (myself included) look upon the orders as a simpler, less threatening, and more ordered way to live out their lives. Of the members of this group, most feel emotionally threatened and insecure by the more chaotic demands of secular life.

I fit into neither group. I desired redemption. I couldn't find it, mainly because I looked in the wrong places. For certain, I couldn't find redemption from the degradation I felt about sex. For me, sex had become dangerous and dirty; it inspired anxiety and fear.

The basic cause of my sexual fear and shame would elude me for many years to come. Certain memories repressed in childhood would lie beneath the surface and fester until other pressures would eventually force them to the surface.

Ten

Hearts and Flowers and Fleurs de Lis

1969 – 1973

English as a Second Language

In April 1969, two separate administrative bodies – French and English Catholic, shared John XXIII High School in Dorval, Quebec. A brand new building, the school boasted a huge indoor swimming pool, fully equipped theatre-auditorium, enormous cafeteria, and classrooms with intercom. Everything was up-to-date and subsidized well beyond any school I'd ever seen.

All was not peaceful, however. The separatist movement was well under way.

I ate with the French teachers and spoke only in French. However, in class, I spoke only English, acting towards my students as though I did not understand or speak French. After all, my assignment was to teach English.

The Language program was taught with tape recorders and earphones. The teacher could switch from pupil to pupil for individual attention or address the entire class.

One senior class consisted entirely of girls.

"*Monsieur, est ce'que vous parlez français?*" (Sir, do you speak French?)

"I'm sorry; you'll have to repeat your question in English."

The girls flicked spit balls and passed countless notes. While I chose to ignore what was not immediately concerned with the task at hand, I began to understand why the former English teacher had gone on leave.

"*Monsieur, aimes-tu les petites filles?*" (Do you like little girls?)

"*Monsieur, veut tu coucher avec moi, chez-toi?*" (Do you want to sleep with me at your place?)

"Would you care to repeat your questions in English?"

"*Monsieur, as tu un gros pitou?*" (Do you have a big penis?)

Over the days, the questions, remarks, and roars of laughter grew.

"*Monsieur, est ce que tu manges les petites minoux?*" (Do you eat little pussies?)

"*C'EST ASSEZ!*" (That's enough!) I shouted.

Shock!

Then I said in French, "*Vous allez tous m'écouter! C'est le seule fois que je vais vous parler en francais.*" (You will listen to me. This is the only time I will speak to you in French.)

Disbelief!

"*Si vous voulez apprendre l'anglais, les leçons seront en anglais seulement. Cette affaire imbécile est fini.*" (If you wish to learn English, the lessons will be in English only. This ridiculous affair is over.) "Now, let us continue in a more serious manner."

Several girls broke out in tears. A couple left the classroom. I continued the lesson.

About five minutes later, the two girls returned with the principal. He addressed the class. "*Mademoiselles, si vous avez de la difficultée avec certaines mots en anglais, Monsieur Bertrand peut certainement vous aider en français. N'est ce pas, Monsieur Bertrand?*" (Ladies, if you have difficulty with certain words in English, Mr. Bertrand could certainly help you in French. Is that not so Mr. Bertrand?)

Every girl was grinning. They had won, or so they thought. However, I continued to teach in English only, but only until the end of the term. The class behaved well and nothing further was said. Fortunately, I had been given a job for the following year teaching on the English side of the school where I reasoned I'd have better support from the administration.

Dorval and Mother

That summer I spent much of my time at Cub Camp with my good friend Peter Dawson and various packs from throughout the Montreal area. In this totally volunteer work, I enjoyed myself immensely.

The following year, I taught Vocal Music, Drama, and Art from grades eight to twelve, formed a mixed-voiced choir for St. Veronica's Church, joined the Lyric Theatre Society and the Lakeshore Players, performing in *The Pajama Game*, *Fiorello*, and several one-act plays, and ran a special exercise class for expectant mothers on the Lakeshore. One evening a week, I drove to Sir George Williams University for Theatre History to complete my B.A. Everything was falling into place.

1970, I directed the school production of *West Side Story*, and in 1971, *Oliver*. While directing *Oliver*, I also took the role of Henry Higgins in *My Fair Lady*, with the Arcadians, a semi-professional group in Montreal. The Director, Alexander MacDougall, did choreography for Les Grands Ballets Canadiens as well as for several groups of modern dancers in Montreal and the West Indies. An agile seventy year-old, he was a master of crowd scenes.

At every performance, I fell in love with Eliza Doolittle, played by Elva Hanson whose husband played trumpet in the orchestra. Jack McCutcheon played a magnificent Doolittle. After the show's run, he moved to Australia for a job with the Australian Broadcasting Corporation. Robert Thorpe, the group's president, played the Major. We were a marvellous cast, a team.

Not only did Alex MacDougall teach me to dance, he taught me to fly through the air as though hoisted by invisible wires. He exerted more influence on my acting and directing than any other person in theatre.

Mother attended the opening night of *My Fair Lady*. She didn't care for the callous Higgins called for by George Bernard Shaw. I took my mother's criticism to heart; the next night, I softened up and played Higgins with a twinkle. Alex MacDougall approved and so did audiences.

I visited Mother often. She helped me decorate my apartment in Dorval. In turn, I installed a pond and waterfall in her back garden, even supplying the water pump and plants. Mother opened up in a way she hadn't done for many years. She shared secrets about her life during the war. She told me why she was absent for such great lengths of time and why Naomi and I had to stay with Uncle Sigvard .

Mother told me that because she had done so well in the Censorship Bureau, because she had lived much of her childhood in Denmark, because she had attended schools in France and Germany, and because of her fluency in French, German, Danish, and other languages, she was assigned to British Intelligence and had to see and do some terrible things.

Married women never got sent on dangerous missions. But Mother wasn't married. Since she had never married my father, my sister and I were illegitimate - and didn't count.

Mother hinted about being parachuted into occupied countries while Naomi and I attended boarding schools. For certain, she fluently spoke six or more languages and possessed the audacity and nerve that such activities required. And for certain, she worked as a censor of important wartime documents. However because records of some wartime activities just were not kept – or were not available, it's difficult to ascertain whether she might have been given other jobs to do, too. But now that she's gone, I'll never know. Anything's possible here.

When Mother met my stepfather, she needed a change of identity and a new life. Her pregnancy, certainly, would provide the secure status of Canadian bride and housewife.

Despite the confidence my mother now showed me, I was still insecure and needed to prove myself to her. So, when Mother confided that she was getting increasingly depressed and that, if she didn't get a car to drive, she'd probably kill herself, I gave her much of my savings to buy a Peugeot from her good friend Jean LeBegue. When she took me for a 100 mph spin in her new sports car, I became motivated enough to trade in my Volkswagen station wagon for a little two-seater Peugeot convertible. Soon the excitement of owning this vehicle made me dream of romance.

> *Vive Montréal! Vive le Québec!*
>
> *Vive le Québec libre!*
>
> – Charles De Gaulle, Montréal, Québec, 24 July, 1967

During the spring of 1971, the movement for an independent Québec grew stronger in the school. The French students and teachers smoked in the hallways, with complete disdain for the English side of the school where smoking was not permitted. They threw garbage and cigarette butts all over the theatre floor. Worst of all, food fights broke out in the cafeteria between the two sides. Slowly but surely, I grew to hate my teaching environment.

Madly in Love

Confident that Harry White, music coordinator for the Montreal Catholic School Commission, would find another job for me, I submitted my resignation in June.

That Summer of 1971, those teaching in Quebec without formal teaching certification were offered the opportunity – through three summer courses at McGill University – to gain a full teaching diploma. My major, of course, would be Music. Meanwhile, I was offered a job teaching music at Holy Names High School, an all-girls school in central Montreal.

I moved to a bachelor suite at Sutton Place, in Notre Dame de Grace, close to Montreal West and took weekend trips into the Laurentians with chorus girls I met through the Arcadians and Lakeshore Players. We swam in the lakes and gathered at friends' cottages.

Nearly everyone talked about sex. And sex, of course, happened. I didn't date – although, through my activities with the Lyric Theatre Society, the Lakeshore Players, and the Arcadians, I became infatuated with several gorgeous women and got involved in petting sessions – some "excruciatingly hot and heavy". Still, I never made the move across that invisible boundary.

I told myself I wanted the right girl, she whom I would marry in sacred union. When girls came up to see my etchings, I showed them my artwork. And I explained the memorabilia on my walls from my years with the Hart Singers.

One snowy night, two of the girls from *My Fair Lady* had to stay overnight at my apartment. I gave them my bed while I slept in the living room on the couch. Knowing they lay naked in my queen size bed, I developed a strong desire to join them.

Well into the night, I heard them whispering and giggling. Maybe they wondered if I was still a Brother. In my mind, certainly, I felt like a Brother.

The sexual revolution passed me by.

Often, during Sunday afternoons, I drove alone to the lookout on Mount Royal, where I parked the car and walked to the pond. When I watched happy couples strolling arm in arm or lying together on the grass necking, I was envious. I wished I had a girlfriend to love as my own.

Mount Royal was a busy place on Sundays when the sun shone. Children floated miniature sailboats on the pond. Other children clamoured around the elderly Italian with the bushy mustache as he ground his barrel organ, sending velvet strains of *Toselli's Serenade* floating across the green grass. Mothers with prams stood listening, or chatted in small groups.

On Mount Royal, the happier the day, the lonelier I felt.

During the final two weeks of my first summer in the McGill Diploma in Secondary Education program, the professor paired off the students for a music assignment. He assigned me to work with a woman who sat shyly at the back of the class. Eloise and I had just two weeks to come up with a major paper.

Funny, I don't recall the nature of the assignment any more. I only remember walking with Eloise up Mount Royal that beautiful summer. When I hummed the major theme from *Rachmaninoff's 2nd Piano Concerto*, Eloise hummed part of the melody with me. Immediately overcome with excitement and feelings of destiny, I told her, "I'm going to marry you."

Poor Eloise. Who was this insane man? When she accepted my invitation to dinner at my apartment, I was so excited, I forgot to prepare a meal. While we laboured on the assignment, all I gave her was a fruit cocktail topped with crème de café. Who needed food when here was a feast for the soul?

Eloise told me she was seriously involved with a Dutch fellow named Willhelm, and that she would be going to Holland at the end of the summer to meet his parents. I replied, "Eloise, I love you. I'm going to marry you."

With ruthless logic, I introduced confusion into her otherwise ordered life.

"My father likes Willhelm. He works for the railway."

"But do you love him?"

"I don't know!"

"I love you."

Eloise lived in a small room near the university. During our first fortnight, I bought flowers and chocolates and left them at her door late at night.

Soon she moved to Montreal West to house sit for some friends off on holidays.

We completed our assignment with an "A".

All too soon, classes were over and the love of my life flew off to Holland with her Willhelm, still confused and overwhelmed. Not only did I ask her to write to me from Holland, I informed her I would await her return.

Not long after she departed, I drove alone, with few stops, until I reached Cape Cod. On Nanset Beach, Massachusetts, about as far east as I could go, I sat on the sand and gazed towards Holland. I wondered if Eloise was thinking of me.

The sea was lonely. And I felt lonely.

In front of me, breakers rolled in long crests and tumbled in silver showers. All about me, the low sand dunes rippled with the wind. In reverent response, the coarse, sharp grasses genuflected as my friend, the sun, bloodied the tide with his farewell to the day. Fishing boats tugged at their moorings with smacks and spanks. As the far shore settled in for a cozy evening of snuggles and hot drinks by family fires, the lights twinkled on.

Later, in the nearby town, I strolled the fishing wharves, and smelled the dead fish and seaweed. And felt dead myself – without the one who completed me.

Just one day after my arrival, I turned around and drove back towards Montreal. I stopped on the way, near Plattsburgh on Lake Champlain, where I visited overnight with vacationing friends. Then I continued nonstop to Montreal.

I couldn't enjoy myself until I received some kind of word from my love. And I got it. In the Monday mail was a card from Holland: "I miss you".

Now the rest of my holiday would be complete. Almost literally, I floated through the White Mountains and on to Virginia Beach. As Mother had piqued my interest in the books of Edgar Cayce, I visited the Institute constructed in his memory.

Edgar Cayce, "the Sleeping Prophet", is reputed to have had the ability to put himself into a sleep state in which he placed his mind in contact with all time and space. Then, provided with the name and location of an individual anywhere in the world he would give answers to questions about that person's medical state. Cayce's answers were written down by a stenographer, who kept one copy on file and sent another to the person requesting the information. Medical doctors were then able to use Cayce's suggestions to achieve amazing cures. By the time Edgar Cayce died in 1945, more than 14,000 of his readings were on file at the Association for Research and Enlightenment in Virginia Beach, Virginia.

Perhaps, I imagined, Eloise was the reincarnation of a long lost love of mine from another life. I rationalized that such beliefs did not contradict my

Catholic Faith. After all, a mystical attraction drew us together. I spent the next piece of forever patrolling the sandy beaches, perpetually gazing out to sea.

My return to Montreal became a pilgrimage of expectation. School would be in session. Eloise would be back. All I need do was see her, hold her, and never let her go.

Then the weather changed. Fog rolled in and rested there, thick as pigs' mud, choking my lungs. This was freak weather in the midst of summer. I had to wait for the road to clear. I pulled over to the side of the highway and slept.

Eventually the sun stopped sulking behind the mist. Rolling out from cover, it bathed me in its renewed smile. Nature, having paid its penance in the chilly morning, shouted out in joyful colours, with paint pots of yellows and greens, reds and oranges, pinks and purples.

My heart became a rainbow of happiness.

Eloise taught Music in Ville La Salle; I had begun my new job at Holy Names. Every night my love and I spent hours on the telephone. Every weekend, we went for long drives in the country or walked up Mount Royal. Frequently, I asked Eloise to marry me. Occasionally, she visited Willhelm; how many times, I'll never know.

One night, while we drove out to Senneville, we lost track of time. House lights flicked out. On impulse, I stopped, picked a huge bouquet of hydrangeas from someone's estate garden, and presented them to Eloise. Fighting back tears, she said nothing; she only gazed in wonder at the blossoms in her lap.

About ten weeks after we first met, during one of our marathon telephone conversations, she remarked, "At this rate, we might as well be married." In excitement, I hung up, sped to her little room on the edge of Mount Royal, and presented her with the biggest diamond engagement ring I could afford. (I had set it aside shortly after we first met.) Eloise cried.

That night, we sat up making plans about meeting each other's parents. I told her I would ask her father formally for his daughter's hand. We agreed to be married at Christmas and spend the two-week break on a gorgeous honeymoon.

Eloise's parents lived, with their elder daughter, within walking distance from my apartment at Sutton Square. After Eloise introduced me to her mother and dad, I said, "Perhaps you should sit down."

They sat. I held Eloise's hand, showed them the ring, and announced I was deeply in love with their daughter. "I have come to ask for your daughter's hand in marriage."

Smiles and shock followed. "Is this what you want Eloise?"

Eloise looked at me and whispered, "Yes."

A confused conversation followed. "What about Willhelm? Kristina's not married yet. Shouldn't you talk to her?"

I told them we'd like to be married at Christmas break.

"Why so soon? We need more time. ...The Church won't let you marry at Christmas."

Finally, grudgingly, I got the answer I wanted: "Well, you're not children any more."

We drove out to Senneville next. Everyone was delighted. Mother said she knew, as soon as we walked in, and welcomed Eloise like a daughter. While we drove off after our visit, we could see the girls jumping up and down and hugging.

When we visited Eloise's pastor at St. Ignatius of Loyola Church, he had other ideas. "A wedding at Christmas? Out of the question! Christmas Eve is a time of preparation." We drove out to Lachine and spoke to my good friend at Immaculate Conception Church, Father Gordon.

For a long time, he spoke about the sacredness and permanence of marriage. Yes, we intended to have children very soon. No, Eloise was not pregnant. At the end, Father Gord decided to obtain permission for us from Eloise's pastor and to talk to us again soon, many times, in fact. He had to be sure we both understood fully what we were getting into. He would also help us prepare for the duties and privileges of married life.

Meantime, because I was in love, my days at Holy Name School were as a rose opening in early summer. Though Sister Superior was very stern – the girls went from class to class, in silence – I effectively began to change this mood. I taught Glee Club in the basement during lunch hour. At the end of our first practice, the girls climbed the stairs singing, "Did I fill the world with love? Did I fill … " One by one the voices cut short.

"Good afternoon sister!" I smiled and continued singing while I walked to my first class of the afternoon. Yes, I was a rabble-rouser. I also taught several of the Sisters to play guitar.

Every morning I greeted the Sister Superior with cheery greetings: "You look beautiful this morning, Sister." I was sincere. Soon, talking between classes was permitted, though no official pronouncement had been made to change the rule.

As Vatican II started taking effect, a few of the Sisters began wearing clothing other than their habits. The staff cheered up a great deal. Teachers exchanged presents. The Sisters gave me a beautiful Crucifix of the Risen Christ and wished me happiness for my upcoming wedding.

WEDDING BELLS

December 24. Senneville. We drove to church in the family car – excruciatingly slowly. I fidgeted in the back seat. But I needn't have worried. We had to wait an eternity before Eloise's family arrived. Then Eloise came down the aisle to meet me. She was Juliet, with flowers in her hair.

Eloise and I had chosen our own songs and readings. At one point, we held hands and sang, "Make of our hands one hand" from *West Side Story* accompanied by a flamenco guitarist. During the love ballad, Eloise wept. My voice quivering with emotion, I completed the last lines alone. "Only death can part us now."

Only a few were present to witness our wedding, including my friends from Lachine. Afterwards, they showered us with tears and congratulations.

My sister, Louise, was in the hospital delivering a son. And my Aunties from Quebec were not invited. (Both sets of parents laid down conditions for the wedding reception to be held at Eloise's family home. Because of space restrictions, our guest list was to be limited.) The wedding dinner was a Beef Stroganoff cooked by Eloise's mom. Eloise's sister threw a tantrum and locked herself in her room, after tossing off, "We all know why you had to get married!" Eloise's attempts to placate her didn't work. Though she told her mother to give her bouquet to her sister, the bouquet remained wilting on the kitchen table a fortnight later.

Vic, Louise's husband, arranged a honeymoon in the Bahamas for us. Mother and Papa François drove us to the airport.

On Christmas morning, we attended mass at a tiny church where little black altar boys stuck their tongues out at each other. During the first week, we took a variety of tours. A couple of times, we got dropped off on deserted beaches. On one such beach, I convinced Eloise to skinny dip with me.

That night, suffering serious sunburn, I could only lie face down on top of the bed. Suddenly Eloise jumped up with a scream. A gecko was climbing up the wall. For the first time, I realized she was terrified of reptiles. All reptiles. So, in great pain, I picked up the little creature and carefully dropped it from the balcony into the bushes below.

We returned to teaching and enjoyed our happy new existence, cozy in our little apartment in Sutton Square, not far from Eloise's parents. Customarily, I drove Eloise to school, then headed to my own school in the opposite direction.

Québec Libre!

During the 1970-71 school year, Harry White and I attended many meetings in Quebec City developing a music program for the Quebec secondary schools. I had also written a detailed paper on the use of creativity in the classroom, which was published in part in an educational magazine.

Towards the end of the school year, Harry White approached me to develop and teach a special program for one of the inner-city schools. "Operation Renewal" would involve a fusion of Drama, Music, and Art and provide special help for new Canadians with mother tongues other than French or English. Classes would run at the new, open-area St. Patrick's Elementary School, in Montreal's inner city.

December 1972, Eloise was pregnant. We lived in a small upper duplex in Ville La Salle to be close to Eloise's school. Our landlady was an alcoholic single mother with a teen-age son. Over and over, she played "Please Release Me, Let Me Go". Desperate for beer, she broke the lock on our apartment door and claimed we had been broken into. Since only beer was missing, we suspected she was the culprit.

During my time at St. Pat's, the *Front de Libération Québecois* (a terrorist group better known as the F.L.Q.) trained openly in the street behind the school. A group of these ruffians, supported by students from a local junior college (known in Quebec as CEGEP), decided to block our noon-hour kindergarten changeover. Tiny children, just out of their cocoons, still fuzzy, moist, and squirmy, were being stopped from running to waiting mums and dads by a gang of screaming oafs. As a result, none of us could leave or enter the school. Soon the police arrived "to keep order". When one child ran towards his father, a demonstrator came forward swinging a chain. The father grabbed the chain and a scuffle ensued. The father was arrested.

The Separatists demanded that all new Canadians moving to Quebec attend school in the French language only. In the suburb of Pierrefonds, marching demonstrators threw bricks through the windows of the homes of Anglophones and some new Canadians.

That December, citing the fact that I'd been teaching without official qualifications, I was declassified by the Department of Education in Quebec City and my salary cut retroactively to April 1969. Since I taught in the Catholic schools, I was represented by the French teachers' union (the C.E.Q.). That union was anxious to see English teachers leave; thus they gave no protection to English Catholic teachers.

Many teachers with education degrees but whose qualifications came from outside Quebec were also declassified and eventually moved to Ontario and further west. First, each declassified teacher would have to repay every penny owed to the Province of Quebec before his or her documents could be released to any exterior department of education. The following summer would see the completion of my McGill Education in Music courses granting me full qualification to teach anywhere in Canada.

I had fond remembrances of B.C. and Eloise had spent many happy years as a child in Nelson, B.C., so we decided to move to the West Coast, despite protestation from both our families.

I wrote letters of application to school districts on the B.C. coast, including Vancouver Island, stating that I would be available for interviews during the Easter break. Eloise would take a leave from teaching.

On the last day of class, we flew to B.C. and stayed with Eloise's relatives in Victoria. Her Uncle Walter was surprised I was not the "hippy bum" he had heard about.

We drove to schools all over Vancouver Island. Everybody was kind and welcoming, and the students especially polite. They opened doors for us and escorted us to sympathetic principals. Applying as a music specialist who also could teach French and Drama, I stated willingness to do anything to move to the West Coast. I determined to move to B.C. even if I had to pick fruit in the Okanagan.

The sun shone every day of our visit. We had come to a green paradise.

A Chill Wind Blows

Our western holiday was too good to last and we had to fly back to Dorval and January classes. The mercury had dropped, and a vengeful winter wind howled. Our Peugeot sat in the airport parking lot covered in ice. Though I managed to get the car started and chipped the ice from the windows, the heater stubbornly refused to work. When we got to Ville La Salle, cold and miserable, the door to our apartment wouldn't open and "Madame" was not in. So I drove to Montreal West, left Eloise with her parents, and took the car to Sutton Place where I waited for it to thaw out in the garage.

Finally, when the ice blocking the heater ducts melted, I drove back to our apartment. Madame was home at last. She informed me that she had to replace the lock whilst we were away. She gave me a new key. I let myself in, and turned on the oil heater. Then I returned to Montreal West to pick up Eloise.

Following our return to Montreal, the weather wasn't all that was vengeful. Eloise's parents had spoken with my parents about our wish to get away. We were being very selfish. They wouldn't get to know their new grandchild. We placated them by promising to spend part of the summer with each family.

In late spring, I was admitted to Jewish General Hospital with a ruptured hernia. While there, hospital support staff belonging to the powerful Quebec Labour Union went on strike. At one point, the strikers cut part of the hospital's power supply. Patients spent several anxious hours in the dark, with no meals. Even some of the emergency power was cut. Doctors and nurses were blocked from entering or leaving and nurses unable to perform their duties. Visitors were neither permitted to enter nor to communicate with patients.

During this same strike, the school janitors went off the job.

Quebec was still smarting from the effects of F.L.Q. terrorism, including kidnapping and murder, and the subsequent War Measures Act of 1970. As a result, the English of Montreal were subjected to bitter resentment, even hatred, by many francophones.

As she did not yet drive, Eloise was dependent on busses while I was in hospital. Her bus stopped a short distance from her school in Ville La Salle where a picketing maintenance worker elbowed her off the sidewalk. The police did nothing but look on in amusement. We were increasingly anxious to leave Quebec.

May 1st was moving day in Quebec. *(Urban leases began on May 1 and ended on April 30. In law, this date had been set in the Civil Code of Lower Canada in 1866 and still carried on by tradition.)* We gave up our apartment and moved to my parents' home in Senneville for the next six weeks of school. Mother had grown cold towards us both, and Eloise spent hours crying in our room. I paid my parents for our room-and-board, and Eloise resented that, even though we'd agreed to pay the same while staying with her parents.

I felt constantly torn between mother and wife. Usually, Eloise won out but I was afraid of displeasing Mother. To move out at that time would have made matters worse as I had promised both my parents and Eloise's that we'd spend time with them before moving to B.C. Furthermore, we'd already sold our furnishings.

When the school term finished, we moved to Montreal West to live with Eloise's parents. Each day, we suffocated in summer school classes; evenings and weekends, we wrote assignments and studied for exams.

At night, in the privacy of our bedroom, I wanted physical contact with Eloise. But the bed, with its protesting iron springs, would broadcast our every move. We couldn't be intimate.

What was it about this one person that caused me to fall so insanely in love? Why had I been so persistent?

Here was a beautiful woman so different from my mother. Eloise was shy, reserved, non-threatening. She appeared to be neither aggressive nor domineering. I felt safe and comfortable.

At the same time, she was obviously an achiever. She loved music and dressed well. She was a teacher, therefore intelligent - educated.

Of all the women I'd met since leaving the Brothers, Eloise was the first I could envision spending the rest of my life with.

I would be the strong one. With my new positive self-image, I would protect her and help her develop her own self-confidence. Where I sensed sadness, I would make her happy. I longed for love. Here she was.

When Eloise didn't fall in love with me, I had to work desperately to convince her and make her love me. I couldn't let her go.

An Explosive Sunday

It was Sunday afternoon. Eloise's parents were with their bridge club. The heat of the day had risen to a brick-red peak. Like a steady hum in the still air, a steaming sauna, it enveloped the house. Stubbornly refusing to find the open window, a fly buzzed angrily between ceiling and screen door.

I perched before my study notes, elbows glued to the sticky kitchen table, sweat trickling down my back to soak the elastic on my shorts. Eloise sat opposite, swollen, looking ill. The two of us struggled to complete our final assignment for the Summer Session at McGill and to prepare for the next day's exam. Eloise's sister droned on at the phone in the hallway. I called out to her, "Kristina, do you think we could all share that fan you've got going in you room? You're down here anyway." She didn't answer.

Ten minutes later, Kristina entered the kitchen and pulled out the chair beside Eloise. "I've invited Aunt Evelyn to supper. You'll have to put that stuff away and start cooking."

"What?" I almost shouted. "You invited her. You bloody well cook the supper. We've got too much..."

Kristina faced me, nearly nose to nose, and growled through clenched teeth. "Mind your own business. I'm talking to my sister."

"Please, Kristina," Eloise said calmly. "We've got to get this finished."

"No!" Kristina shouted. "You have to cook supper. You know I'm not well." Her voice rose to a shrill whining crescendo and shattered like slivers of glass in my ears.

"Well, then. You shouldn't have invited Aunty Evelyn. You certainly didn't check with me." Eloise was surprisingly calm.

Her face bloated with temper, Kristina pushed the chair into the table. It squealed and thumped unhappily. "Get your junk off the kitchen table," she hissed, spittle flying everywhere. Then she pushed Eloise's papers onto the floor.

At this point, I jumped to my feet. "Oh, Kristina, for Christ's sake, will you fuck off and leave us alone?"

Kristina screamed as if sliced with a knife. She tore down the hall and out through the front door. Running pell-mell down the city street, she screamed again and again. Her screams were long and piercing. Murder had been done. Blood spattered the kitchen walls.

"He told me to fuck off! He told me to fuck off!"

Neighbours opened their front doors and windows. "Poor Kristina." Someone walked out and took her in.

When Eloise's parents returned from their bridge club, they told me what they thought of me. My mother-in-law, her voice cracking into splinters of indignation, opined, "You are absolutely disgusting, treating poor, sick Kristina in such an unChristian way."

With a grimace of disgust, Eloise's father shook his head at me. "Filthy, filthy mouth." His voice sounded like a burnt, breaking twig, brittle and dry.

Though shaking, I was unrepentant.

Running Late

At last, Monday August 6th arrived. It was time for our final exam at McGill. Though the baby was due at any moment, Eloise was not excused from writing if she wanted her certificate. Labour pains started in earnest while she was still plugging away. She had barely finished the last question before I rushed her to the hospital. Even then, I had to argue with the exam supervisor who said it was too early for us to leave the room.

I had taken the prenatal classes with my wife. So I dressed in a hospital gown and got ready to assist. Eloise's labour was long and difficult, and I huffed and puffed with her for several exhausting hours. At last, a tiny head appeared, elongated from the process. In horror, I thought the baby was Mongoloid. But I kept my fear well hidden. As soon as I saw the baby, I told Eloise with tears of joy, "It's Hanna!" We had chosen the names Alexander and Hanna shortly after Eloise became pregnant.

I telephoned both families to tell them the good news. They had a granddaughter, Hanna Anne. Mother decided not to come to the hospital. "Why would I want to visit a baby I'll never get to hold?" I had difficulty understanding her bitterness. I took my little daughter, cradled her in my arms, and sang, "My little girl, soft and sweet, as peaches and cream is she..." Hanna smiled. Eloise's mother said it was gas pains. But I knew different.

From all my applications to teach in B.C., I received just one offer. I would have to report to the west coast and sign my contract prior to August 15th. This meant leaving before the end of the week and driving west, with whatever belongings remained. Eloise would fly out as soon as it was safe for the baby.

I drove out to my parents to say my good-byes and to ask sheepishly to borrow a few dollars until I could get settled in my new job. I was turned down. "We just do not have any money at present. But do enjoy your trip."

As I departed, I noticed the new dishwasher waiting to be installed. I felt cheated. I hadn't asked for a gift, merely for a loan. But Mother was angry we were leaving with her new granddaughter. The rift never healed.

Eleven

NEW HORIZONS

Trans-Canada Highway

Early Friday morning, August 10th, I packed the little Peugeot two-seater until it resembled a Norris cartoon. After pushing and prodding some of our meagre belongings into every imaginable niche and cranny around the driver's seat, I piled up the rest until I could no longer use the car's canvas top. To protect everything from the elements, I had to rely upon an ill-fitting tarp, one corner or another destined to flap at fellow motorists until I reached Vancouver.

I had just four days to travel almost 4800 kilometres. Leaving Mother once again, I would begin a new life as father, husband, lover.

Almost dusk on day two, hot and sweaty, I stopped for a dip in a warm, shallow pond just off the road. Dug around in my gear. No luck: Couldn't find my bathing suit. Trees masked much of the pond from the highway. I skinny-dipped while a brace of geese winged their way across the flaming sky. Then I heard the sound of young voices. Quickly, I dried off beside the car. A busload of campers pulled up, hooting and whistling.

In the clear night, I stopped to stretch. Gazing up at the expanse of stars, I allowed my imagination to float freely through time and space. The same stars that looked down upon me looked down upon the two loves of my life in Montreal West.

"Lord, keep them safe this night."

A dog barked "Amen!"

Day three. At the crest of a rolling hill, I watched the world gradually open up as light broke through, harbinger of another scorching day. A short distance ahead, a dusty road led to a small grove of trees and a couple of picnic tables. I pulled over, turned off the ignition, and got out to stretch. A few lights still twinkled in far-off farmhouses.

Body ached. Temples throbbed. Eyes burned for want of sleep. I got back into the car, drove to the grove of trees, yanked my sleeping bag out of the jumble of luggage, spread it out on the stubble beside the picnic table, and stretched out, face down. Immediately, I fell asleep.

Several hours later, I awoke, with the sun almost directly above my head. Nostrils dry with the heat; body hot, heavy, and stiff. If it weren't for the glare, I would've slept most of the day.

At the edge of the grove of trees, a deer glanced up from her grazing, watched me shake out my sleeping bag and fold it, and nonchalantly resumed its tugging at the tufts of low bush.

In Saskatchewan, the sun turned the highway into a liquid, rippling mirage. My eyes burned – visual indigestion.

Then, "Thump, thump, thump."

To change a tire, I had to unload nearly everything while the sun beat down with white-hot blows. Trucks whizzed by. A colony of inquisitive gophers chattered from a nearby hillock.

Job done, dripping with perspiration, I pulled out a can of warm pop, leaned against the car, and contemplated the countryside. Lonely stands of scrubby trees panted for rain. The skies heaved. Flickers of lightning teased the parched prairie.

In the mountains at last, the little Peugeot puffed up steep inclines, summer traffic honking at her tail. She sang down precipitous stretches of open highway, only to join conga lines, bumper-to-bumper holiday campers. When I'd almost despaired, we reached Hope. Two hours to go. The weather had been perfect.

Oops! I'd forgotten Murphy's Law. Rain and more rain. In the Fraser Valley, motorists flew past drenching me in their spray.

Just before noon, Tuesday, August 14th, 1973, mere hours before the deadline, I signed a contract to teach at North Drummond Secondary School. I was to report to my new principal, the following morning. As I departed, the school superintendent observed, "You look as if you've just come in from the Klondike." My face was scarlet, and my beard bushy and windblown.

A week later, Eloise arrived with tiny Hanna.

New Beginnings

Until my first paycheque, Eloise and I couldn't look for a home of our own. I commuted from Richmond where we stayed with Eloise's Aunt Rose, a hearty first generation settler from the Ukraine via a Saskatchewan homestead.

In early October, Eloise and I began looking at rental housing. We had no furniture, no curtains, nothing. We had only a few eating utensils. On the strength of my teaching contract, I obtained a bank loan for furnishings.

Several teachers were discussing investments. Real estate was rapidly increasing in value. It would be advisable to buy rather than rent. All I needed was the down payment.

We had looked at several ugly rental properties. Then the agent showed us a house for sale not far from the school, priced at forty-nine thousand. With a down payment of five thousand, it could be ours.

Back at the bank, I convinced the loans manager that I could manage both loan payments and a reasonable mortgage.

The house had no appliances. Worse, it needed cleaning, repairs, and a good paint job. Still, it gave us a roof. And it was ours!

After several days of scrubbing and carpet cleaning, we moved in mid-October, taped newspaper to the windows, and slept on the floor in sleeping bags. Eloise cooked on a camp stove and stored perishables in our camping cooler. I cadged ice from our neighbours, fruit and vegetables from Aunt Rose's huge garden, and bought baby formula on credit. Hanna slept in a plastic bathtub until my principal provided a crib his grandchildren had outgrown.

After a month, I bought a bed, fridge, stove, unfinished table, and four chairs – all second hand. In December, a second-hand clothes washer. Meanwhile, I laundered in the basement sink and hung rows of diapers on clothesline stretched across the back yard.

Our back yard was solid clay with sparse patches of grass. I found a shovel and a rake. A neighbour gave me an old wheelbarrow and I began collecting bags of leaves, which I spread over the entire ground surface and dug in row by row. The following spring, I would mark off a couple of sunny areas for vegetable and flower gardens, then rake the rest, spread grass seed, and rake again.

Throughout the winter months I sanded, painted, and built an extra room in the basement.

The Drummond School Board was completing a "state of the Art" theatre auditorium at North Drummond Senior Secondary School. The facility would be available to the community when not in specific use by the school. My job was to build up a Theatre Arts program.

While touring at a similar auditorium in South Drummond, I encountered potential problems and suggested modifications for our school, which could still be made without adding to construction costs. For example, whereas I asked for a covered pit, which could be opened for musicals. The principal told me the area under the stage was to be filled with sand. I saw that the wing curtains "legs" at South Drummond were fixed. Moveable wings would be far more flexible during productions. I made notes and asked if I might speak with the architect and building superintendent. The principal shrugged his shoulders, "The same architect is in charge of the new auditorium. I doubt he'll consider changes in his plans."

My greatest concern regarded stage lighting. One of the teachers, an electrician in his spare time, was acting as lighting consultant but obviously knew nothing about stage lighting. Lights were already being set to permanent positions, with reflective lamps containing bulbs of red, blue and yellow – primary colours for pigment.

It would take a couple of years to convince the authorities that we needed moveable lamps on bars that could be lowered and that frames could hold red, green, and amber gels to produce a multitude of interesting effects. As for front lighting, no allowance had been made to install it – ever. The administration was intransigent. I was ordered to stay away from the auditorium until it would be ready for use.

I taught my first semester drama class in a small room in the school basement. We built a puppet theatre and worked on voice, movement, and creative dramatics. My students and I produced a series of puppet shows on traffic safety for elementary school children. Using a hand-held camera, we made a video, "This is Your School". The film, complete with sound over, began with almost the entire staff appearing to arrive in one Volkswagen. A skeleton office staff was on hand as – you guessed it – skeletons. The principal obliged by hiding in a cupboard, to be caught smoking a cigarette. The usual lunchroom hubbub was accompanied by appropriate barnyard sound effects. The school band played "Twinkle, Twinkle Little Star", off-key of course. Most teachers and students were very cooperative when we asked to film them in ridiculous situations. We aired the tape in the school cafeteria during lunch for two days running. After school, we rehearsed *Oklahoma* on the gymnasium stage amidst basketballs, piped music and cheerleader practices.

Home was close enough that I could return for lunch most days. Eloise, pregnant with our second child, couldn't stand the smell of soiled diapers, so I'd change Hanna first thing in the morning and, when I could get home, just before lunch. Then I'd pick her up after school and return to rehearsals. Drama club students made fantastic baby-sitters.

That first semester, I also taught French. The vice-principal, a Francophone, attended one of my classes. Following his forty-minute visit, he expressed amazement that not one word of English had been spoken. We sang French-Canadian folk songs and conversed in small groups. The only rule was that no English was to be spoken during class time; a rule not always kept.

The head of the Art Department was a super teacher who encouraged experimentation. My students and I painted with melted wax crayon applied with old electric irons and made several large collages. When the class occurred during fourth period, we sometimes took paints and sketchpads to the river to draw and paint boats and old buildings. Other times, we scattered about the school to observe perspective, tone, and shade. Those who chose to skip class still had to find ways to complete their portfolios.

With the success of *Oklahoma*, I had full Stagecraft and Acting classes for the second semester. My fourth class was Art. I felt fulfilled on every front. By the time the auditorium stage was completed, I had won my case regarding an orchestra pit although the remainder of the area under the stage was still filled with sand depriving us of much potential storage space.

By the beginning of the second year, the demand rose enough to allow me to teach full time Theatre and I began to integrate Acting, Stagecraft and Writing/Directing. As a body, we worked on main stage productions, student scenes, student productions, fashion shows, classical plays, and musicals.

Diapers and Scrounged Materials

On the eve of Thanksgiving Day, 1974, our second baby was coming. I rushed next door to ask our neighbour to baby-sit Hanna. Then I drove Eloise, emergency flashers blinking, through red lights, pausing every so often for contractions. After accidentally missing the Emergency Entrance twice, we arrived at the Maternity Ward – Riverside Memorial Hospital.

I parked the car, scrubbed up and donned the green gown and mask to be present for the delivery of Alexander.

Each day, as soon as classes ended, I dashed home, changed diapers, picked up two babies, and brought them to rehearsals. Hanna and Alexander became "stage brats" with no end of willing and capable sitters. They took part in productions whenever toddlers and young children were required.

Students and I scrounged lumber from school building sites and built enormous sets. The stage was a giant canvas, ready to be filled with form and colour. Future directors and actors learned to use every area and level possible. We planned with miniature models of balsa and cardboard. Often learning as I taught, I helped young thespians perform magic with lights and make-up and gain experience in making their own decisions about costume colours and stage movement.

To overcome fixed stage lights, we built our own lighting boxes for the floor and hung other lights from scaffolding. Because we were constantly calling school board electricians to change ceiling lamps, I finally got my way and a movable lighting grid was installed. While they were at it, I had the electricians put up extra railings for side legs.

The set for *A Midsummer Night's Dream* comprised a huge discarded fishing net, obtained from a student's fisherman father. The net filled the entire proscenium. Another student obtained discarded plastic flowers and greenery from her Zellers employer. Lighting helped make the set magical. Characters entered and exited, appearing and disappearing through the foliage.

Two years later, we used the same netting and plastic flowers for *Romeo and Juliet*. Romeo climbed confidently amongst greenery and roses.

For *Man of LaMancha*, we built a full-size dungeon with steps leading up to a clanging gate that fell shut with a heavy roll of chains, as prisoner Miguel de Cervantes tumbled down to the convicts below. Rats scurried as lights came up on the opening scene while inmates scratched for lice or tussled over bits of rag and crusts of bread.

We made all sets and costumes with scrounged materials and rampant imagination. Stagecraft became an exciting part of the school's Theatre Arts program.

To raise money for our productions, we showed Disney movies on Saturday afternoons and split the proceeds with the Physical Education Department. This kept me on the good side of the Phys. Ed. teachers and scored brownie points with school administration. Sports always took pride of place. For one school Annual, I had the Drama Club pose as a soccer team; the picture was included with school sports teams.

Shortly after Alexander was born, I taught Eloise to drive. When she had developed enough confidence to drive on her own, she became a teacher on call for Drummond and Riverside . Not only did "subbing" get her out of the doldrums, she regained self-esteem being back among professionals.

Eloise taught French in junior high schools. But she liked teaching Home Economics best, so she began taking Home Economics courses at UBC during summer sessions. She took a room on campus while I stayed at home with the children.

We became involved with a lively new parish and took on a children's choir and parish youth group, holding meetings and practices in our basement rumpus room.

Six years after moving to B.C., we found a larger house in a much more upscale neighbourhood, a ten minute drive from my school. After clearing a number of overshadowing alder trees, I built a playhouse and sandbox in the back garden. We had enough alder firewood to keep us warm for years to come.

Life was beautiful. My past was packed carefully away; childhood trauma banished to the deepest recesses of my subconscious. I could live on, forever basking in my successes. Teacher – father – husband.

Marriage Encounter

The demands of Church upon our lives grew. Of those, the most significant turned out to be Marriage Encounter. One day in 1974, a couple, whose children were members of our Youth Group, invited us to a Marriage Encounter Weekend. Baby sitting arranged free of charge.

Three team couples and a priest presented the "Weekend". The lead couple was a dynamic husband and wife team from Seattle. I liked the content of their presentations, their deep introspection, and their ability to explore their partner's feelings.

Emotions out in the open, I got swept away with enthusiastic participation. On Sunday night, the team couples invited Eloise and me to join the organization and become a team couple.

At this point, I need to backtrack. A few months before, I had been diagnosed with skin cancer, requiring two weeks of radiation treatment on both shoulders. Since my weight had gone down to about 115 pounds, Eloise was convinced my days were numbered. I was more optimistic; however, we kept the news to ourselves – not to upset my mother.

Marriage Encounter is a crash course in communications for married couples. The weekend, because of its strong Roman Catholic perspective, also renews the faith for many.

When Eloise and I started working as team members, we wrote and rewrote presentations. Many nights I stayed up typing until almost time to leave for school. Before long, we became a lead team couple also in charge of scheduling for B.C and Alberta.

Within two years, we helped present twenty-one "Weekends", frequently rewriting while also workshopping other couple's talks. During our weekends away, Hanna and Alex became part of several Marriage Encounter families.

Beautiful things happened in Marriage Encounter. The most outstanding occurred one Friday afternoon, while we were driving in our Peugeot to Seattle with Father Tom Nicholson. Our engine blew a gasket, and we had to pull over to the side of the highway. "Grab your bags!" said Father Tom. Immediately, he stuck out his thumb, and a car stopped. Our Good Samaritan helped push the Peugeot further onto the side of the interstate, then drove us to his farm. With no more than a few words, he asked for the key to our car and told us to take his vehicle until Sunday night. We arrived in good time to present the Weekend.

On Sunday night, when we returned to the man's farm near Bellingham, the replacement gasket had not yet been found. "Take my car and call me at this number midweek. We'll see what we can do."

A few months later, Eloise and I were invited to a Marriage Encounter Convention in Los Angeles. While there, a Beverly Hills couple invited us to fly down with our children during the 1980 spring break. With Hanna and Alex, we attended every attraction at Disneyland. Then our host drove Eloise and me over a maze of twisting five-lane highways to Hugh Hefner's Playboy Club and other adult attractions. Our host was a professional gambler. Broke on one occasion, he took twenty dollars and left us in his car for less than half an hour, while he turned the twenty into several hundred.

Since my visit in the early fifties, Los Angeles had changed. As the plane began its approach for landing, I saw a straight line of thick, grey fog – a huge blanket of smog.

At lunch we sat among imitation shrubs and flowers on plastic chairs at a plastic table, ate cardboard sandwiches tightly enshrouded in plastic wrap and drank plastic coffee from styrofoam mugs.

Like zombies in oversized sunglasses, celluloid people in celluloid shirts, shoes, and slacks butchered their feet on concrete slabs beneath imitation palm trees. Even our host's teenage daughter wore a plastic see-through dress – the latest adolescent rage in Beverly Hills.

Angeleños wore sunglasses not to avoid the sun's glare but the plague of smog, which made eyes water copiously. Broken hearts and hangovers may also have been reasons for watery eyes of course. But in Los Angeles with dark sunglasses, how was one to know?

At home, though surrounded by a Marriage Encounter community, our own relationship was strained. I desperately attempted to make things right. I redoubled my endeavours to keep the house clean. I increased my efforts in the kitchen and did all the laundry. But Eloise was seldom satisfied. Invariably, she found dust and dirt I'd missed. I shrank sweaters, washed the spring out of elastic waist bands, left streaks on newly washed drinking glasses, and overlooked grease in hidden corners of the kitchen.

I took to buying flowers for no particular reason, but to say, "I love you". Almost daily, I made it a point to tell my wife, "I love you". But she no longer returned my endearments. Instead, she merely said, "I know". This drove me to near-desperate efforts to please, to rekindle the fire of her affections.

Surely, I prayed, since we have helped so many other couples, God will not permit our own marriage to wither and die.

Meanwhile, Eloise had been supply teaching. In September 1984, she was offered a full-time position teaching Foods and French in Riverside .

Time came for a checkup of my skin condition. Doctors were amazed. I'd been too busy to think about being ill. My weight had come back up to about 155 lbs. I felt healthy. Apart from the occasional bit of light surgery – and with my new awareness of the dangers of being out in the sun without full protection – cancer became the furthest thing from my mind.

Finding My Father

In 1982, Father Tom planned to combine a trip to Rome with a visit to his sister in Northern Ireland. As he had been a lawyer before entering the priesthood in Vancouver, he knew how to access documents and investigate legal matters. So, when he asked if he could do anything for us during his trip, Eloise replied, "Father Tom, could you locate Paddie's dad?"

"Of course," he replied. "Jot down his address and phone number for me."

I told him my father had been "killed" in North Africa and that the British Red Cross had been unable to find any trace of him. As far as I was concerned, he was buried somewhere in the deserts of North Africa and long forgotten. I merely wanted to find out.

Six weeks later, Father Tom returned to Vancouver and telephoned from the airport. When I answered, he asked me if I was sitting down.

"Paddie, your father is alive and well and living in a Franciscan friary in London."

I was in shock. How could this be true? Almost in a whisper, I asked Father Tom, "Could you please come over?" Within the hour, our good friend knocked on our door. We had a long, wonderful talk.

In London, Father Tom looked up the name Milne in the telephone directory and found one John Milne, Jr., living in London. He telephoned and left several messages. Then, receiving no reply, he travelled on to Rome. On his way to Ireland, he tried again but still no reply. Finally, with one day left before returning to Canada, he called once more. My cousin John answered. When Father Tom asked him about my father, his response was immediate: "Poor Uncle Freddie. He's a Franciscan Friar in East London."

Father Tom got the number, telephoned the friary, and was told: "Brother Freddie is in bed. Could I take a message?"

Father Tom explained why he was calling and promised to telephone back the following morning before heading to Heathrow Airport.

The next morning he talked to my father. "Paddie, his voice is identical to yours. I thought I was talking to you."

My priest friend had just told me the most amazing news of my life. Tears streamed down my cheeks. My heart beat so fast I thought I'd explode. The many lost years streamed back. Where had he been? What had kept us apart so long? Why had he stayed away?

I wrote my father a lengthy letter. Almost right away, he replied. His handwriting was shaky and hard to decipher.

We made plans to visit the following summer. We would stay at my Uncle John's estate in Essex. Meanwhile, I sent pictures of Eloise and the two children, told him about my years with the Christian Brothers, that Naomi had died of cancer, and about his other grandson, Naomi's child, Freddie. I also sent copies of the poems I'd written while in the Christian Brothers Noviciate.

We were excited about the coming trip. Having rediscovered a piece of myself, and after conferring with Eloise and the kids, I applied to have our names officially changed to Milne.

We met my paternal cousin Janet on Vancouver Island. Her father, my Uncle John, had been a paediatrician in Nanaimo for years. In all the time I served at Naden, I never had the wildest idea that an uncle lived so close to me. In fact, not only did I have a cousin Jan living in Parksville, I had six uncles, one aunt, and many cousins. But the greatest surprise of all was that I had a sister, Anna, only two years older than myself.

Anna is both my sister and my cousin. Her father was my Uncle Alex in New Zealand and Mother's first husband. After her marriage to Alexander and the birth of Anna, Mother had run off to Africa with my father, Freddie, while Anna Louise remained with Granny and Grandpa Milne in a large house in Oxford.

Years later, Mother told my sister Anna how, in her late teens, she got permission to attend art school in London. There she met Anna's father. Nine boys vied for the attention of this lively beauty but Alex caught her eye.

The two were wed at St. Ansgar's Church in Copenhagen in September 1929. Alexander had a withered leg, which young Alicia soon found repulsive. Thus she began to dislike the leg's owner.

Uncles in England told me the rest.

Shortly after Anna was born, in fact, while a German nurse, Nollie Holk, was nursing her, George's younger brother Freddie took a shine to his sister-in-law. He had been newly assigned to the British diplomatic corps. Mother ran off with him to Tanganyika, British South East Africa.

Quite literally, I was born on safari. My birth was registered in the town of Tabora, only shortly before Naomi was due. Consequent to my mother's second pregnancy, Freddie was reassigned back to London. In January 1934, George divorced my mother. As for Anna, my grandparents held on to her. Mother told me she was only permitted to see her daughter on occasion and that she was never allowed to hold her. While visiting in England I learned other boys in the Milne family had also run off with one another's wives. To sum it all up, my grandfather, the Reverend George Milne was the grandson of another Reverend George Livingston Milne, all originally High Anglicans from Glasshouse, just outside Dublin. The family, descended from Puritans, awarded Glasshouse for their service to Cromwell during the suppression of the Irish rebellion in 1649-1650.

Although known by their moral severity, the actual Puritans of history were the radicals and revolutionaries of their era. Under the rule of Oliver Cromwell, they spread hatred and destruction and very little peace, love, wisdom, or humility.

My Uncle Pat told me their father, my grandfather, was severe and that my father was afraid of him. Having fathered seven sons and one daughter, my grandfather was quoted to have declared that God's one mistake was having created sex. Perhaps he had to be severe to control so many boys. Whether or not his severity came from Puritan roots, I wasn't told.

An Old Wrong Righted

Our official change of name came through just before Christmas, 1982; immediately we applied for passports and arranged to leave as soon as school let out at the end of June.

Cousin Cecilia met us at Heathrow Airport and we boarded a train for London. At Paddington Station, we transferred to another train for the final leg of our journey. From the train, I saw the odd pillbox, left over from the war. The sky was low. Suddenly, I experienced terrifying flashbacks of planes diving from clouds. I had to pull myself to the present and hold on to my emotions.

Uncle John met us at the railway station, accompanied by an old man, just over five feet tall, who looked a lot like me, even to the smallest detail. For a year or so previously, I had sported a short beard – not a goatee, just a short beard. This man wore the exact same beard. Uncle John repeated, over and over, "Oh, my God! Oh, my God!" I couldn't even manage that. I hugged my father right there, on the open railway platform. We shared tears with the drizzling rain.

Uncle John's wife had inherited a massive mansion with a costume room in the tower. Here Hanna and Alex spent hours dressing up. The house was filled with ancient paintings, sculptured busts, and suits of armour. We were shown an original charter from King Henry VIII. The grounds consisted of acres of well-kept lawns, fishponds, and great sculptures done by family members.

The atmosphere was formal. We visited my father in the main house and occasionally took tea with everyone. Apart from those visits, Eloise, the children, and I were given a basement suite. We did our own housekeeping and cooking, and shopped at a greengrocer nearby.

Uncle John showed me a photograph of my grandfather. Of all the family members, I was his double, and the double of my great-grandfather, too. I learned about another Alexander, my cousin in Africa. Another cousin had a son named Patrick, the same age as our Alexander. Patrick is an artist in London.

When my sister Anna came for a visit, we planned a trip to stay with her in Oxford. Anna looked like my mother and had identical mannerisms. She favoured the same brand of cigarettes and held them the same way. She even told the same stories and jokes. Eloise remarked that many of my sister's jokes and songs were already familiar to her, having heard them from me over the years.

I rented a car and drove all of us with Freddie to Finchingfield, my childhood home, where we managed to get ourselves invited inside Willets Cottage. Naturally, electricity and indoor plumbing had been installed but the low doorways hadn't changed. I remembered the many times my father had bumped his head. (In my memory he had been very tall.) We climbed up to the tiny room where Naomi and I had danced with the little people.

The farm where we visited the "piggies" was still there, but now the yard was filled with chickens. The old witch's house looked all too ordinary. The church on the hill and the graveyard looked the same. The windmill still stood in the field behind the house. We were told Willets Cottage had been featured in an issue of *This England* magazine. On that visit, I was unable to find Mrs. Turner's greengrocer shop.

I wanted to find the house where we had lived after Dad went off to war. But Dad – everyone but I called him Freddie – was getting tired and did not wish to visit "that evil place". Nor would he show us where the ack-ack gun placement had been. In fact, my father was grumpy all the way back to Uncle John's home and complained loudly about my driving.

We enjoyed a beautiful stay at Aunt Penny and Uncle Pat's home in Cadgwith, Cornwall, high on a hill overlooking the Atlantic. I had suggested renting another car, but Freddie insisted we go by rail.

Aunt Penny produced short films for BBC Television. Uncle Pat worked with ceramics. Hanna and Alex were more interested in Penny's ponies.

For me, one of the greatest thrills of the trip occurred in a Cornish pub in Cadgwith. Fishermen sang in four and five-part harmonies. Many of the songs were identical to those sung in Newfoundland, but with the original Cornish references. Their harmonies wove a multicolour tapestry of sound, sometimes soft and gentle as lamb's wool, at other times like wind in the trees, rising and falling in volume.

We borrowed Uncle Pat's car and drove to Land's End and Saint Ives where we saw more palm trees and warm, sandy beaches. Who'd have thought there'd be palm trees in England?

During our stay at Uncle John's, I asked my father what he thought of the poems I sent him. I was shocked by his answer: "I burned those poems when I was in the Noviciate. I had a terrible Novice Master named Father Francis." About my poems, he had nothing to say. I was referring to the poems I'd written in the Christian Brothers' Noviciate. He was referring to poems he'd written in the Franciscan Noviciate and, under orders of his Novice Master, had destroyed. I'd hidden mine. The parallels were astounding.

When I told my father how I had wanted to commit suicide by falling through the ice, he was quick to reply, "There was never a day I did not pray for you and your sister Naomi." Was that angel on the ice sent in answer to my father's prayers?

On July 15th, the Superior of the Anglican Franciscans in England came to visit. I asked him if it was by intention that he had come on the feast day of St. Bonaventure, the first Brother to join Saint Francis. Of course, my question had to do with my name, Brother Bonaventure. This was another amazing coincidence. I saw all of these events as mystical. My life had been so full of miracles.

The Brother Superior told me how my father returned from the war in North Africa and, after searching everywhere for his wife and children, entered the Franciscan friary and asked to work with the Blacks on the London docks. For many years, he lived as a man without hope. He said our reunion had awakened "dear old Freddie", brought him back to life but I witnessed only an embittered man who showed little warmth about our reunion – the most enormous hurt and disappointment of my life.

We left Freddie with Uncle John and went off to visit Anna in Oxford, where we stayed with Aunt Katie at King's Mill, her home. It was an ancient mill on the River Cherwell, a tributary of the Thames. King's Mill was listed in the "Doomsday Book" (*a census of the whole of England commissioned in December 1085 by William the Conqueror*). For the last three or four hundred years, King's Mill has been owned by Magdalen College, one of the more famous colleges of Oxford University.

When we were there, the building comprised a living room with a low-beamed ceiling, a huge open fireplace, a tiny passageway of a dining-room, and a jerrybuilt kitchen and bathroom – added on when Katie and Ralph moved in. Because of the war, they had to use all sorts of second hand building materials - plumbing, bricks, flooring, wooden window-frames and doors – none matching, and all hastily cobbled together. Up a narrow, steep wooden flight of stairs was the big bedroom overlooking the River Cherwell and the millrace. Up one more floor were two tiny attic bedrooms. That was all – apart from numerous outhouses and sheds, including an old generator they'd used before being connected to municipal electricity.

The house was down a muddy lane, far from neighbours, and at one of the entrances to the University Parks. The murmur of the mill race, flowing incessantly over the sluice-gates, rose to a roar in winter when the rains had swollen the stream; it offered a constant soothing, relaxing and soporific background to everything that happened at King's Mill.

We went punting on the Cherwell and ate at The Trout Inn up the River Thames just outside Oxford. Close to The Trout stands a ruined convent called Godstow Nunnery – the source of many romantic historical legends. In the evenings, we all visited with Aunt Katie, who told humorous stories and jokes and related anecdotes about the Milne family.

On one of our day excursions, we went to Stratford-on-Avon, where we visited Anne Hathaway's Cottage and the schoolroom where Shakespeare studied. Unfortunately, we couldn't attend a play; bookings had to be made too far in advance. But I did enjoy walking through the many buildings and walkways where the Bard had spent his youth.

On still another visit, we went to my grandfather's manse, the house in Oxford where the Milne family had been raised. Anna showed us an idyllic, tiny cottage, just down the lane from the Milne home where her father and our mother had lived the two brief years of their marriage. We looked at my grandparents' gravesites in an overgrown churchyard and wandered through churches in the Cotswalds where my grandfather had been pastor. Every day brought new surprises.

All too soon, the time came to return to Canada. I could have spent weeks, even months more, rediscovering my childhood.

In the end, I wrote a long letter to Mother telling her I loved her and that I accepted the life she had led. I even asked her to forgive and love me as her son. Years later, I learned from Louise and Jackie how Papa François was angry that I had changed my name. I hadn't explained to him, or to Mother, why this was so important to me. All I knew was that I now understood who I was.

In-laws and Outlaws

Shortly after our return from England in 1982, Eloise's father retired. Both parents came to join us on the west coast. They bought a house in North Drummond and added a basement suite complete with kitchen so that Kristina, who had Multiple Sclerosis, could live with them yet be independent.

Almost every Sunday, we either had dinner with them at our home or theirs. This was not always a pleasant experience for me as I now found myself having to be very careful in what I said, even to my children. When Eloise and I disagreed, she invariably had her mother and dad on her side, preventing us from working things out on our own.

Kristina's M.S. worsened until she was admitted to extended care at Riverside Memorial Hospital. Her parents sold their house and moved closer to the hospital but within a few months, Kristina was transferred to a Salvation Army group home closer to Vancouver. We visited often, usually picking up Eloise's parents on the way. I brought my guitar and entertained patients and staff both. This made me feel special and that I was making amends to my sister-in-law for having sworn at her in Montreal so many years before.

We also picked up Kristina and drove her either to our home or to her parents' home. Having been a hospital orderly, I was able to lift a paraplegic to and from the car. I emptied her colostomy bags, changed her, and cleaned her up when accidents occurred. "Close your eyes, Kristina, we're going to change you". When her parents objected to my performing this service, I quietly suggested they do it, but they were unable for a variety of reasons.

Farewell to Mother – Alzheimer's Hospice

For two years following our trip to England, I received no news from any member of the family in Montreal. Phone calls and letters went unanswered. When I finally reached my half-sister, Louise, she told me Mother had become impossible to manage at home and was in an Alzheimer's hospice in the country. As soon as school was out, I flew to Montreal.

I barely recognized Mother. She sat upright in her wheelchair, a tiny bird with feathers plucked.

While she folded and refolded an imaginary serviette on her lap, Mother's silver hair seemed to float, like little downy feathers. "Send those lawyers home. No more questions. No more questions." Her eyes lit up. "Thank God you're here."

"Hello, Mom."

"Did you come to feed my birds?"

"We came to see you."

"Who are you?"

"Paddie… your son." The words choked in my throat.

"Hello, Mom."

"Did you come to feed my birds?"

"We came to see you."

"Who are you?"

"Paddie… your son." The words choked in my throat.

She puckered her lips and made bird-calling sounds.

"Would you like to go for a walk? I'll take you."

Mother narrowed her eyes.

Other patients sat, babbling. Some drooled, open mouthed. One woman beckoned to me. "Allo. Allo. Allo." She was tiny, sweet, and ancient. She brushed imaginary cobwebs from her face. "*Quel heure est il?*" (What time is it?)

I turned back to Mother. "You know me, Mom. I'm your son."

She sounded annoyed. "Of course I know who you are. I'm not … I'm not"… She lost her train of thought and gazed off into space.

"I know, Mom. I know. Let's go for a walk."

I pushed her out into the courtyard. Mother watched a robin on the path. For years she'd kept a budgie and fed the wild birds that came to her garden feeders. "Allo bébé. Pretty bird."

I looked at my mother's knees. Tucked over sideways beneath the blanket, they looked all bone and wrinkled flesh. The eggshell skin on Mother's bird-boned wrist glistened with large, blue veins. Her body's hunger signals no longer connecting with her brain, she was slowly starving herself to death.

For most of my life, I had been unable to face Mother as an equal member of the human race. Rather, I had carved her in mythic proportions, installed her on a pedestal, and propitiated the goddess in all her volatile moods - even the unloving and the wrathful.

Now, here she was, meek and unthreatening, a frail human being. The mother I had known was gone. No more did I have to sing for her.

I should have felt emancipated. I felt only great sadness and terrible loss.

A few weeks later, I flew to Montreal and then boarded the train to Saint Anne de Bellevue to attend Mother's funeral. She lay in a coffin at the funeral home. I gazed at the wrinkles at the sides of her eyes and remembered the love I'd sought and seldom found. Then I closed my eyes and smelled her perfume and lipstick, from the days when I'd loved her in Finchingfield. I tasted her mashed potatoes and mushroom gravy and heard her singing Danish nursery songs.

At the church, I asked permission to sing from the choir loft. No one saw the soloist who sang Cesar Franck's *Panis Angelicus* – my final, emotional goodbye to Mother.

ALZHEIMER REFLECTIONS

Mother painted nymphs in the woods

free as Chagall's women floating over houses,

her own spirit freed by dementia

danced in childhood innocence

nurses confiscated paint and brushes

to prevent splattered bedding.

she soiled sheets anyway,

laughed at the irony.

pale as butter, soft as peaches

a candle waiting for a match

memories wash up through fungicidal fog

like seepage on a stagnant beach

road map legs

hands hung limp as rope ends

she traced imaginary journeys

through varicose highways on her hands

she seemed embarrassed

merchandize fondled in a lingerie shop

her look softened – a lamp turned down

a carnival of bedclothes and jerseys

the week dragged on,

feet lugging the hours like convict chains

she chased her breath inside an oxygen mask

I run my memory along the razor's edge of those last days

a drenching of regret

Goodbye, Goodbye

The next summer we vowed to fly to England again to visit my dad. We bought plane tickets for the two of us as well as a Brit-Rail Pass. Eloise's parents agreed to look after Hanna and Alex. We planned to leave for one month, as soon as school let out, and combine a visit with my dad with an overdue holiday on our own. But after hearing that my stepfather, Papa François, was in hospital, we decided we should stop over in Montreal on our way. I wanted to make the peace with him that I had failed to make with my mother.

Meantime, my own father died two weeks prior to our scheduled departure. His body was cremated. After I called them, the Brothers agreed to postpone the burial until we could be there.

When we arrived in Montreal, it was obvious that Papa would not last long. He had difficulty breathing. I talked the matter over with my sister, Louise, and her husband Vic, and asked if we should stay.

Our visit clearly upset Papa François. He waved me off. "Fuck off! You're not wanted here." I moved away, embarrassed and angry but kept my feelings to myself. I hoped no one had overheard and never repeated what my stepfather had said to me.

Vic promised to contact us should Papa's health situation worsen.

Arriving in England, we traveled to the Brothers' house in East London but my father's remains were at the Mother House in Dorset. We were invited to stay at the retreat centre and catch a train to Dorset next day. The following morning after prayer service, I spoke with several Brothers who had known my Dad well. They all said how he had changed since we found him. He had become happier and more gentle in his temperament.

Late the following night, Vic phoned the Dorset Mother House. Papa Bertrand had passed away. Vic suggested we remain in England and continue with our plans. However, Eloise insisted we return to Montreal right after my father's burial.

Following a brief prayer service for my father, we tagged behind the procession of monks as they carried the small casket down a gravel path to the cemetery. I heard the birds sing in the trees. I saw the Brothers in their bare feet and had an overwhelming feeling of déjà-vu. Bare feet on a gravel pathway had been a form of bitter penance. I did not remove my shoes. Not wishing to interfere in the humble service, I did not sing for my father. Later, I regretted my omission.

The return flight to Canada was silent. My emotional cup was brimming and I didn't know how I'd react to my stepfather's funeral. His recent rejection had stung me deeply. I pulled myself together to support Louise, Jackie, and my aunts – especially my aunts. In the same church where we'd had Mother's funeral, I again sang from the choir loft. This time Mozart's *Ave Verum*. As before, no one knew I was the soloist.

Then I eulogized Papa François in French and English. I said he always had wanted a son and that I had tried my best to fulfill that role. Speaking of his devotion and good example, I asserted that my life had been blessed by having known him. I couched everything I said in diplomatic phrases, which, I convinced myself, were as truthful as I could make them.

How did I honestly feel about my stepfather? His parting words to me, as we left to bury my own father said it all. He rejected me. And probably, in his mind, I had rejected him by reclaiming my own father's name. Never, in the years I'd known him, had he shown me any love. So how could I feel love for him? Perhaps he sensed the burden of guilt I had always carried. And most likely he was not able to identify what it was he saw in me. Thus, I believe, my childhood shame poisoned our relationship. Now I felt guilty for my lack of love.

As for my own father, at first I regretted the years I had been deprived of him. Then, when I met him once again, a bitter old man, I was disappointed and angry. I felt as though I had reached out to him in love, and he had barely recognized me, and appeared uncomfortable in my presence. Perhaps the children and I reminded him too much of what he had lost. As for my own reaction to him, maybe I was still blaming him for having run off to war and having left me to the mercy of all the monsters I would later meet.

In Dorset, I buried the "Daddy" I knew at Willet's Cottage. With him, I also buried the only happy part of my childhood. At my father's burial service, though I felt sad and cheated, I felt locked-up and kept silent.

I had yet to experience two other emotions about my dad: devastation and emptiness. These didn't rise to the surface until much, much later - when I was able to deal with them better.

Spanking

I was not very good at disciplining my children. My own father had never spanked me. He left that task to my mother. Since she applied a hairbrush to my bare behind, her spankings were painful. As time went on, I learned to cry and sob until I received hugs, even if the wait took forever. Quite simply, the cuddling made the paddling worthwhile; at last I received the love and attention I craved. Pain and love went hand in hand for me; I didn't know one without the other.

When my sister also got spanked, that proved much worse for me. I'd have to wait outside the bedroom and hear her screaming as the sounds of the slaps of the hairbrush on her bare behind turned my legs to jelly. Then it would be my turn. The waiting was a greater torture than the paddling. Mother would sit on the edge of the bed, hairbrush in hand, and make me take my pants down and I'd feel as though I'd wet myself as I did so. Sometimes she'd spank, then hold me across her knee for a few moments and remind me why I was being punished. Then she'd spank some more. I don't think I heard her explanations because I was too unhappy holding on for the next onslaught.

I never associated caning from my teachers with love. The cane was always cruel. The cane blistered. Straps and rulers used by teachers all through my primary and elementary school years hurt the hands so much they made writing difficult. Yet often we were too proud to cry. Sometimes, we didn't dare cry. Sometimes we couldn't help ourselves.

The threat of the pointer at the blackboard inhibited my thinking. Oftentimes, I remember my mind going numb when a pointer slapped at the board in front of me.

Hairbrush, paddle, hand. These stung but somehow said to me: "I care!" I don't believe that anymore, of course. These weapons terrorized my childhood. When we grew older, Mother switched her focus from our bums to our faces - and we got slapped hard. To that act, no love was attached, only frustration. When I ducked her smacks, she got angrier. When I think back to those days, it seems Naomi and I lived in constant terror.

So here I was, forty years later, with my own children. Since my father never spanked me, I loved and respected him. I obeyed him because I loved him. It was that simple. Or was it?

As I loved my children, I did not want to behave like my mother. Often, in frustration, Eloise shouted, "When will you spank that child? Be a father."

I could hug my children. I could change their diapers. I could bathe them. I could love them in countless other ways. But not by spanking them. There was no love in spanking. Spanking was from a very distant and unhappy past.

"You have no backbone. Are you afraid to be a real father?"

Though these words hurt, they didn't change me.... However, under constant pressure I did give in and spanked my children. Did I do it in frustration and anger? Yes, I did get very angry at my wife. And yes I did get very angry with her parents for interfering. And yes, I did get upset at the increased demand for me to do something I did not want to do. Inevitably, I didn't agree with the reasons given and judged them petty. Frustration grew. When in anger, I caved in and spanked my children I felt terrible shame for weeks afterwards. Of course, I sometimes felt anger towards my kids when they misbehaved or were disrespectful, but I hated hitting them.

Alex was the one, according to Eloise, whom I consistently failed to discipline. When Alex rebelled, I rebelled at Eloise's pressuring. "You are too old to be a father. The damage you do in spoiling your son will never be undone."

Today, I'd never spank a child. The thought makes my stomach turn. I feel a shuddering in my back and a weakness in my legs for the pain and fear I caused them. And yes, I have apologized to both in later years.

Fresh Air and Country Living

In the fall of 1982, I registered for a Master's program in Theatre at Western Washington University. We sold the old Peugeot and bought a new Sprint Chevrolet and a Honda Passport scooter which I drove in all weather. At school I parked in the theatre storage room. On Saturdays and some evenings I drove from Sunshine Hills to the University campus in Bellingham, about seventy kilometres. The trip took almost two hours each way allowing for delays at the border. The following summer I attended seminars, took part in productions, and drove home late at night.

In 1983, we saw a beautiful two-and-a-half acre hobby farm with Tudor style house on a hill in South Langley. Sunshine Hills, where we had been living, was becoming increasingly rough, with young bullies ruling the streets and parks. I didn't want Hanna and Alex subjected to bullying. Country living would be good for the children. We sold our house and moved to the country.

Though we already had a Siamese cat, I also wanted a dog to help look after the property. We selected a Doberman pup and named her Esther after the heroine in the Old Testament who guarded her people. Ester was a gentle dog, but Eloise didn't want her in the house, so I built a doghouse on the side of the tool shed close to the house. In winter, I gave Esther plenty of straw and old blankets. She was a good guard dog and affectionate and accompanied me through all my farm chores.

The property was covered in weeds, thistles, and brambles. So I hired a farmer to plow the front field down to the bottom of the hill. Then I got him to bring in a backhoe and dig out a pond, with an island for ducks in the middle. For several weeks, Hanna, Alex, and I raked from top to bottom, carrying rocks and debris to the sides in a wheelbarrow. We planted a mixture of grass and clover and soon had the greenest acreage for miles around.

I paid a young friend to help fence the entire two-and-a-half acres. The two of us pounded in every post with a two-by-four and sledgehammer then stretched and stapled a four-foot sheep fence, placing rocks along the bottom to keep coyotes out. We dug a ditch for electric cable and ran electricity down to the barn where we raised a yard light. At the front entrance, I built stone light posts and installed a set of iron gates.

Finally, I winterized the barn with insulation and plywood and picked up several bales of hay. With everything ready, I bought three doe lambs from my farmer friend, a dozen Golden Comet chicks, and six ducklings from Buckerfields. I was a hobby farmer in my glory.

Soon we had fresh brown eggs to eat and sell to fellow teachers at school. One year I raised plump meat chickens, the best we'd ever eaten. Our deep freeze was full. I was less successful with turkey chicks. They grew to be stupid, messy, and hard to contain. However, when finally butchered, they were fat and delicious and well worth the effort.

During an all-night downpour, one of our favourite sheep slipped into the pond and drowned. Alex and I had to pull her out and bury her. I borrowed a ram from a friend. Almost five months later, we had four new lambs.

In winter, Alex and I cleared the driveway with a plow loaded on the front end of our tractor lawn mower. I always had an eager driver in Alex, both for snow clearance in winter and grass cutting in summer.

One summer my sisters Louise and Jackie, their husbands and all the nieces and nephews came to visit. They found us living in Paradise. We threw weenie roasts on our hill. My Brother-in-law, Vic, was so enthusiastic I think he would have sold his airline and moved to the West Coast. The following Thanksgiving, I sent him a homegrown turkey.

Meanwhile, I continued my courses and wrote a double thesis on Creative Dramatics as well as a musical adaptation of *Treasure Island*, which I directed as "Involvement Theatre". Prior to the production, my Stagecraft students and I built a huge, workable ship's deck with wheel and sails.

On production nights, as youngsters arrived, they were permitted to sign on to the ship's crew. Others were secretly recruited as pirates by Long John Silver and given "the mark" secretly stamped on the palm of the hand to be shown when the signal was given. The entire audience got involved with singing, making thunderous ocean waves and scary jungle noises, and shouting warnings.

With children in the play, we never could be sure which side would win. At the end, whatever the outcome, we provided buried treasure for one group and emergency supplies for the other – small bags of candy for all.

Finally, after thirty-six years, the boy (me) who had been pulled from high school in the middle of grade nine graduated. A little voice called out: "Way to go, grandpa!" It was my Alex with my sense of humour. I was fifty-two – old enough to be a grandpa!

Thorns Among the Roses

No matter how involved I got with schoolwork and university studies, I made sure to take Hanna and Alex to school concerts, music and ballet lessons, and birthday parties. Both loved their school and made many friends. I lined up before dawn to register first Hanna, then Alex in the Langley French Immersion School. With limited spaces, children were accepted on a first come basis. For the second year, some parents even camped overnight. In no time, my kids became fluently bilingual.

As Langley offered string classes, we bought a violin for Hanna and a cello for Alex. Eventually, however, with government cutbacks to education, their instruction became available only through private lessons.

We enjoyed our local church and got involved with the parish youth. I directed a youth group production of *Godspell,* enlarging the cast to accommodate all wishing to participate. The rehearsal process brought me closer to those young people than any other activity I had ever done in the Church. We hosted bonfires on our hill and toboggan parties. Eloise and I were still involved with Marriage Encounter, taking part in occasional "Weekends" and team meetings, but without the extra hours of organizing.

Belonging to such a large parish family was one of the greatest benefits of living in Langley. We had many friends.

At school, not everything was rosy. For several weeks, the auditorium was broken into; expensive equipment was stolen or damaged. Prophylactics and sex toys were left on the stage for my students to find. Someone was playing a terrible practical joke. The administration accused me of inadequate supervision. When I suggested people were gaining access from the roof, the vice-principal said that was impossible.

I discovered several grade twelve students painting a grad slogan on the roof that was "impossible to reach". Investigation by a school board maintenance man revealed workmen had left a roof hatch unlocked. The hatch got locked and incidents ceased.

Some weekends, the principal asked me to supervise rallies and other gatherings in the auditorium. Usually I agreed to do this. And usually I experienced no problems.

There was one occasion though, when militant and moderate Sikhs held a rally in the auditorium to resolve their differences over whether or not chairs should be used in their temple. Some men began a punch-out. Others jumped onto the stage to attack the speakers. I sent my student assistant to a payphone with a quarter to call the police. Fearing accusations of racism, the police decided their involvement could only make matters worse. Not only did they decline to show up, they sent my assistant home. I was on my own not knowing when or if the police would arrive.

When several men struggled to get at the microphones on the stage, I cut the sound. One of the organizers came to the sound booth. I told him the problem had to do with the main power box and that I would fix it right away. Then I locked the booth door, walked down to the power room, locked the door behind me and flipped the main breaker. I stood in the dark room, knees shaking, until everything fell silent. After what felt like hours of waiting, I opened the power room door and peered out. All was quiet. Everyone had left.

When I described the incident to the school administrators the next day, they dismissed my concerns. Later the same day, a radio report stated: following arguments at a meeting the previous night, a man had been killed with an axe in a nearby restaurant.

I asked for a telephone to be installed in the auditorium. Request denied.

Essays and Dead Poets

In September 1989, cutbacks threatened the arts in education. Ostensibly to protect me from losing my job if Drama and Music were cut, my Chorus class, with more than fifty students, was awarded to a young lady recently transferred to our school. I was switched to full-time English and Communications (remedial English).

The new drama teacher had experience acting in professional theatre and television productions and many of the students knew him from junior high school. When they stopped to speak with him in the hallways, he called them all by their first names. I resented the man all the more since he failed to acknowledge me in any way. Worse, contrary to my own experience, the new man never lacked support from the school administration. Within weeks, he had a telephone in his Theatre office.

To add insult to injury, all the photographs and posters of my past productions disappeared from their display cases, seemingly overnight, to be replaced by materials from those junior high school productions that many of the new grade eleven students "could identify with".

No longer was I recognized for my successes. Except when I absolutely had to be there, I avoided the school auditorium. It was no comfort to me to hear that the same was happening to the Theatre Arts teachers in the other Senior Secondary schools in our district. A teacher I admired in particular also ended up teaching full-time English. I sank into a deep depression. My classroom became my hermit's cell.

Communications 11 and 12 were designed for students who had difficulty with the regular curriculum, providing them with such skills as writing resumes and letters of application. Those students were often anything but "students" and tended to be restless. It's hard to share one's enthusiasm for poetry and good writing with youngsters who hate school and find any topic boring before it has begun, especially after the enthusiasm of my Theatre students. Still, I vowed to accept the challenge and make the best of the situation.

In my regular English classes, I shared my love of Literature bringing Shakespeare to life. Sometimes, we shouted out scenes: "Double, double, toil and trouble / Fire burn and cauldron bubble." Students prepared at home to present individual ingredients for the potion. "Fillet of a fenny snake / in the cauldron boil and bake." "Eye of newt and toe of frog." with extra marks for enthusiastic delivery.

On occasion, our noisy sessions elicited the attention of roving administrators, and I was instructed to quieten down and get back to work. "You're supposed to be teaching English, not Drama."

I have always enjoyed poetry and reading dramatic poems aloud. I closed the blinds, lit candles and played a recording of Bach's *Toccata and Fugue in D Minor* as I read Edgar Allan Poe's *The Raven*. I preceded such poems with vocabulary exercises so that students knew the meanings or backgrounds of such words as "Lenore", "nepenthe", "quaff", etc. I shared modern poems that speak of the environment, such as *And the Seagulls Were Dying* by Gary Dunford, or poems by Lawrence Ferlinghetti, such as *The World Is a Beautiful Place*. I also motivated students to write poetry with mixed results.

Students frequently worked in groups with projects accomplished through teamwork. We often exchanged and corrected tests and quizzes immediately upon completion so that correct answers were reinforced. In most cases, an atmosphere of trust prevailed, even though some cheating did occur. But then, who was the cheater fooling? Still, my methods were criticized. I lacked discipline in my classes.

One day, several of my students urged me to see *The Dead Poet's Society*, starring Robin Williams. They said I would see myself. When I did, I felt vindicated.

When I hear of continued strife between teachers and government and about cutbacks that end up enlarging class sizes and increasing work loads, I remember the late nights and long weekends spent on school work, while teaching a full semester of English. With four classes, averaging thirty students in each, and one essay per week, requiring at least seven to ten minutes of marking apiece, a teacher would have to spend a minimum of sixteen hours correcting essays alone. Then there are tests to correct, lessons to prepare, reports to fill out, students to give extra help to, extra supervisions to do, and school clubs to supervise.

Good teachers, of course, are accustomed to burning the midnight oil. One either must love teaching or go crazy. Or both.

Whenever I needed to let off steam and relax, I worked in my garden. I pulled weeds and tossed rocks against the fence. My love of plants extended to the classroom; most times the window ledge sported a pot of mums or aloe vera.

One year, right after the Christmas break, boys in my Communications 12 class presented me with a leafy plant. My plant grew bushy and tall until it disappeared. One of the quiet girls in the class told me I had nursed a marijuana plant while students ran a betting pool as to when I, or the school administration, would discover the joke. What a contradiction! For quite some time, I had tried, unsuccessfully, to convince the school's administrators that several students came to class stoned and smelling of pot. Yet I couldn't identify a marijuana plant when I saw one!

Away From the Farm

During the summer of 1986, Hanna, Alex, and I spent many days at Expo in Vancouver. Eloise had been struck with a flu bug that later turned out to be full-blown pneumonia. She spent most of her time in bed and sent me off with Hanna and Alex, thus assuring her peace and quiet to rest. Friends visited regularly, always within reach, should she need them.

Eloise's parents, however, were less supportive. Her mother found the farm "dirty". A twenty-minute drive from their Riverside home was too far. They had come to the West Coast to be close to their daughter and grandchildren, yet we had moved "into the wilderness". Eloise, they said, should be more readily available to her sister and parents who needed her.

Hanna, Chris, and I were happy in Langley and didn't want to move. But with constant pressure, I finally capitulated. The summer of 1988, we put the house up for sale. It was soon gone, at considerable financial loss. While deciding where we would live next, we rented a house in the city – White Rock. On our first Sunday at church there, Alex pointed out how old everyone was. The pastor rambled about golf and terrible teens. There were very few young people at church.

We took Esther for walks on a lead, and she tripped Eloise. Too big for the city, the dog had to go. We gave her to a lonely old man in the country. A few weeks later, the cat was gone as well. I felt cheated, overruled by Eloise and especially by her parents.

In an attempt to make my wife happy, I suggested we have a new house built to her specifications. We chose a builder and bought a lot in one of the new subdivisions near White Rock. Then we drew up a plan and presented it to the builder. Architect and builder helped us choose a plan similar to our specifications, although much larger. Since we couldn't afford landscaping, I took my wheelbarrow, spade, and rake to the mounds of earth and created a lawn, dug flowerbeds, and built rockeries. The house looked beautiful. But we had bitten off far more than we could chew.

I suggested we sell the house, without an agent, to recoup our losses. Then I made up sales contracts on the computer and placed a "For Sale" sign on the front lawn. I told Eloise that St. Joseph, my patron saint, would help sell the house and began a novena – nine days of special prayers. It would be a tough job; we were asking top dollar. Eloise was not willing to budge one penny.

On Sunday, the ninth day of my novena, I attended Mass with Hanna and Alex. Eloise didn't feel well and stayed home. After Mass, I lit a candle at St. Joseph's statue and said a silent prayer. St. Joseph gave up his home to move with Mary and the infant Jesus to Egypt. While I was in church, Eloise received a call from people who had driven by and wanted to view the house. She told them we wouldn't be ready for viewers until later in the afternoon.

Shortly after I got home, another couple phoned to say they liked the house from the outside, and asked to visit right away. I suggested Eloise take Hanna and Alex out and offered to show the house myself. Instead, Eloise stayed and put cinnamon buns in the oven. She was happy that we might sell the house after all!

The couple walked through and left without a word. I waited in agony; I couldn't sit down. About an hour later, they phoned to say they wanted to make an offer. A few minutes later, the couple that had telephoned earlier, came through the house. After spending time alone in the back garden, they said they wanted to make an offer. Now we had two couples interested! Both had sold homes in Vancouver and wanted to move to the suburbs. As each couple presented an offer, I told them about the other party. Eventually, the people who telephoned while I attended church offered full asking price.

Many people don't believe in miracles or help from patron saints, but I thank St. Joseph. He always helps when asked.

Not far from where we had been living, we found a beautiful English-style house on a quiet street. I loved the house right away. Eloise wasn't so sure. Finally, days later, she agreed. Again, I created a garden, built a back deck, and surrounded it with roses. Inside, I sanded, painted, hung wallpaper and put up moulding – ceiling and wainscot. After several frustrating weeks with changes of colours and even wallpaper, my wife was happy. The house looked beautiful. When Eloise invited her parents to come and see, they approved. All was well again.

For a little while.

Travels With a Trailer

Since we had recouped our real estate losses, Eloise told me I should trade in my scooter in for a new car. We bought an Oldsmobile Cutlass Ciera and a camper trailer. I felt compensated for the loss of our Langley farm and dared to hope we would draw closer once more. Eloise told me she was happy to be living in a more civilized world, away from animals, farmers, and loneliness. I accepted that. At last, I thought, we were back to smooth sailing.

With beautiful summer weather, we all went camping at Silver Lake in Manning Park. Hanna met a boy from Ireland who played guitar. They went canoeing together. We could hear our daughter's laughter from far across the lake.

The following summer, we drove through the mountains to Saskatchewan and visited Eloise's cousins. We saw old abandoned homesteads and walked the farm where Eloise's dad had grown up. In Regina, we walked around Eloise's high school and drove up and down streets where her girlhood friends had lived. This was her summer.

On the way back through the Rockies, we stopped in Nelson, and drove to the house where my wife had spent the happiest part of her childhood. We visited her old school and the cathedral where she had made her First Holy Communion and talked to the monsignor who had been her pastor.

The summer after that, we drove through the Midwestern United States to Salt Lake City. We visited the Mormon Temple and heard part of a choir practice. Then we continued southeast through New Mexico, Texas, and Louisiana, to New Orleans, where we parked the trailer and stayed at a small hotel. Oysters in the half shell in New Orleans taste unlike anything one could eat anywhere else. We took a short boat trip on the Mississippi and toured some of the sites I remembered from my navy visit.

In the evening, we strolled through the narrow streets of the French Quarter absorbing the music. When naked girls swung out from bars on trapezes, Eloise was scandalized. We went to bed early to a jazz trombone lullaby.

Next morning, we returned to our car and trailer and headed away from that sinful, but exciting city. We travelled along the Gulf of Mexico but skipped Florida. Eloise was terrified of snakes. We drove directly north from Mobile, Alabama, up the Atlantic seaboard. How much the South had changed since my previous visit. Blacks had a new dignity, and people behaved politely and very hospitably. Still, I felt an old terror but said nothing to Eloise about it. I had never told her about my misadventure in Mississippi.

When we parked for the night Eloise had to visit the facilities and asked Alex to go with her while I set up the trailer. When she walked out of the washroom, Alex pointed out a warning sign about snakes being drawn to the washroom areas in dry weather. Eloise insisted we raise the camper and block every possible entry area. In our hothouse quarters, I tossed and turned all night.

Farther up the coast, a terrible storm struck. About midnight, Alex and I walked outside, hauled in towels and swim gear, and tied our trailer to surrounding trees.

A blinding shaft of pure white light zigzagged across the bay and backlit the boats anchored in the harbour. The powerful clap of thunder heralded a downpour. Wind howled; trees swayed.

Throughout the night, we tossed and turned, slapped at mosquitoes, and said very little. In the din, conversation was impossible. The next morning, damp and groggy, we folded the camper and drove almost non-stop to Washington D.C.

Two days sightseeing in the Capital City impressed and saddened me. At the long black Vietnam Veterans' Memorial and the Kennedy Memorial Flame many paid tribute with flowers and mementos. Some, full of emotion, traced names on the stone with their fingers. Many visitors were veterans with missing limbs.

We walked through endless cemeteries and visited the Lincoln, Washington, and Jefferson Memorials. Then we browsed the Smithsonian. I could have spent several days in Washington. How wonderful it would be to spend a lot of time in one place and just explore. We were running – hurry, hurry, hurry. This time, it wasn't I who was in a hurry.

The highway in New Jersey was rough and the sun blazed down. We blew a tire on the trailer and replaced it with the spare. The rim was damaged, but we were unable to replace it. Then, while bypassing New York City, we blew the spare. All we could do was park at the side of the highway. A couple of Spanish-speaking men stopped and offered to take us to a repair shop. A police cruiser pulled over, and the Spanish men took off. The two officers advised us to trust nobody. They called a tow truck for our trailer. We ended up in a repair shop where the mechanic said he would have to send to Quebec for a new rim. As that would take a couple of days, we stayed at a hotel, paying one night at a time – in advance.

Two days later, we received a phone call that our trailer was ready. The bill for repair: $500 U.S., included storage fees. When I protested, a big man walked out with a crowbar in his hand. I had no choice but to pay in full – Visa happily accepted. Eloise wanted me to be more of a man and stand up for my rights.

We spent several days with Eloise's Brother and his wife in Pointe Claire just outside Montreal. Next, we drove to Toronto to visit my sister Louise's family. Eloise told my sister I should at least have one of my mother's paintings. I was uncomfortable discussing Mom's paintings or her will. Still, Louise gave me several pieces of Mother's pottery including a couple of ceramic lamps Mother had made.

After Toronto we were anxious to get home. From Thunder Bay, we crossed to the States, where gas was less expensive and the roads in better condition than the Trans-Canada Highway. Then, from Grand Forks, Minnesota, we detoured north to visit my sister, Jackie, and her family in Winnipeg.

Jackie offered me a ceramic tile collage of St. Francis – made by Mother. Both she and I believed Mother had made it as a way to remember my father. Since Jackie had several of Mom's paintings, Eloise asked if we could have one of them. Once more, I preferred to accept what I was given without discussion. We left with the Saint Francis.

After Winnipeg, we returned to the States and drove, without further sightseeing, through North Dakota and Montana, seeing the Badlands from a distance. The holiday was over. Six weeks of cramped trailer living had frayed our nerves.

The following spring, we sold the camper.

Twelve

Broken Promises — Shattered Dreams

Running, Still Running

The years in South Riverside flow together in a mad jumble of events and activities. Eloise returned to U.B.C., this time for a Master's degree in Counselling Psychology. Again she spent her summers living on campus while I remained at home with the children. Sometimes, I went to her residence to type her papers.

Hanna and I took part in a Christmas pantomime. Since I needed to drive my daughter to rehearsals and pick her up, I decided to get involved playing the Wicked Wizard.

Eloise and I ran the parish youth group, but the pastor showed only minimal support. We had to conduct our meetings in the church basement while smoky meetings of Alcoholics Anonymous were held in an adjoining room.

Because we had to keep the noise level down, there could be no games. Too often frustrated, we finally gave up.

We were also involved with church music. Eloise played the piano and I directed choir with practices held in our home. More and more often, the Sunday music at the little church in Crescent Beach was just myself with guitar and Hanna, Alex, and three or four other voices. In those days, younger families attended Mass there while older parishioners attended the main church in White Rock.

The day in July 1987 when Eloise's sister Kristina died, we had all been to see her in the White Rock Hospital. After supper, Eloise returned alone and witnessed her sister's last moments. Death terrified her and with grieving, she fell into a bad depression.

I plunged deeper into schoolwork. Eloise gave me a reconditioned computer for Christmas and I became enthusiastic about recording class marks and projects. I also volunteered to make English Departmental Exams computer friendly for easy marking by assembling dozens of quizzes with multiple answer keys and devising crossword quizzes based on the English Literature program.

I began keeping track of household accounts, learning early on to back up files on floppy disks. By getting lost for hours on my new toy, I escaped much of the increasing tension at home.

In an effort to get my English students more interested in poetry, I read poetry aloud then asked them to find their own poems to share with the class. One student chose to read *St. Paul's First Letter to the Corinthians, Chapter 13*, "Though I speak with the tongues of angels and of men..." Lickety-split, a parent complained to the principal that I had allowed Bible reading in class. I argued that *The Bible* is an essential element of English Literature but he told me *The Bible* is forbidden by the School Act.

Another boy in the same class chose to write a book report on *The Satanic Bible*, by Anton Szandor LaVey. I said, "No!" If *The Bible* is not permitted, neither is *The Satanic Bible*. This time, the principal told me I was not permitting freedom of choice. I refused to mark the paper so the principal marked it and awarded an "A+".

In the staffroom, I avoided any discussion of religion, whether negative or positive. Unable to ward off unwarranted criticism, I felt the sting of anti-Catholic barbs, especially from a couple calling themselves "recovering Catholics". One teacher told Virgin Mary jokes. I pretended not to hear or quietly left the room. Media had begun to cover the news of sexual abuse by religious Brothers at the Mount Cashel orphanage in Newfoundland. I had made no secret of the fact that I had been a Christian Brother. Suddenly, of all those dedicated and caring men, every one was branded a pedophile.

The Brothers at Mount Cashel had been members of the Irish Christian Brothers. My order had been the De La Salle Brothers. That didn't matter; we were all branded. I felt guilt by association and became increasingly angry and fearful about it.

My turn came to be inspected by the principal, a process every teacher underwent once every five years. Normally the visits were brief and simple with follow-up notes and suggestions. Since my inspection was scheduled for the beginning of the semester, I barely knew my students.

For the visit, I chose to teach an introductory lesson on *Macbeth*. Rather than announce to the class that we were going to study Shakespeare – groan – I asked the students to close their eyes while I recreated the two main witches' scenes. With the principal sitting at the back of the class, I began with sounds of wind and rain and cackled the three hags from memory. Only a couple snickered. Next, I instigated a discussion on witchcraft – past and present. I asked the students to consider:

Are there witches' covens in the Langley woods?

What do witches do?

Do they really steal babies from maternity wards at Halloween?

I asked the class to consider the fear people had of witches in the age of King James. I described the politics of James of Scotland concerning witches and spoke briefly of life in Shakespeare's England. I explained that women were not permitted on stage; therefore, men played women's parts and rough characters, possibly sailors, played the witches. Then I asked who had recognized the scenes I'd portrayed. A couple answered "Macbeth". Nobody groaned. I handed out the text and uncovered blackboard notes indicating their home reading assignment with questions that would be posed on a quiz for the following class.

A couple of days later, the principal handed me a negative report. In his verbal explanation, he told me he found me too "artsy-fartsy" and off topic. He "encouraged" me to learn the U.B.C. method of lesson planning and presentation. "Tell the students what you are going to teach. Teach the lesson. Ask questions."

He told me he would return for another class taught according to his instructions. I taught a lesson on faulty sentence structure with oral examples I asked the students to correct. This followed with written exercises. The principal was not happy with my second presentation, even though he acknowledged some improvement. The negative report remained.

I sought consultation with the president of the Drummond Teachers' Association. We met for breakfast one day before school. On her advice, I returned the report unsigned.

The following year, the same principal inspected me again. This time I taught a lesson in grammar, which, under normal circumstances, would be very straightforward. Although couched in softer language than my previous report, this one made reference to my age and "apparent lack of organization". I shared this with Eloise and with our principal friend. Both found the wording inappropriate; however, I felt compelled to sign, to get the principal off my back. Meanwhile, my enthusiasm for teaching English was waning.

In May 1989, the vice-principal, aware of my qualifications and experience in Drama, Music, Art, and French at all levels, encouraged me to apply for a position of "district helping teacher" in Fine and Performing Arts being advertised in the district. After several weeks, a young art teacher was given the job. My application was not acknowledged.

As time went on, our vice-principal went on to become the principal of a junior secondary school. A new man filled the position of vice-principal. One of his responsibilities was to monitor supplies. Although paper was becoming increasingly expensive and in short supply, every department in the school used reams for class assignments, quizzes, and tests. I also ran off my share of tests and notes, but recycled as much as possible by having students put answers on their own paper and copy notes for homework.

When interim report card time came, I used a new computer reporting-program including comments, marks for assignment and test marks. The new vice-principal told me I was using too much paper, and my reports were too long.

The Gun Incident

On Wednesday, December 6th, 1989, Marc Lepine entered the University of Montréal's School of Engineering building and shot fourteen women. A year later, Thursday, December 6th, 1990, as I sat at the back of my class listening to student presentations, a young man entered the classroom dressed in army boots and fatigues and wearing a balaclava over his head. He pointed a black submachine gun and shouted, "I want the women!" Pandemonium broke out as he sprayed several girls sitting at the front of the class with water from his gun. Angry and shouting "Stop!" I darted after him, amidst screams from the girls. Bright lights flashed before my eyes; my head swam as I chased the boy down the stairs and past the vice-principal.

The V.P. called after me, stopped me, and ushered me into his office to "cool down".

"Who's looking after your class?"

I told him what had just happened.

"Why are you making such a fuss over a silly prank?"

"He had a gun."

"You were yelling in the hallway."

"I tried to stop him."

"You were disturbing classes."

The next morning, I went to school early enough to see the principal. But he was busy. When I did get to see him at the morning break, he told me to take it easy over the weekend and talk to him on Monday. On the Monday, nothing was done. The gun incident was not important. I was making a "big thing out of nothing."

"Forget about it." Even the girls who had been sprayed seemed to have forgotten the incident.

Nobody ever found out who the young "terrorist" was. My memory became a confused nightmare. The following weekend, I related the incident to a family friend, a principal in an adjoining school district. He advised me to report the episode, in writing, with a copy to the School Board and one to the Municipal Police Department. But I was too frozen in fear to act. I'd allowed too much time to pass. Worse, I got to the point where I couldn't recall the date of the occurrence. Soon, the entire incident became a blur in my memory. And then I forgot it altogether until I remembered it, with horror, many months later.

In the weeks and months to come, I became increasingly confused, until I could no longer identify my students. In October, 1991, on the recommendation of my family doctor, I underwent a battery of tests at the University Hospital Alzheimer Clinic. A follow-up examination was scheduled for January, 1992. The doctors found no specific organic cause for memory loss, which was growing steadily worse. Noise was increasingly troublesome. A soft drink machine in the hall outside my door irritated me with its constant jangle. I had dizzy spells. Doors slamming made me jump. Tinnitus caused me to hear a constant hissing sound that grew louder and louder. A hearing specialist prescribed hearing aids. In class, they amplified surrounding noise, causing further discomfort and confusion. Pranksters dropped books behind my back.

Keeping attendance records became almost impossible in one remedial English class of thirty. Students exchanged seats so that seating plans were ineffective. One by one students disappeared until there were but a handful in class. I gave spot quizzes, hoping to use the results for my attendance register but when I collected them, signatures were often missing or illegible.

One lunch hour, I fell in a school hallway and broke my ankle. While students gathered around, I got up and hobbled into the staff lounge, then stubbornly returned to class for the afternoon sessions. After school, I visited my doctor, who sent me for x-rays. Sure enough, my ankle was broken. I returned to school the next day with crutches and wearing a cast.

The Prince of Tides

On a Saturday in January 1992, Eloise and I went shopping across the border in Bellingham and ended the day with dinner and a movie. *The Prince of Tides* starred Nick Nolte as a trauma patient and Barbara Streisand as his psychiatrist. At the point where Tom Wingo [the protagonist as a boy], his mother, and his twin sister Savannah are violently raped by three armed ex-convicts, I experienced such a vivid flashback I sank down in my seat. I did not see, thus I did not recall the remainder of the movie. I simply sat in shock and cried, audibly. When the lights came on in the theatre, Eloise went to the lobby. I was the last to leave.

I controlled myself enough to begin the drive home. Neither of us spoke. Just north of Bellingham, I could no longer contain myself. I pulled over to the shoulder of the highway and cried.

"I was the boy in the movie." I whispered again, "I was the boy in the movie."

Without a word, Eloise got out of the car, walked around to my side, and motioned for me to shift over. She drove. At home, she told me "I don't want to hear about it. Go see a shrink."

I slept alone on the downstairs couch.

The next day, Sunday, Eloise and the kids went to church and visited friends for the day. I remained at home. On Monday morning, I phoned in sick, called our family doctor, and asked for an emergency appointment. He made an appointment for me with a Vancouver psychiatrist.

Eloise and I discussed the matter no further.

In April 1992, I started regular appointments with a psychiatrist. As in so many recovery scenarios, I had to feel the worst before I experienced anything better. I had nightmares of burning schools, bombings, snipers, and lost classes.

A student had behaved disruptively with another teacher and was transferred to one of my classes. When he arrived, I assigned him to a front seat. He waved to some friends in the back, put his feet up, and farted loudly.

I said, "Excuse me, would you kindly leave the room."

He mimicking me, "Excuse me, would you kindly leave the fucking room." Then he said, "Make me."

I shouted "Out!"

He stood, waved to everyone, lifted his middle finger and walked out, slamming the door.

A short time later, he returned with the vice-principal with whom I was having a bad time. The V.P. said, "Mr. Milne, this gentleman tells me you swore at him."

I smiled and shook my head. "I'll come and see you both after school."

The boy interjected, "I can't stay after school, I have to work."

"Go back in and sit down." the V.P. said to the boy, indicating him into my classroom.

"You might like to ask the class what happened," I suggested angrily.

"Oh, I couldn't do that. That would embarrass the child."

So upset and angry I was shaking, I told the class to continue with quiet study or homework for the remaining fifteen minutes of the school day.

As soon as I closed up, I went to the office. The boy did not show up. I waited for about fifteen minutes, then the principal ushered me into a small storage room adjacent to the office where he and the vice-principal stood facing me. After telling me to sit down on a stool, the V.P. began a lecture on the evils of "child abuse".

"Yes," the principal told me, "swearing at children is child abuse."

Confused, angry, and in tears, I protested that I did not swear at my students and certainly not at that boy. The vice-principal responded, "I have known this student for years and I know his parents. He is not the kind of child who would lie."

I was outnumbered. I no longer could protect myself. In tears I rushed from the office. I sat in my car for nearly an hour before I was able to drive home.

That evening, in despair, I sat alone in my back study. I didn't know how much longer I could hold on.

During the following week, the same boy became increasingly hostile and disruptive. On May 6th, 1992, I spoke to one of the school counsellors who referred me back to the vice-principal. In turn, he called in the principal who, instead of offering support, asked me if I'd considered retiring. I broke down. That was my last day at school. I didn't retrieve my personal belongings; I couldn't return to class.

Post Traumatic Stress Disorder

Under doctor's orders, I was placed on medical leave. For a long time, I couldn't read. My mind was so overloaded, I'd read a passage and not remember what I'd read. I spent much time sitting in silence, watched little television, unable to listen to the radio, and only skimming the newspapers. Sometimes, I'd pick up a video only to realize, upon viewing it, that I'd already seen the film weeks earlier.

For no apparent reason, I'd burst into tears and sob audibly. In the end, I had to get Eloise to drive whenever we went anywhere. After church one Sunday morning, I blacked out and was disoriented when I came to. Panic attacks and blackouts increased. Eloise became more and more frustrated.

When the disability insurance company asked for a letter from my psychiatrist, he told me the charge for such a letter was a little more than one hundred dollars. Eloise said that was too much and I should discontinue the visits. Furthermore, she didn't believe in Post Traumatic Stress Disorder. I paid the doctor.

The fear, anger and helplessness associated with earlier trauma are re-experienced when a person is faced with a similar situation in the present. Highest rates of Post Traumatic Stress Disorder are found among survivors of rape, military combat, captivity, and genocide. Individuals with this disorder may describe painful anxiety and guilt, feeling implicated and responsible for the violence that has happened to them. Resulting depression and avoidance patterns may interfere with interpersonal relationships and lead to marital conflict and job loss when the person has not been assisted, through therapeutic experiences, to understand and learn to cope with emotions.

A boisterous family bought the house next door and erected a basketball hoop on the edge of their driveway, almost right under our living room and bedroom windows. Stray balls pounded against our wall and windows. Since the new neighbours refused to stop, Eloise insisted we go to the police.

The police informed us "Basketball is a popular sport. You cannot deny children the right to play, especially on their own property."

The situation became unbearable. I stood on the neighbours' driveway and begged the kids and their mother to stop banging balls against our house. The father threatened to have me reported to "his friend", the Attorney General. "They have places for people like you."

The battle escalated. Our front lamps were broken repeatedly. Eggs were thrown against our house. I found bits of copper piping poisoning our cedar bushes. Once, while Alex helped me remove a dead bush from our front hedge to replace it with another, the mother from next door came out and confronted him. She charged that he had threatened her with his spade. I knew this wasn't true. I had been pulling at the shrub at the same time Alex had the spade beneath its roots. Once again, the father came out. We picked up our tools and went inside. Then, two police constables arrived to check on the "attempted assault". Next followed a series of police visits back and forth between the two houses. In the end, one of the constables told us we would have to keep the peace and allow children to play without harassment.

Feeling under constant attack, I hid in the back study, listening to the drip, drip of the kitchen faucet while I waited for the troubles to go away. No matter where I sought refuge, basketballs resounded – thump! thump! thump! The sound terrified me. An enemy pounded mercilessly at my walls. There was no escape.

Alex, the only one who appeared to understand, hugged me whenever I broke down crying. Eloise grew increasingly annoyed and suggested one of us had to leave. Sometimes she stayed with her parents for the evening and left me alone in the house. The phone would ring, but when I answered, there was nobody on the line. Hanna and Alex spent more time with their friends. When Alex stayed out past curfew (ten or eleven o'clock), Eloise locked the door and forbade me to let him in. She said she was practicing "tough love". Our son had to spend the night at a neighbour's house.

I joined my wife for brisk evening walks but couldn't keep up. She'd arrive home well ahead of me. The boy from next door would be standing in my way just before I reached home. "Hey, mother-fucker! How about me and you?" he'd say to me. His father stood at his front door, watching. While I hurried into the house, the kid laughed loudly. Deeper, ever deeper, I slipped into the whirlpool. I couldn't claw my way out. My chest ached. I couldn't breathe.

I had frightening nightmares that the school was on fire. I couldn't find my classroom. Snipers in the hall were shooting at me. I dreamed of jungles and little men with sharp jagged teeth.

Between horrific nightmares and apparent and imagined threats, I sat day after day through the month of June, praying for peace, and waiting for my troubles to go away.

Handyman's Delight

One weekend in July 1992, Eloise and I took a ferry and drove up the coast to Sechelt to visit a couple we had known since our youth group days in North Drummond. Mike and Maureen had been on one of our Marriage Encounter Weekends and their boys baby-sat our two when they were little. Though Mike still worked in town, the couple had bought a new house on Porpoise Bay, just outside Sechelt, two hours beyond Vancouver and accessible only by ferry. They told us how much they enjoyed the community, the nature walks and the fresh air. They showed us around Sechelt and as far as Tuwanek, a tiny fishing village, north of where they lived. I fell in love with the area and suggested to Eloise that Sechelt would be a wonderful area for our retirement.

After some thought, she agreed to have a realtor show us around. We viewed an old house on a hill in West Sechelt with a fantastic view of the ocean and I pictured a home I could renovate and paint, and a garden with endless possibilities. The house, occupied by an elderly couple in poor health, was in desperate need of repair and a paint job. I told Eloise I could spend some of the time I now spent feeling lost at home, fixing up the house and property. "If nothing else, it would make an excellent investment for our retirement. We could rent out most of the house to cover the mortgage. And it would be fun to fix a small suite for us in the basement until we'd be ready to move in."

We drove around looking at other houses for sale – many in areas too remote for Eloise's liking. Then we returned to Sechelt to make an offer.

The following day, Eloise's parents returned with us to see what we were buying. Her father was enthusiastic but her mother refused to step out of the car. When Eloise's dad suggested looking around Sechelt for a place for them too, her mother hissed, "Don't you even think it."

They never returned to the Sunshine Coast.

Eloise and Hanna had been taking singing lessons for a couple of years. I decided it would now be a good time for me to learn piano. But Eloise told me she needed to excel at the piano and didn't want me to compete. As usual, I gave way.

"Furthermore," she added, "I want to open my own bank account. What if something happened to you? How would I manage?"

Eloise transferred the balance of our savings to a savings account in her name alone. From then on, we would live solely on my medical insurance payments. Her salary would be saved for our retirement when she reached sixty.

September 1st, I packed my car with tools, sleeping bag, a cooler, canned food, Kraft dinners, and moved to Sechelt and set to work. I hardly knew where to start. Mice and larger rodents had taken up residence everywhere. The garden ran amok with tall hay, poppies, lavender, thistles, dandelions, and tangled blackberry vines. The ditch contained pages from old newspapers, cigarette packages, Coca-Cola cans, and broken beer bottles.

I walked up crumbled wooden and cement steps through the rockery to the kitchen door. A couple of pigeons protested my intrusion. They fluttered uncomfortably, made small complaining sounds, and sat perched above the door. A snail drew its albuminous trail across the path while a line of ants climbed the one cement step to a crack at the base of the wall. I made a mental note to pour hot water along their trail, and block their access to the house.

I walked to the gazebo at the top of the tumbling rockery. Wood bugs scuttled from a rotting container wall. Toward the ocean, a flock of starlings dive-bombed a crow above the arbutus. Everywhere, climbing plants rambled. Roses grew wild – luscious pink, crispy white, silky yellow, and long-stemmed, hardy red. Other flowers rioted in profusion.

I almost stepped on something. Just a short time before hatching, a baby bird had plunged to its death leaving scattered bits of shell, a shapeless smudge of feathers, and dried red flesh.

Beyond the ragged palm tree, I could see the ocean, the islands, and the distant mountains of Vancouver Island. Almost immediately, I felt new hope, took a deep breath and rolled up my sleeves.

I cleaned the upper level, then set to work clearing drains, repairing the front deck, cleaning an old oven and refrigerator, and building a suite in the basement with a separate entrance from the laundry room.

On the day my advertisement appeared in the local paper, a young mother-to-be contacted me. Her husband was a roofer. Since the ad stipulated: No smokers, No pets, the woman told me that they both intended to quit smoking and promised they'd keep their big shaggy dog outdoors. With a baby on the way, I was sympathetic. I continued patching and painting the upstairs and preparing my basement suite so they could move in November 1st.

I began attending Holy Family Catholic Church in Sechelt. One day, a group of men gathered by the church with paintbrushes and ladders. They were painting the exterior of the church a pale blue with white trim. When one of the men asked who would climb up to paint the cross, I volunteered and climbed the long ladder onto the roof and then scaled another ladder to the spire.

From the spire, I looked down – and discovered my fear of heights was gone. When the church painting was finished, I returned to the house in Sechelt and painted all the white areas under the eaves that previously I'd been unable to reach.

Once the renters moved in, I returned home to South Riverside but would visit Sechelt every two to three weeks to keep the winter garden under control and spend quiet time in my basement hideaway.

One weekend just before Christmas, Eloise came to see the improvements I had made and to inspect the basement suite. Mike and Maureen came over. Maureen saw a huge rat in our basement flat and screamed. While Eloise and Maureen stood on the far side of the lawn, I seized a shovel and killed it. I had to convince Eloise that the rat had run in from the outside because the door had been left open. Rodents in the house and snakes in the garden would be sufficient reason to convince my wife that country living would be out of the question. Still, she did agree to come up with me once in a while, if only to see what I was doing with our investment. She didn't think she'd want to stay overnight. But over time, when no more incidents occurred, she changed her mind.

For the balance of the winter, we visited our new home the occasional weekend and met several neighbours whom we invited to visit our tiny flat. When summer arrived, a second-hand hide-a-bed, a small refrigerator, a two-ring stove, and a microwave turned out to be sufficient to help furnish our summer place by the sea. Eloise and I renewed plans for eventual retirement. She picked a colour for the house's exterior, and I began painting. Already, I had chipped and repainted the white trim and was labouring hard to pull the grounds out of chaos.

During the week in South Riverside , I wrote poetry, cleaned house, and began to feel much happier, despite the noise from next door.

That summer, Hanna and Alex took restaurant jobs to help pay for college. Hanna would enter her second year at Douglas College. Alex won a first-year scholarship for Journalism School at Carleton University in Ottawa. I planned to spend more time during the week on the Sunshine Coast, and join Eloise and Hanna in South Riverside on weekends.

My first job outdoors, after a general cleanup, was to rebuild and enlarge a shattered rock garden. I cemented stone steps and walls, rebuilt a lawn and cultivated berry bushes and fruit trees on the far side of the house. The ditch and banks were smothered in blackberry vines, which I cut and pulled until the entire property began to look civilized. The neighbours were delighted and brought me pies and soups.

Remembering my own homesickness as a child, I sent Alex fare to fly home for Christmas. Eloise was upset that I'd done so at a time when we had decided to be more frugal. Then she suggested we sell the big house and move into something smaller. I saw this as a possible escape from the problem of the next-door neighbours. Once again, I put out my sign – "sale by owner" and, despite repeated vandalism to the outside lights, managed to keep the place presentable.

While all this was going on, we looked at many smaller houses. I suggested we look for a condominium, where the two of us could live. Eloise agreed. I would spend part of my time in Sechelt, and we would alternate weekends between Sechelt and South Riverside .

After much searching, Eloise agreed to a brand new, two-bedroom, two-bathroom condominium being built in White Rock. After the sale of our South Riverside house, we would rent storage for the good furniture and take temporary lodging until the new condominium was ready. Naturally, the older furniture would serve our country home.

Packing and Sorting

While I stayed in Sechelt, Eloise's parents helped their daughter pack our belongings into boxes in preparation for the move to the new condo. Eloise said her dad would look after all accounts and that the bills I had kept in file folders would be better in his care. I was no longer to worry about such things. She would sort photographs and albums later.

On moving day, a van took the household furniture to storage and a rental apartment. Alex and his friend helped me move the balance from our basement to Sechelt.

Planning to move upstairs, I had given the tenants the customary thirty-day notice and, without inspecting, returned their deposit with interest. We placed my belongings in the basement. I needed to clean the upstairs and paint before moving in.

It took me a while to realize the entire upstairs was damp, mouldy, and smelled of dead skunk. With increasing trepidation, I saw the house would require a drastic overhaul.

For those first few weeks, I sat in the basement at night and listened to the scurrying of rats in the walls and around the furnace, which had been turned off for the summer. I sat in silence, absolutely alone.

One day I tried using my credit card to buy groceries but the transaction was refused. Embarrassed, I went to the bank to learn the account was maxed out. I tried withdrawing cash instead but the joint account had only a few dollars. I tried telephoning

Eloise but she hung up so I returned to the bank, closed the joint account and cancelled credit card, although I would still have to pay the outstanding balance. Then I telephoned the disability insurance company to have my cheques sent to a new Sechelt account.

The next payday, Eloise telephoned to say I'd broken our agreement and she'd never trust me with money again. She reminded me that the previous Christmas I'd sent money to Alex against her wishes and that this Christmas was proving more expensive than Christmases past as she'd had to buy numerous new items for the condo. Then she informed me she would spend the holidays with her parents and I should not try to see her.

Hanna came to Sechelt for a visit. I drove her back for Christmas Eve, to be with her mother. On the way, I bought two large bouquets of flowers. When we arrived at the condominium, I asked Hanna to take in the flowers while I waited in the car. I waited for more than an hour but didn't have the courage to walk up to the new apartment and knock on the door.

I drove back to Sechelt, so lonely I cried all the way. Unable to get out on the ferry because I didn't want to bump into anyone on Christmas Eve, I huddled in my car.

Christmas day, Alex joined me to cook dinner. But I couldn't eat. Patient and loving, my son spent several days with me. To help me get out of the house, he drove with me to points of interest further up coast. When he left for a skiing trip, before returning to school, I sat, silent and lonely in my living room

Before long, I pulled myself together and got busy renovating the upstairs. I wanted to forget my loneliness. I removed heavy drapes and sent them to the Salvation Army, leaving only sheers, which I washed three times before they were ready to rehang. I pulled up shag carpet to discover part of the floor was damp and beginning to rot. One by one, I called in help where needed, to change plumbing and update wiring, paying and buying supplies as I could, when I could, charging to my new credit card account when I had to. I pulled out the old, cracked bathtub and completely redid the bathroom with a deeper tub and shower enclosure. The weather turned cold and the electric furnace burned out. I phoned a heating contractor and arranged for natural gas. With a new furnace and hot water tank, I installed a gas fireplace in the living room.

Gaining momentum, I hired a carpenter and together we pulled down and moved walls, enlarged the kitchen, and opened up the house to the bright southern view of the ocean. I covered the front of the living room fireplace with wallboard. Eloise had not liked the brick facing; I was sure she'd approve.

I built a large mantel and installed marble facing. Then I found matching material in a composite, for the kitchen countertops, and, with the help of a plumber, replaced sink and piping.

With fresh paint, vertical Venetian window coverings, carpeting, and paintings on the walls, I was finally ready to return outside and complete the rockery with a grotto, waterfall, and fishpond. It was spring.

My next step was to have the house blessed by the parish priest. I invited several new friends from Holy Family Parish. One lady baked and decorated a cake.

A week after the house blessing, Eloise paid a brief visit. She was not happy with what I had done. The grotto had to go as well as the fishpond. The stone steps were too rough, and the cement statue of Mary did not belong in the garden. I had used granite gathered along the highway. Eloise preferred smooth beach rocks and commercial cement rounds.

While she stood by, I moved the statue into the house and took a pickaxe to the grotto, fishpond, and to the steps. I was in a rage. I did not destroy my work because I agreed with Eloise, or even because I wanted to please her. I didn't stop to think. Despite my obvious anger, which would be very frightening to anyone close by, Eloise appeared controlled as I blindly followed her directions.

When I had exhausted myself and sat with my head in my hands, Eloise informed me she was not happy living in an apartment. She needed me to sign the condominium over to her so she could sell it and buy a house.

That was her last visit for a long time.

Shortly after Eloise went back to White Rock, I wrote to her that I thought I understood her reactions and pleaded to find a way to get us back together. I begged her to forgive me for the many hurts and suggested we sell the Sechelt house and the condo, and buy a house in Riverside for the two of us.

I received no answer. A few weeks later, Alex came up. He was shocked and angry that I had destroyed so much of my work in the garden. "Mom's not living here, Pops. You are."

Then he helped me to start rebuilding pond, grotto, and steps.

When the second Christmas approached, I determined we should all be together, at least for Christmas dinner. Eloise agreed to have dinner at "her place".

I felt nervous as Alex and I parked in the guest parking lot. Alex carried in two bottles of wine. I carried our wrapped gifts for Hanna, Eloise, and her parents.

The apartment was stunning, very up-to-date. Eloise's parents were already there, as were Hanna and her boyfriend. Eloise received the wine and gifts without a word. Her mother said she was sorry they had "forgotten cards" for Alex and me. As dinner wasn't served for quite a while, we all sat uncomfortably making polite conversation with the grandparents while Eloise continued in the kitchen.

Following the traditional turkey, Eloise told us dessert would take a while, too, as it was not quite ready. Eloise's mother reminded us, "We should always wait awhile, to allow our first course to digest." I was worried about the time. There was no place for us to stay and Alex needed to return to Sechelt on the last ferry. I wanted to remain and try to find healing with Eloise. I told Alex to take my car.

Since he would have to leave within the next few minutes, I asked if Alex could have dessert ahead of us. Eloise told Alex to be polite and wait, like everyone else. I suggested he take some plum pudding on a paper plate. Grandma replied, "Those who do not have the good manners to wait should go without."

In the end, Alex left without plum pudding. Hanna had words with her mother and Eloise went into her bedroom and slammed the door. Hanna and her friend left. While Eloise's mother remarked that children today have neither the respect nor the morals of the children of their day, I sat in silence.

Finally, the parents left. Eloise threw a blanket on the couch. She told me the other bedroom was full of boxes and I couldn't use the shower in the second bathroom since it too was stacked with boxes and she had no guest towels. The couch was too small for me to sleep on so I stretched out on the floor in front of the gas fireplace, fully dressed, and pulled the blanket over me. I lay there, listening to the faint sounds of music coming from a nearby apartment. Perry Como was crooning, "Oh, there's no place like home for the holidays." Oh, sure! Eventually, I got up and undressed. Folding my clothes neatly beside me on the floor, I got into my pyjamas and tried to sleep. I regretted not having left with Alex. Tomorrow, surely, I'll have a chance to talk one on one with Eloise.

The following morning, I awoke to sad reality. I slipped into my clothes and folded the blanket. Eloise's parents arrived just before she got out of the shower. Like a martyr, I helped my mother-in-law clean up the dinner dishes. Neither of us spoke. Eloise came to the kitchen and made coffee and toast for them and for herself. I helped myself to coffee. There was no sugar.

After breakfast, we all went for a walk. Eloise walked with her mother and father. I followed, alone, like a bedraggled puppy. Later, we ate cold turkey and went out in the evening to see the lights in the park.

The entire day had been taken up by Eloise's parents. They gave me no opportunity to talk to Eloise alone. When they finally left, Eloise went into her bedroom and closed the door. She didn't even say "goodnight". She treated me as though I was not there.

Again, I slept on the floor, this time with a small cushion in a pillowcase. The next morning, I walked to the bus and made my way back to Sechelt.

Handyman's Delight

i chose to live high on that hill

above the ocean, in that tiny house

that needed so much care

top to bottom,

where rats sat glaring

from basement corners.

they ran across my bed at night

and tickled with their whiskers

while i tried in vain to sleep

to the cough and sputter and squeak

of the oil furnace reek,

while centipedes and spiders

crawled across my pillow in the dark.

smoky rays of morning sun

peeped through the rickety blind

that hung by a thread,

over the sliding glass doors

that led to the patio with cracked cement.

ants marched single file,

in snaking columns,

under the door to the Coca Cola can

that sat in front of the dusty brick fireplace

full of soggy newspapers

and rusty tins.

Keeping Busy to Forget My Troubles

After the holiday season, I arranged to give a benefit performance at the Raven's Cry Theatre, in Sechelt, ostensibly to help get the Management Society out of the red. An old friend, Dorla, from Langley, and her two friends, formed the "Aldorio Trio". They agreed to come up from White Rock where they usually rehearsed and join me in a program of music and poetry. Dorla played the cello, Celia played violin, and Alicia played piano. I read poetry. The program combined excerpts from classical and old favourite musical compositions, with a variety of poetic readings, presented in the style of the Palm Court Trio. This style recalls the elegant hotels and restaurants of late 19th and early 20th century Europe, where such groups popularized the themes of classical music for the general public and where young poets often introduced their writings.

Two weeks before the concert, I wrote Eloise, with hopes she would attend, which she did. Then, with my wife in the audience, I aimed love poems directly at her.

> I love thee with a love I seemed to lose
>
> With my lost saints, – I love thee with the breath,
>
> Smiles, tears, of all my life! – and, If God choose,
>
> I shall but love thee better after death.
>
> – Elizabeth Barrett Browning.

Eloise was unimpressed. Immediately after the concert, she informed me she wanted to sell the condominium as well as the house in Sechelt.

Shocked and in agony but, once again, trying to please, I replied, "We should be able to do that without much difficulty and find a really nice house together."

"Not with you, I won't."

"Where will I live?"

"I really don't give a damn. There must be an apartment you could rent in Sechelt."

"I can't do that!"

While well-wishers gathered around me, Eloise disappeared to catch her ferry. I stood there, heart pounding, totally devastated.

LIVING IN DENIAL

Once again, trying to rescue myself and/or prove my strength to Eloise, while attempting to keep the inevitable at bay, I joined the Sechelt Legion. When the executive learned I could write, they asked me to publish a monthly newsletter. Before long, I wrote a weekly column for the local press about various Coast veterans or about historical events of interest to the Legion.

I joined the Sunshine Coast Music Society and played Tevye in *Fiddler on the Roof*. I sang with the Belltones Chorus and with the 59ers, an all-male chorus. Twice, I acted as Master of Ceremonies for the Coast Music Festival.

Volunteers are always in demand. I entertained for "Over Eighties" teas and for the White Cane Society. I wrote and directed four short folk tales for the visually impaired. This was performed at a luncheon during a Sunshine Coast Story Festival.

On another occasion, my son made a video of a Legion program I wrote for Remembrance Day, "Then and Now". As the production was televised, a copy of the tape was sent to Legion Headquarters in Ottawa.

Jimmy Paul, a Native Canadian veteran who had been wounded during World War Two, was a constant visitor to the Legion. He had received no recognition from the Department of Veterans Affairs and no government pension. Like so many Native veterans, lost his Native status. Jimmy wasn't bitter; in fact, he was an active volunteer at the Legion.

I wrote a feature story on his plight. A copy of my article was sent to the Senate Committee on Native Affairs in Ottawa. Some time later, Jimmy was given back his Native status and provided with a small house on the Sechelt Band Land. More than fifty years after he had lost part of his right hand in Germany, Jimmy Paul received a lump sum payment amounting to just five years of the pension that had so long been denied him. The following

November 11th, Alex spent a day with Jimmy Paul and helped to produce a special edition of *The Ubyssey*, the U.B.C. newspaper, on Veterans and Remembrance Day.

Divorce and Annulment

Seven or eight months had passed since the concert when Eloise had told me she wanted to sell both the condominium and the house in Sechelt. I'd not heard from her since. I telephoned and, as soon as she answered, asked her if she would ever consider making a "Retrouvaille Weekend" – a weekend based on Marriage Encounter, aimed at marriages in trouble. She replied, "With you? Never!" Then she hung up.

A few days later, I received a letter from her, stating she wanted a divorce and an annulment from the Church. I was no longer surprised. Just numb. However, the more abuse she hurled at me, the more I fantasized the punishment was deserved and that I'd win her over no matter what.

My friends on the Sunshine Coast advised me to see a lawyer in order to protect myself. I refused to listen or consider even talking to a lawyer. Eloise's and my friend Maureen urged me to see a lawyer she knew who worked in Sechelt two days each week. According to her, a financial settlement would resolve any arguments over money matters and clear the air for both of us. She said it had worked for her and Mike. This gave me hope. I certainly did not want a divorce.

The Sechelt lawyer told me I should pay my wife the money she would be awarded by the courts anyway, and save myself the expense of a dispute. The Sechelt home would have to be sold as well as the condominium. She said I had no choice in the matter. I could not win in court. I'd be lucky to keep my pension. I felt desperate. How would I live?

My son put me in touch with a lawyer in West Vancouver. Then, I rediscovered my old Quicken back-up disks and ran off the same financial records Eloise had presented through her lawyer. My records were more inclusive and computer dated.

With the lawyer's help, I soon discovered how I'd allowed myself to be led around like a puppy on a leash. I would not have to lose my home.

Divorce proceedings turned out to be lengthy and bitter. However, in the end, Eloise won none of her demands. I not only retained my Sechelt home and my pension, I was awarded a fair portion of the family savings too. And Eloise got her divorce.

Shaken but relieved, I was now free to live my life. There'd be no more threats, no more upsets, no more false hopes. With money in the bank, I paid off my debts, added an art studio to the ground floor and bought a hot tub for the back deck.

Months later, I received a copy of a document from the Archdiocesan Marriage Tribunal granting Eloise an unconditional annulment. I visited the Chancellery Office in Vancouver and asked to speak to the Monsignor. A young lady came to the counter – the Church advocate assigned "to act on my behalf". I had not been informed that such a person existed and she had certainly not tried to contact me. Neither did she wish to talk to me now. I was not to know on what grounds the annulment had been granted. "The Church has very strict rules in these cases, to protect the innocent victim."

My own church had betrayed me. Since the Catholic Church does not recognize Civil Divorce, what right did she have granting an annulment? It was as if to say I'd committed some grievous sin that Eloise had to escape from. At one point, in the midst of divorce proceedings, my pastor had interviewed me regarding grounds for annulment. I told him I saw none. As potential witnesses on my behalf, I listed the clergy in whose parishes I had served since being married. Was the annulment granted based on a lie or on lies? I was never to know.

Damn them all!

Thirteen

"Recovery is the process of discovering who we are"

My Healing Garden

Much of my time in Sechelt turned out, in the manner of Thoreau's *Walden*, to be a closed, silent retreat – and the venue for my healing. Manual labour and the sorting out of memories and emotions dominated my waking hours. I ate sparingly, slept briefly. I heard no radio, watched no television, and read no newspapers.

Past, present, and future coalesced into ever-present now.

Western culture permits little silence. We are constantly bombarded by voices, music, and traffic – noises that surround us even when we sleep. In losing silence, we lose the opportunity to face our inner selves, to find out who we really are. We float along in the general hubbub, afraid to be alone, happy to be "part of" something, yet unable to define what that "something" is.

Even with sound all about us, we seek distractions – television, movies, games, parties, and recreational drugs of all sorts. We are afraid to face the silence, in which our spirits may commune with our minds and bodies. We are afraid to face ourselves.

At some level, I needed to hear God's voice in the silence. Only then, I knew, could I work through my inner turmoil and find peace and healing. To begin that healing, I would have to face my demons.

My garden was my chapel. I looked around at God's beautiful nature. I saw Him in the flowers, in the many birds by my waterfall, in the deer that came freely to munch and doze in the shade beneath my Arbutus.

* * *

Like children at recess, spring flowers and shrubs tumble about in laughing chaos from every nook and cranny. Reds and pinks, blues and yellows giggle in bunches. Beneath a stem of Bleeding Heart, purple crocuses caress the garden fern with water droplets, crisp, fresh, clean.

Here and there, the odd weed sneaks in and tries to masquerade as something sweet I dare not pull. Their roots are deep and they cry out to be left to live in peace. I feel their pain. I once was ugly and rejected but held on. With so much beauty all around, how can I cast them out? They too have tiny buds. I'll let them stay.

I'm on the fireplace mantle, happy to be the centre of attention. He turns me over and pulls down my pyjama bottoms.

Striped prince of the underworld slithers past my shoe. Vivid stripes of almost blue blend with the leaning lavender. Poor creature so maligned. Surely, it was

Eve who tempted you. I know you've snatched a goldfish now and then. You also swallow snails that eat my water plants. Pass in peace. Enjoy the evening shade. You'll not be banished from this garden of plenty.

Uncle Sigvard carries me to his bed. He puts Vaseline into my bottom with his finger. It feels nice. Like my mother's love.

Snails still draw albuminous trails across garden paths. Ants run conga lines near the kitchen door. I've asked them to stay outside and they obey. We made peace years ago. Wood bugs scuttle where wood bugs must scuttle. Roses, luscious pink, climb the kitchen wall. Wild flowers riot in profusion before the compost boxes, which sprout new potatoes grown from last year's peelings. I'll harvest white and red gems before the fall turning of older compost onto this year's collection of lawn clippings, kitchen peelings, crushed egg shells and coffee grounds. On the front bank by the driveway, my palm tree, no longer ragged, announces the sparkling bay.

Burning pain – can't breathe. I throw up all over the bed.

"What will your mother say when I tell her what you've done?"

My two pigeons are back again this year. They've moved to the top of the gazebo where they perch in the sun, no longer complaining when I approach. I guess they've decided to let me stay. The same flock of starlings strafes the same crow above the arbutus.

A pair of barn swallows have built their nest of mud and straw beneath the highest eaves, above my bedroom window. In graceful flight, they twist and turn in search of flies and wasps then swoop back to their home – then out again. They're feeding their nestlings bluebottles and horseflies. I hear the chirping from three hungry mouths as parents come and go from before dawn until well after sunset. What devotion. I wonder if the parents ever rest.

I try to wash but can't get clean. I'll never be clean.

So far the ground below the nest is clean but soon I'll need to quietly place a box of soil to catch the droppings as the baby birds back up and defecate over the edge of the nest. Last year I collected quite a pile of fertilizer before the second brood had fledged.

Other swallows have also nested nearby. Like neighbourhood watch, they appear to work together and look out for one another's young. One morning, I watched a flock of angry birds mob a neighbour's cat with aerial acrobatics to make an air ace envious. The attack sent the old hunter running for cover behind my patio flowerpots. My cat Oliver has learned in seasons past to stay well clear of swallows while they feed their babies.

My uncle's not pleased. God is not pleased. Mother will not be pleased. It's all my fault. Mother will be furious; she must never know.

In winter, my bag of birdseed feeds Steller's Jays, finches, Oregon Juncos, Rufous-sided Towhees, starlings, chickadees, Yellow Warblers, crows, and Red-winged Blackbirds. My seeds feed raccoons, squirrels, and various other rodents. I'll happily feed whoever comes.

I cry because I feel so dirty I want to die.

While the birds take turns at the bird feeder, and bees tease the rhododendrons, my cat Oliver and his feline friends frolic around the grotto rocks and roll in the catnip at the Virgin's feet. Now I gaze at the grotto – a work of love built from beautiful chunks of blue and green rock.

"We won't say anything about this to anyone."

Between 1990 and 1998, sections of the Coast Highway from Halfmoon Bay to Pender Harbour were blasted from some of the most beautiful granite on Canada's west coast. Day after day, I drove that highway picking up treasures – rocks formed in the dawn of time then buried, pressed and pushed beneath mile thick ice and finally covered with moss, Douglas Fir and Arbutus. Western Sword Fern, Sorrel, Salmon Berry, Thimbleberry and Wood Rose with large fragrant pink flowers spread out beneath the trees. Then, that beautiful piece of coastline, home to deer and raccoons and bald eagles and owls was stripped, blasted and broken so that commuters and tourists could speed to their destinations, no longer pausing to see the beauty by the roadside.

Here, along that scar, were pieces of rock in all sizes, shapes and colours, jagged gems in shades of blue, white, pale yellow, dark green, light green. Here were boulders to be wrestled from the bottoms of ditches, pried out, rocked out, rolled out end over end and lifted into and out of the trunk of my poor old car, ruining my poor old back.

"*Our little secret. You must promise.*"

All one spring, I hoisted and carried, rolled and pushed small mountains and monuments into place. Pieces with clean cut edges I positioned just so to contain fishponds and steps. Jagged edges were perfect for waterfalls, for the Virgin's grotto and for highlights between rhododendron and azalea.

My back may never forgive me but my spirit rejoices in the Creator's materials and in my own handiwork.

"I promise."

Nature's dream catcher hangs suspended between grapevine and garden shed. A rainbow shines through each dewdrop – a million diamonds sparkling in the morning sun. Plump spider vibrates her web as I draw near but pass with care.

Mother is never pleased. If she finds out, she'll hate me forever.

Just below the garden shed a colony of ants scurry back and forth with eggs so big I'm reminded of the weight of the slab of rock beneath which they've built their home. Just as I carried and placed that hunk of granite near the top of my garden, so do these ants carry enormous weights far greater distances and perhaps far heavier in their perspective. Oh, how sorry and ashamed I am for once having poured scalding water on their homes and on their babies. Now I apologize in deep respect to these oldest residents of our biologically diverse planet. I've read that ants have colonized and mined almost every landmass on earth for almost sixty million years and constitute 15 to 25% of the total animal biomass. Now I stand in awe of this colossus.

Maybe there'll be an air raid, and I'll be killed and Mother will be sorry.

My garden contains the graves of one stray cat, a friend's small dog, several birds and a hamster. Three young friends, and I celebrated a beautiful funeral for Charlie, the hamster. I don't recall the cause of Charlie's demise but I do remember the ceremony when we laid him to rest with full honours in the little flowerbed at the foot of the Virgin's grotto. The deceased was laid out in a handsome shoe box coffin appropriately painted mahogany brown with my best acrylic paint and lined with Kleenex tissues. Following a homily of suitable words proclaimed by Jamie, closest to the deceased, three children sang "All things bright and beautiful, all creatures great and small..." I, the organist, played accompaniment on the harmonica. Either I, or the choir, was slightly off key but no one in the congregation seemed to mind. Following the interment and planting of a small head stone of plain description, we all retired to the vicarage (my patio) for chocolate chip cookies and lemonade.

I close my eyes tight and let him do what he wants.

My cat spends most of the day sleeping. But then, he spends the long night hunting and carousing with other night hunters in the neighbourhood. Only occasionally do I hear his night songs although another tom sometimes comes to howl outside my bedroom window. Oliver doesn't howl. He's been neutered. Non-neutered and non-spayed younger cats howl. It's part of the mating ritual.

He forces my mouth open and I try not to gag when he does his stuff at the back of my throat. I don't want him to slap me again. "Swallow. It's good for you. You'll soon learn to like it, I promise. Swallow!"

No need of mouse control in my garden. Oliver catches one or more each week. I'm glad he's such a good hunter when it comes to rodents. They burrow nests beneath the clematis and chew the roots. I'm not so happy when he catches birds. I've managed to rescue quite a few this year. Oliver forgives my interference. He knows I encourage his mousing skills.

"If you tell anyone, you and I will be put in prison."

With cats, cleanliness is next to godliness. What better place to groom than perched atop the grotto in the noonday sun? There, paying little attention to the stone Virgin below, Oliver licks paw and fur, fur and paw, until his coat befits his perch.

Oliver is fastidious, but there are some cleaning tasks he cannot perform himself. So I'm there from time to time to clip his claws and clean inside his ears. He loves to be brushed with a stiff cat brush at least once a week. I place the brushings neatly in a corner of the garden for birds, squirrels, and mice to line their nests.

If he finds someone else, we'll have to live with the lost children in the London underground.

A bright orange monarch with black wing veins flits and settles on a yellow rose to drink and sun and then to flit again. He lands to share the space where my cat lies. Oliver looks up but does not pounce. He knows a butterfly will make him sick with milkweed toxin. Butterfly knows the orange cat and flutters in the sun.

"You're my Special Boy." I wish I could be Mother's special boy. Then she'd take me away from here.

My three deer spend whole afternoons beneath the Arbutus. No longer able to reach the raspberry canes, they're content to nibble grass along the bank and doze in the shade. They did chomp off all my tulips although they don't bother with the daffodils and I'm happy to see they don't eat my Western Sword Fern which look rather like the tops of palm trees in tight dark green bunches. I found those beautiful plants when collecting my rocks just past Halfmoon Bay. They require a daily watering and love the shade of the Arbutus.

The man at the veterans' school pulls me into a shed slams the door shut, grabs me by the arm and yanks down my pants. He throws me over a greasy table. I can't cry out.

This year, the lilac bush has given me the best blooms ever with glorious perfumed purple flowers which I present in bunches with clippings of pink and white clematis when I go to entertain my friends at the seniors' lodge. In fall, I'll do the same with hydrangea flowers which bloom in great blue bunches. They were growing wild among the evergreens when I moved in. They love the acid soil and dappled shade.

I go limp. Old wounds rip open.

I don't dare leave. It's dark when I finally do. My whole body throbs with pain. Too terrified to say anything or they'll find out what I promised never to tell.

From my trellis, I snip pink roses for another elderly shut-in who mourns the loss of her husband after sixty-five years of marriage and beautiful gardens. Then I arrange treasures from my garden in ceramic pitchers and small blue glasses. At Christmas, my son makes wreaths from homegrown cedar and holly, and winds grapevine about them. I put lavender in paper bags and scatter it about the house. Not only does it smell wonderfully, it offers year after year insurance against moths.

I'm sick and stay in bed. Blood soaks my sheets. "What did you do to yourself? You're disgusting!"

Even in fall and winter, this garden is beautiful, and I know death will be followed by nature's promise, a promise forever kept. The goldfish disappear among the pots at the bottom of their pond. They'll come back to life on the first warm days of spring and eat the mosquito larvae to keep my evening garden almost free of those pests.

I dream of little men with slobbering lips and sharp, pointed teeth. Their breath smells of sour milk. I fly, but never high enough; people chasing me grab my feet and pull me down.

I'll not remove the dead lily pads until the spring but add a log or two to keep the top from freezing solid in the coldest weather. I'll also leave fallen leaves and many dead plants in my garden beds to protect fragile roots and dormant insects from the heaviest frosts of January. In spring, after the snowdrops and crocuses have dropped their petals, I'll carefully rake the debris to expose new growth. Only then will I weed and dig over the vegetable patch in readiness for the few greens I love to harvest fresh for summer salads.

In a dream, I sit naked on a toilet in the middle of a large room. I try to hide but little men jump out from hiding places and grab me. In another, I sit in my classroom and have to pee. I leave the room but can't find the toilet. I pee by the blackboard while the other boys point and laugh.

Though I try to keep my herb garden contained, the plants run wild. Their roots crawl beneath stone barriers. They spread at will among the irises. They even find their way into the goldfish pond. The worst of these horticultural wanderers is mint. Oregano also gives me a run for my money. As does lavender. So, should these tasty herbs be classed as weeds, just because they run at will? I too believe in freedom. Welcome friends. There'll be no harsh discrimination here.

I get up several times, only to find I'm still in bed, having another dream. I wonder if I'll ever wake up, or if I'll continue dreaming until I die.

When I wet the bed, I lie here shivering, afraid to get up. I dare not move.

On the high terrace, bamboo sprouts through patio rocks and beneath the greenhouse floor. And English ivy thrusts its way through greenhouse walls to smother shelves and cover windows. If I fail to remain ever vigilant, the jungle will obliterate all signs of civilization.

Maybe that's the way God intended things to be.

One day I sat in the garden feeling sorry for myself. All about me the birds sang: "Pull yourself together. You can do anything you set your mind to."

I looked up and saw a squirrel jump from one high tree to another. He aimed for a limb so far out of reach that the leap looked like suicide. Though he missed, he landed safe and unconcerned on a branch several feet lower. Then he climbed to his goal.

If a squirrel can succeed in this way, I can, too.

CHELSEA TERRORS

In 1941, I left my teddy bear behind.

You smothered all my faerie dreams,

drowned my childhood

in Gold Leaf, London Dry,

and flickering silver screen promises.

You oozed over me,

an albuminous silver streak of spotted slug.

You immersed me in your cobwebs and sour sweat.

Night after night after night,

you drove your poison dart deep, deep, deep –

and no one heard my sobs.

Outside your lair,

the Chelsea world screamed another agony.

Before the moaning sirens ceased,

the shrieking metal fell.

it filled the crumbling streets with flames –

and running,

running,

running.

No place was safe

to hide away.

Healing Friends

Those flashbacks in the garden marked the true beginning of my recovery. At last, after so many years, it seemed I had uncovered the root of all my problems. With marital troubles and school worries out of the way, I knew, at last, what even the psychiatrist had failed to uncover: keeping those horrendous secrets and repressing such horrifying memories of sexual abuse had caused a lifetime of nightmares and running.

In Sechelt, a male support group helped with my recovery. Five of us met once every two weeks in members' homes. Those who were married arranged for their wives to absent themselves. In this way, we obtained complete privacy to share our deepest concerns. The rule was that nothing said within the group was to be repeated or discussed outside the group. We observed that rule faithfully. One of the men had been sexually abused by his mother but was unable to describe the abuse. Suddenly I realized how angry I was at my own mother and I jumped in instead of waiting my turn. This caused a third member to become very angry with me, almost to the point of blows. In tears, I apologized. Then, given permission, I began to share tiny fragments of what my uncle had done to me. The man whose anger I had caused had been abused by his minister and, like me, had kept the secret hidden all those years. His mother had defended the minister against the accusations and, as usually happens, the victim clammed up. We all had so much to tell and so little time to pour it out. We increased the frequency of our meetings to once a week. Sessions were frenetic, but we supported one another through childhood nightmares, anger at abusers and parents and regret over wasted years and lost loves.

The chief thing the men's group taught me was that I was a good man. I continued with the group until I moved away, long after terminating my visits to the psychiatrist.

After the divorce, I resolved to get off antidepressant medications. One day, I quit "cold turkey". Two days later, while visiting some friends, I felt cold and clammy. My heart raced and breathing became difficult. As soon as I lay down, my skin paled and my hands shook.

My friends were concerned. When I told them I had taken myself off my medication, one of them gave me an antidepressant. Eventually, symptoms subsided. In this way I learned it is inadvisable to discontinue meds on ones own, but only with a physician's guidance.

Over the course of several weeks, with my doctor's approval, I decreased my dosage to one tablet a day and, later, to one every second day. Sometimes panic attacks returned and I had to take an extra pill.

Eventually, I went off antidepressants entirely. Sleeping and appetite improved, I learned to prepare healthy meals, with fresh fruit and vegetables. I grew less dependent on pastas, baked beans and cans of stew.

Writing poetry, writing my memoirs, singing, acting, painting in oils, and receiving recognition from the community restored my self-esteem.

Before long, I covered my walls with my own paintings. I bought and refurbished a grand piano and began to take lessons. I continued my avid involvement in the community.

When I look back, a great many people contributed to my healing. There was my son, who telephoned almost daily and visited often when he lived in Vancouver. It was he who convinced me to shout out my anger and frustration on a mountaintop. Then there was the men's group and my many good friends on the Sunshine Coast.

INSIGHT AND LOOKING BACK

I do have regrets concerning my children. While just a teenager, Alex, especially, helped and supported me. And Hanna tried to advise me. Yet, when they needed me, I was busy trying to rescue myself. Since I couldn't support and defend them, our relationship evolved into a reversal of what's normal. Fathers are supposed to help their children, not the other way around.

Clearly, both Eloise and I carried from our past significant feelings of rejection – in some ways remarkably similar loads. Maybe that's part of the reason why, in the end, we could not help each other.

This process is never complete. Over time, I see how I blamed my ex-wife for the breakup of our marriage and see more and more how I made life unbearable for her.

Who is there who can retain sanity while spending day after day in the company of a man who cries morning, noon and night, and who experiences difficulty defending himself and his loved ones? How Eloise managed to remain calm and keep the household going during those earliest months of my Post Traumatic Stress breakdown is a credit to her.

My recovery has turned out to be a roller coaster ride. Oftentimes, I'd announce to all and sundry that I was fully healed. Then another memory or incident would pop up to knock me down.

In the early fall of 1999, the CBC aired The Sheldon Kennedy Story. Kennedy played for the Boston Bruins of the National Hockey League. After undergoing much agony, he finally exposed his own childhood abuse at the hands of his junior league coach. During the part of the film when Kennedy's beautiful wife, Jana, loved and supported him, I descended into an abyss of sadness and self-pity.

I spent the majority of my years trying to please important people in my life. People-pleasing also motivated me to try teaching in the southeastern United States and to seek heroic sanctity with the Christian Brothers. Then, when I married, I transferred this impulse to Eloise. Deep down, I thought of her as another mother, someone I had to please. I also wished to rescue her from her own, similar feelings of rejection by striving constantly to make her happy.

My mother had been abandoned by her mother, just as her mother had been abandoned before her. In Eloise, I found a woman who, I felt, would not abandon me. Yet she "did so". Laying blame, either way, leads nowhere as it is carried by futility.

While I was a counsellor at boys' camps, we would sometimes sit around a campfire and write out the negative things in our lives on little slips of paper. Then we would throw our troubles into the fire. In doing this, we resolved to get rid of past hurts, to forgive, and to make new friends.

One day, thinking back on this, I tried to put my divorce with all its wrangling and bitterness behind me. Time to get rid of old files, memories of past hurts, and the rubble and litter of the marriage feast. It was time for fresh pages. I needed to make room for positive memories of those early marriage days.

I took down my boxes of documents, manuscripts and assorted junk. Out went old letters, bills paid, examination papers, notes and exercises from courses taken and taught, pamphlets and catalogues, empty cheque books, old financial records, court documents and dusty folders.

Out went so many sad memories.

For one long evening, I fed the stove. My back ached from hours of bending over boxes and bags. The whole house glowed. The years gazed back at me and laughed.

At last, I had begun to jettison the pain of the past.

* * *

My recovery continues. One may never be totally healed, especially from childhood sexual abuse. But one can learn to live with the ghosts.

Now that I have stopped living a lie, I have cleansed the poisons and have begun to leave the past behind. I have come to terms with the injustice and pain of my life. By feeling anger, re-experiencing the pain, and mourning the loss of what I might have become, I've been able to forgive myself.

Now I can accept who and what I am and enjoy those positive people in the here and now.

I had no healthy role model. So I tried to be a saint.

Much more often nowadays, I feel my mother and my wife were just fellow strugglers, as I am, who did the best they could with the hand they got dealt.

In truth, any reasonable person would view my ex-wife just as I now would have people view my mother: as a complex person with many, many grey areas, just a fellow struggler in the pain and travail of this earth. Also, any reasonable person would say I am not – cannot be – without blame where the breakdown of my marriage and the consequent pain suffered by my children are concerned.

When I first met Eloise, she was a gorgeous, near-celestial being, the object of my poetic impulses. She was my lover and my friend. Most importantly, she became the mother of my children. The problem is, I put her on a pedestal; I saw her unrealistically right from the get-go. Pedestals are difficult spots for women to stand upon for long. Most women want their mates to see and accept them, as they are, warts and all. It is on the basis of such emotional honesty that they build up feelings of intimacy toward their loved ones.

A New Song — Finchingfield,

May, 2002

Here I am, at last, returning to Finchingfield! On this sunny Sunday in mid-May, I walk the nearly two miles from Brook Farm, my bed and breakfast in Wethersfield, Essex, to Finchingfield – where my entire story began, close to seventy years ago.

While I stroll in fields bordered by wild flowers, I stop to contemplate sheep and long-horned cattle. I rejoice in the shrill songs of birds – nightingale, willow tit, bluebird, finch, skylark, and thrush. I haven't heard these since my childhood.

Strangely, maybe not so strangely, I even welcome the aroma of fresh manure.

By a stream, I sit and gaze at tadpoles. Everything brings back moments of a happy childhood. Here, it's so peaceful. Water rushes by in creeks and streams. The breeze blows in the trees and bushes. Disturbed by my presence, grey squirrels scurry away, scolding.

As I walk by thatched-roof cottages and ancient churches, my mind flashes back to those wonderful walks, when I rode horseback on my dad's shoulders a lifetime ago. At last, the upper village of Finchingfield flashes into view. I have returned to an old world, comforting and safe, a world defined by centuries of slow motion. On my left, I read a plaque proclaiming "The Nurse's Cottage". Would she have been the nurse who came to Naomi and me and kept the little people away when we had the measles? Or would she have been the one who started the rumour about German spies? Either way, what a lovely wee cottage!

On this visit, I must take the time to talk to people and to ask questions. Lots of questions. This time I will have no one to hurry me on. I head straight to Willets Cottage where I gaze up at the gable windows. There, at one end, overlooking the common, I see the little window Naomi and I peered through when our mom and dad went out in the evenings to play tennis. Left alone with fairies and little people, how happy we were then. And now, I miss Naomi.

Throughout the years, we became strangers. If only I could have listened to her long, long ago, shared her pain, recalled the happy days of our early childhood, told her of my love for her.

Though other things and people had changed – certainly, the war had changed us all – here is Willets Cottage, almost unchanged. I look up and notice its roof for the first time. No, it is not thatched; by the looks of it, it never was. So much for birdies in the thatch! They must have nested under the eaves instead. How I teased my little sister about this.

I knock at the little door. No answer. Before long, a neighbour ambles over. Agreeably, she answers my questions.

"Ah, yes, there were tennis courts right over there. Removed years ago."

The little gate invites me. We stroll over to look at the back garden. How small everything appears. It was such a big back garden when I was little. I remember the privy and its mixed smell of excrement and Dettol. Automatically, I hold my breath in disgust although the little shed is long gone.

After the neighbour leaves, I stroll up the little path to the windmill, now fully restored. Even though it's Sunday, the mill is open for visitors, courtesy of one of the many regional restoration societies. I ascend the tall steps and gaze a long time into the mill's interior. Here are the ghosts of villagers with their sacks of grain, of millers and farmers and farmers' children, some busy, some not so busy.

My thoughts flash about everywhere. Are these the shadows of those I knew when children talked with spirits, as though they were part of our every day? All is ancient and all is oh-so-sturdy. If I return tonight, will the children still be dancing with the little people?

From the top story, I peer down upon Willets Cottage. It looks so close I feel I can reach out and touch my past. Here are the fields, once wide open for boyhood ramblings, now crowded with tall hedges, shrubs, and houses, houses, houses everywhere, in places where nothing but grass and dreams once grew.

Where is the hill Naomi and I rolled down on afternoon picnics? I long to touch that part of my past that lived hermetically sealed, beyond tears. I walk away.

Soon I stand before the little lane that led to Duck End, nearly opposite Willets. I recall the bully who lived there. My memory shuts out his name. I speculate: I dared not remember it then; therefore, I cannot remember it now.

Could that boy now be the old man shaking his cane at the little barking dog? I want to think so. I feel the bully twisting my arm behind my back. "Swear to Jesus..." I wouldn't swear. I wouldn't swear.

The crack of a breaking twig brings me back to the present. For a moment, I don't know where I am. Then I remember. This place is where I once played. The grove of trees was populated with imaginary tribes. I was Robinson Crusoe. I made a den with a secret entrance that only I could find and crawl through.

Tears come to my eyes.

A tap on my shoulder brings me back to the present. Unhappily, I see only a tangled mass of thorn bushes and brambles.

"Are you all right?"

"Thank you, I'm fine. Just reminiscing."

I smile at the young lady. Such a gentle face!

After what seem a few moments – but really an hour or more – I walk over to the village. The pump? Where is it? It's no longer there. I enquire. An old-timer tells me, "Yes, there were pumps. Two of them! Gone now." I feel cheated, robbed of another tangible. I remember my dad walking home with two three-gallon cans, one for us and one for the old lady across.

I stroll past the butcher shop – once the village workhouse where orphans and the homeless were housed in Charles Dickens' time, now a private home – and over the footbridge, past the post office, and toward Swan House, the place of mixed memories, the place I wanted to explore with my father who refused to go farther with me. There it is! Looking just as I remembered it; even the garage is unchanged. There, under the leaning roof, old Bessie, the family car, sits on blocks. I blink. No. Old Bessie has vanished, a mirage generated by my overheated brain.

I pluck up my courage and ring the doorbell. "Hello. My name is Patrick Milne. I'm visiting from Vancouver, Canada. I lived in this house more than sixty years ago." My last words fade off in a wave of emotion and my voice catches.

Michael and Lynn Bethell prove to be delightful. Yet I wonder. How can people so young live in this house? And the house ... It looks even younger than they, recently renovated, in fact.

 The back garden has diminished in size. It is much smaller than the field where Nellie and Joyce once grazed. The apple tree has moved to the same magical memory realm as the barn – the one that an incendiary bomb destroyed decades ago.

For a moment, I see the flash of bursting bombs above my head. I hear the humming, whining sound, like a swarm of bees.

I shake myself back to the present.

My only reminder of years gone by turns out to be the horse equipment hanging on the garage wall, lonely and tattered. I feel lonely and tattered too. I sense an unlucky ... what? Omen? It was here, certainly, that my world began to change so drastically.

I philosophize a little. If I had known what lay ahead, would I have been able to go on? Probably not! For this reason, it may be God's special gift that most of us cannot see into our own futures. If we could, the results could be devastating.

I ask to see the little cellar window, the one that plagued so many of my nightmares. I look around the back and at the sidewalls. And see no window. Am I mistaken? Is this the right house? Then Lynn Bethel shows me, partly covered in the sunroom, the old cellar window.

Finally, I see it clearly.

It seems so ordinary. So unthreatening. So incapable of admitting a host of demonic creatures!

A tidal wave of relief drowns my momentary panic. All the vampires, with their razor-sharp teeth, disappear in the cataclysm. They will invade my sleeping hours, to suck my blood in endless nightmares, no more.

It doesn't take long to see all I need to see. I thank my hosts and carry on, instinctively, towards the anti-aircraft placement on the hill.

I walk up a minor incline along lanes between country houses. Though I think I know where my destination must be, I turn out to be wrong. Eventually, when I give up trusting my own memory, I encounter a middle-aged lady out in her back garden, with apron and gloves, cutting stalks of rhubarb.

"You must mean the wartime machine gun post, which used to be in Wincey Chase. Just a moment, I'll fetch my husband. Maybe he can help you."

A very pleasant chap, Ron Hawkins reminds me of a retired military officer, just like the people one sees in country gardening magazines. He welcomes me into his garden and introduces himself as president of the Finchingfield Heritage Society.

Together, we set out on a short walk. "There, where that small mound is. That's where the gun sat. It was removed a short while ago. It's being restored."

All that remains is a small, grassy mound. To ease my disappointment, Betty Hawkins invites me in for a slice of fresh rhubarb pie and coffee.

Indeed, Ron remembers "The Witch of Finchingfield – the kindly old lady who lived opposite Willets Cottage." He tells me that, after Miss. Timms' fiancé was killed in the Great War, she found no one to replace him. So she remained a spinster until her death. When she got old, the children made up stories about her as "the witch".

When I mention the German parachutists, Ron Hawkins offers the most significant information. "Ah, yes. One landed on the war memorial, and the second became tangled in a tree in a farmer's field. The third came down some distance away. He was frog-marched into the village at the end of a pitchfork. The local first aid people looked after them all until the Home Guard took them away."

Excitedly, I tell Ron of my mother's involvement as a first aid person and translator. I also tell him that my sister and I met the German pilot who spoke fluent English, that my mother spoke to him in German, and that, as a result, our maid refused to join us for tea.

I soon form the opinion that everyone knows everyone else in Finchingfield. Furthermore, the people have a keen interest in British history, especially in Finchingfield's role in it. Ron, for example, had researched much of what went on during World War Two. One of his stories, about the very raid I remembered, already had been published in the village newsletter.

After coffee, Ron drives me three quarters of a mile to look at Spains Hall, an Elizabethan manor house where, if memory serves, my father played cricket. Its owner during those days was Sir Archibald Ruggles-Brise, a Member of Parliament. Its gardens had been beautiful, its trees tall and shady. In fact, the Manor of Spains Hall had been mentioned in the "Domesday Survey".

Sadly, on this visit, I only get to see the Manor from a distance. Therefore, I must continue relying on vague memories of events past.

After bidding farewell to Ron and Betty, I visit the Guildhall, built in the late 15th Century. Here I'm shown an embroidered commemoration of the German parachutes coming down from the sky, following England's first air raid. I feel a sense of history now – I'm truly a part of it. Yet I feel a little, niggling ... something. Where, on that tapestry, is the little boy climbing down from his apple tree?

On my way back down the hill, I rediscover Mrs. Turner's greengrocer shop – now a craft shop, closed on Sundays. I stroll through the yard of the Church of St. John the Baptist, with its large Norman tower. The building was constructed mainly in the 14th Century. Like so many Christian churches in England nowadays, it is locked shut. I would have loved to explore its interior. Still, I'm not all that disappointed; I never dared venture inside as a child. So no memories are present, urging me on.

The sun is warm as I search amongst the gravestones – many indecipherable – and lean for a while against a chest-high tomb dedicated to the memory of someone who died in 1742. A tomb nearby features a skull and crossbones and anchor. I wonder if this old sailor could have been a pirate?

In a quiet spot beneath the trees, I contemplate a stanza from Thomas Gray's Elegy Written In a Country Church Yard:

> *Perhaps in this neglected spot is laid*
>
> *Some heart once pregnant with celestial fire;*
>
> *Hands that the rod of empire might have swayed,*
>
> *Or waked to ecstasy the living lyre.*

There's still more to see. I walk back down to the pond, across the road bridge and past "The Fox" – now undergoing flood repairs – to the United Reformed Church, built in 1799. Next door, is the old schoolroom, presently owned by an architect and remodelled as his private home.

Was it here that Naomi and I went to school for a while? I can't recall! So many memories flood my mind. I only remember a big room, divided by a windowed partition, and classes taught by two matrons. Was it from here that I got sent home in disgrace having dared to add a penis to the horse I had been commissioned to draw?

Yes, here's the schoolyard. But it was so, so long ago. My cloudy memories easily could be wrong. How I want to connect. Here is my past; here were my happy days. If only I could step back in time! But could I undo the pain and just keep the happiness? If I could perform such a miracle, who would I have become? And would I like this person any better than I like myself as I am now? Who knows? Is pain God's way of moulding us into better, more loving people? If so, why would I wish to avoid it?

Up beyond the church on the hill, I see another old school. Is this the one I attended? If only my old father had come with me to answer my questions, twenty years earlier. On the green, I stop at the War Memorial. Twenty-seven men from the village – I count them – perished in the Great War. Six in World War Two. Many of their descendants still live in the village.

Down by the village pond, I stand on the footbridge and gaze at the River Pant, now a mere trickle. The river had flooded the previous year and caused considerable damage to houses and shops.

I remember the fish that got away so many years before.

Four weeks after my visit with him and his wife, Ron Hawkins reaches me by e-mail:

> Dear Paddie,
>
> After asking around the village, I found two people who remember you: your sister and your mother. Firstly, Flo Hardy. She helped your mother in the First Aid Centre. She remembers her as a fine, upright woman with blonde hair down to her shoulders. Flo remembers the name of your dog; not only that, she recalls Paul Robeson walking around the village. Her husband remembers your old Morris car.
>
> The second woman who vividly remembers you and your family is Floss Halls, who used to 'do' for your mother sixty-four years ago. I met her in the post office the other day. After saying, "Of course I remember the Milnes", she immediately recalled your name, Paddie, as well as your sister's name. She, too, remembers your dog, a Springer spaniel named Buller.
>
> In April 2000, I wrote a story for 'The Villager', which I called "The Germans Have Landed". It was based upon reminiscences, told to me by Chris and Flo Hardy, about a 'dogfight' (aerial combat between two aircraft) that resulted in a German Dornier bomber of the No. 7 Staffel Bomber Group getting shot down by a pilot of the Royal Canadian Air Force. As a result, four German airmen had to parachute into Finchingfield.

Unfortunately, following the encounter, the Canadian lost his life when his aircraft crash-landed in Little Hydes, Little Bardfield. Much of my data about the RCAF pilot [Flying Officer Christopher Leonard Edwards of No.1 Squadron] has been taken from official RAF records. Edwards arrived in England on June 20th, 1940. His craft was a Hurricane Mark 1 [serial number P3874]. His body is buried at Brookwood Military Cemetery.

One of the German parachutists injured himself, ironically, on the War Memorial itself! Alicia Milne, Cecilia Ruggles-Brice, and the Rev. Paul Walde, who all possessed language skills, interviewed the four Germans, firstly in Swan House, then later in the first aid centre. The first aid centre, located in Spring Mead, is now the home of Pam and Michael Shaw.

On Friday the 31st, I spoke to Mrs. Kemp. She remembers the "witch woman". Her name was Miss. Timms, a lady bent double with advanced age. Mrs. Kemp also remembers you. She also recalls your sister, who occasionally visited her home to play with her daughter.

I called upon Rhoda Cornell [née Hardy], who lives in one of the cottages opposite Willets. She told me that Miss. Timms was one of three sisters. Another was Rhoda's grandmother. During the early part of the 1900s, all the sisters moved to Canada. When Rhoda's grandmother died, her grandfather, and Miss. Timms moved back to Finchingfield, leaving the other sister in Canada.

Rhoda remembers Miss. Timms as having an abrupt and abrasive manner. Could this be why the children thought her to be a witch? Miss. Timms died in early 1942.

Rhoda also remembers that your mother gave Miss. Timms "some small wooden figures".

About two years ago, I interviewed Rhoda about her life, etc. At that time she mentioned "a foreign lady who lived on the causeway and gave some figures to Miss. Timms." I know now that we were talking about your mother.

The more I speak to older residents of Finchingfield, the more I'm surprised concerning how many remember your family. In fact, I only have to mention 'Milne', and they remember both yours and your sister's names.

– Ron Hawkins, Finchingfield Heritage

Epilogue

No More Running

While I carried emotions from my past, I hid them like soiled underwear, all tucked away. I went through much of my life in fear that the shame of my youth would be found out. I repressed traumatic memories until they resurfaced, to cause depression and chronic fatigue. I sought means of not remembering in all manner of distraction.

As a child, I often lived an imaginary life to escape the trauma of my abuse. Fantasy was more comfortable for me than reality. Fortunately, as an adult, I managed to escape two of the most common consequences of a dysfunctional childhood: alcoholism and drug addiction. But I did not escape workaholism, an even more common consequence.

Sigmund Freud describes what he calls "the repetition compulsion", where people repeat the patterns of their parents and the torments of their past. For example, children raised by depressed parents will be more likely to grow up depressed unless, that is, they have healthy outside influences and activities which distract them and bring them much-needed fulfillment and self-esteem. I can only pray that my own children are able to survive the potential damages caused by my emotional baggage.

It is so easy to be a victim, to wallow in self-pity, to decline to face reality, and to become adaptive and compliant. It is so much harder for the victim to face reality; this, after all, involves facing down one's victimizer. One has to become assertive about one's legal and moral rights. Such assertiveness is not to be confused with selfish aggressiveness.

Cycles, once recognized and understood – awareness is the key to it all – can be broken. Though raised in an atmosphere of shame, hostility and intimidation, I have faced, dealt with, and even forgiven most of my tormentors. I feel no need to continue submitting to those who attempt to victimize me, in order, selfishly, to release their own inner demons.

I have been able, with some professional help and through writing, to make peace with my past. In humility, with God's help, I face it now. No longer do I need to run away. I can survive and thrive.

In January 2003, I sold my home in Sechelt, got rid of most of my belongings, sold or gave away most of my paintings, and bought a condominium in Vancouver.

Then I met my new love, and my life started over. Together, we attend concerts and symphonies, plays, art galleries and museums. Together, we travel and enjoy our golden years. She is an accomplished artist. With her encouragement, I continue to paint, better than ever before. She is also my primary editor and not only knows me better than anyone ever has, but has helped me to know myself. We are very open with and respectful of each other.

Most important of all, I have learned to forgive my mother and my ex-wife, as I have had to forgive myself. In forgiving, I have found true love – healthy love.

My life has come full circle.

Finchingfield, where my memories began almost seventy years ago, sits in the same peaceful part of England, grown up-to-date yet essentially unchanged. Here the older people live on with their memories, and all are connected.

In Finchingfield, I rediscover and confirm the love of a father, the love that has sustained me through a lifetime. In rediscovering this love, I rediscover my stolen identity.

In Finchingfield, the name Milne is remembered with fondness. This is the source and confirmation of my art. Here, in my childhood, I know the love and joy of music. Here is beauty and spirit, regeneration and connectedness. All the things I tried to pass on to my children.

Here also is sadness revisited, and anger. How could a mother deliberately keep a son from his father? How could she even tell her son his father is dead? Yet now I know the answer: Mother had her own way of dealing with a difficult life.

How did I – better: how do I, despite the many years – survive the abuse I suffered? In a different context, Sir Winston Churchill said it best:

> *If you are going through hell, keep going.*

To the many victims of sexual abuse, afraid to speak up because they still fear someone might accuse them of the same unspeakable crime, I offer only this: Eventually, one has to speak up. In revelation is healing and redemption.

I'd like to say my shame is gone. But, I still must remind myself that I am clean, whole and innocent. I always will have to remind myself of this.

When I was a child, I lost my sense of innocence and beauty. This resulted from the actions of my uncle, and the man in Saint Paul l'Hermite who pushed me into a shed and raped me. And myriad other bullies.

I washed and washed; yet I couldn't rid myself of the filth I felt inside. Dirtiness is lost beauty. Loss of an inner sense of goodness and purity (self-esteem) is lost innocence.

My scrupulous, lifelong desire for cleanliness, especially in the bathroom and kitchen, is a continuation of my need to regain externally that which I've lost internally – my inner beauty.

My delight in children represents, at least partially, my need to regain memory of my own beauty and innocence.

In this wondrous world, flowers and birds and beasts live easily and naturally. And they teach me to do the same. Thus, my appreciation of nature.

I'm healed of the sickness that plagued me – the anger, the shame, the bitterness, and the pain.

On a beautiful Sunday evening, my dearest friend and I were enjoying the nostalgia of some long-play recordings. One was of themes and commercial jingles from radio programs of the 1940's, which I recalled so vividly from my first years in Canada and which took my friend back to her happy days with her parents and grandmother. The second recording was titled *George Formby Souvenir*. My friend hummed happily along.

Without warning, I grew painfully uncomfortable and felt increasingly agitated until I wanted to scream "Shut up! Shut the f… up!" George Formby's high-pitched voice irritated me beyond belief. My friend's happy humming made me angry. My reaction embarrassed me. I could see no reason for it. Fortunately, she noticed my discomfort and turned the music off.

We sat silently reading but I was unable to concentrate. My chest grew heavy, my breathing laboured. I closed my book. She reached for my hand, and the tears began to trickle down my face.

Only then did I remember. George Formby movies had been my reward for "being good". My Uncle Sigvard took me to see the singer with the ukulele to help ensure my silence in those darkest days of my life. I was feeling the anger and the unspeakable revulsion that I had been unable to express for most of my life.

Fortunately, I was now with a person who not only understood, but also was not fearful or distancing. Instead, she was able to support me in that moment. She reaffirmed my goodness and I recovered quickly.

One may never be totally healed, especially from childhood sexual abuse. But one can learn to live with the ghosts.

www.ingramcontent.com/pod-product-compliance
Lightning Source LLC
Chambersburg PA
CBHW071228070526
44583CB00017B/2089